BEYOND THE DECADE OF THE BRAIN

Volume 2

*Dopamine agonists in early
Parkinson's disease*

Editors:

C. Warren Olanow, MD, FRCP(C)
Professor and Chairman
Department of Neurology
Mount Sinai Medical Center
New York
USA

José A. Obeso, MD
Professor of Neurology
Clínica Quirón
San Sebastián
Spain

Published by:
Wells Medical Limited, Speldhurst Place, Speldhurst Road,
Royal Tunbridge Wells, Kent TN4 0JB, UK

ISBN 185939048X

This publication has been sponsored by
an educational grant from
SmithKline Beecham Pharmaceuticals

CONTENTS

Section IV – Search for Consensus

PARTICIPANTS

Professor A. Albanese	Università Cattolica, Rome, Italy
Professor A. Aquilonius	Akademiska University Hospital, Uppsala Sweden
Professor P.J. Bédard	Hôpital de l'Enfant Jésus, Québec, Canada
Dr. D. Bentue-Ferrer	CHRU de Rennes, Rennes, France
Professor U. Bonuccelli	University of Pisa, Pisa, Italy
Professor D.J. Brooks	Hammersmith Hospital, London, UK
Professor T. Brücke	University Hospital, Vienna, Austria
Dr. E.R. Brunt	Academisch Ziekenhuis, Groningen, Netherlands
Dr. D.B. Calne	Vancouver Hospital and Health Sciences Centre, Vancouver, Canada
Professor J. Chacón	University Hospital of Virgen Macarena, Seville, Spain
Dr. P. Damier	Hôpital la Pitié Salpetrière, Paris, France
Professor P. Delwaide	Hospital Citadelle, University of Liège, Liège, Belgium
Dr. R. de la Fuenta-Fernandez	Biomedical Research Centre, Spain
Professor J. Garcia de Yébenes	Ciudad University, Madrid, Spain
Dr. C.R. Gerfen	NIMH, Bethesda, Maryland, USA
Professor O. Gershanik	Centro Neurologico, Buenos Aires, Argentina
Professor S. Giménez-Roldàn	Gregorio Maranon Hospital, Madrid Spain
Professor P. Jenner	Kings College London, London, UK
Professor P. Lamberti	Instituto Di Clinica Delle Malattie Nervose E Mentali, Bari, Italy
Dr. J.P. Larsen	Rogaland Central Hospital, Stavanger, Norway
Professor K.L. Leenders	Universitätsspital Zürich, Zürich, Switzerland

FOREWORD

Levodopa has been used to treat Parkinson's disease (PD) since the 1960s. It was the first effective treatment for PD and has revolutionized the welfare of patients suffering from this chronic, progressive, neurodegenerative disorder. Levodopa provides long-lasting efficacy in treating all of the cardinal features of PD and is considered the gold standard against which other treatments must be measured. Indeed, benefit is so universally obtained that a good response to levodopa is considered one of the diagnostic features of PD, and failure to respond raises questions as to the accuracy of diagnosis. Nevertheless, despite these benefits, chronic levodopa therapy in PD patients is associated with the development of adverse events that limit its long-term utility.

Levodopa adverse events primarily consist of motor fluctuations and dyskinesia and tend to develop after five to 10 years of treatment. In the early stages of PD, patients enjoy a long-lasting response following a single dose of levodopa. With disease progression however, patients begin to experience motor fluctuations, which initially manifest as a gradual waning of the motor response with worsening of parkinsonian features at the end of the dosing period ('end-of-dose deterioration'). In more advanced stages, patients may develop the 'on-off' phenomenon in which they rapidly and unpredictably fluctuate between being 'on' and functional and 'off' and parkinsonian. Patients may also develop dyskinesia or involuntary movements typically characterized as choreiform or dystonic. These uncontrolled movements occur in response to a dose of levodopa and may prove as unpleasant to the patient and their family as the disease itself. Furthermore, as the disease progresses, the dose of levodopa necessary to induce a motor response approaches that which induces dyskinesia. Eventually, the therapeutic zone narrows to such a degree that a dose of levodopa sufficient to induce a motor response invariably causes dyskinesia. Thus, in the extreme, patients cycle between having 'on' periods complicated by dyskinesia and 'off' periods in which they are akinetic and frozen. Further, with disease progression, patients may develop new problems such as freezing, postural instability, autonomic disturbances, and dementia which do not respond to levodopa and may reflect degeneration of non-dopaminergic neurons. Accordingly, alternate treatments are being sought that can delay or prevent the progression of parkinsonism and the development of levodopa-related adverse events.

The basis of levodopa motor complications is a matter of debate but appears to involve both presynaptic and postsynaptic mechanisms. Younger patients are particularly susceptible to the development of motor complications which appear to relate both to disease severity and to the duration, dose and method of administration of levodopa. There is additional concern that levodopa, because of its oxidative metabolism, may promote oxidant stress and accelerate the rate of neurodegeneration and disease progression. This raises the possibility that agents such as the direct-acting dopamine agonists may prove beneficial because they delay the need to introduce levodopa or may be combined with levodopa to reduce the total levodopa load that a patient receives over the course of their illness. In animal models of parkinsonism, dopamine agonists have been demonstrated to attenuate the motor complications associated with levodopa therapy. Additionally, dopamine agonists have been shown to have antioxidant properties and to provide neuroprotective benefits for dopaminergic cells in tissue culture and in animal models.

Clinical trials of dopamine agonists in patients with early PD have demonstrated that they are effective in treating the cardinal features. Moreover, many studies indicate that they produce a reduced incidence of motor complication in comparison to levodopa. In addition, they have a levodopa-sparing effect which may offer putative neuroprotection. Thus, a rational strategy for the treatment of patients with early PD who require symptomatic therapy is to initiate treatment with a dopamine agonist. Once more potent therapy is required, the dopamine agonist can be combined with low doses of levodopa with the aim of providing clinical efficacy coupled with a low incidence of motor complications. Patients treated in this way may thus be expected to experience satisfactory relief from the symptoms of PD and to maintain a better quality of life over the course of long-term treatment.

In October 1996, a panel of expert clinicians and basic scientists with a special interest in PD met in Barcelona, Spain, to review the current state of science and clinical therapeutics as they pertain to the use of dopamine agonists. This event was underwritten by SmithKline Beecham on the occasion of the introduction to the market of their new dopamine agonist, ropinirole (Requip®). This volume represents the papers and discussion that took place at this meeting. Collectively, they represent an authoritative review of the current state of knowledge regarding the use of dopamine agonists in PD. In particular, there are extensive reviews pertaining to the mechanisms that might underlie motor complications and strategies aimed at treating and preventing these problems. The culmination of this effort was the development of a consensus on the use of dopamine agonists in the early stages of PD.

It is evident that many clinical questions are still unanswered and the ideal way to treat a parkinsonian patient remains to be defined. Nonetheless, a body of scientific and clinical data now provides a rationale for introducing dopamine agonists as early therapy, and perhaps as the first drug in the symptomatic treatment of PD. Based on this new information, and the occasion of the introduction of new dopamine agonists into the marketplace, it is hoped that this will provide the opportunity to initiate clinical trials to define, once and for all, the best way to treat PD in the present era.

C. Warren Olanow, MD, FRCP(C)
José A. Obeso, MD
Editors

SECTION 1

Introduction

CHAPTER ONE

Complications associated with chronic levodopa therapy in Parkinson's disease

José A. Obeso[1,2], Gurutz Linazasoro[1], Arantza Gorospe[1], Maria C. Rodriguez[1] and Gabriel Lera[3]

[1]Centro de Neurología y Neurocirugía Funcional, Clínica Quirón, San Sebastián,
[2]Departamento de Neurología y Neurocirugía, HOSPITEN, Tenerife, Spain,
[3]Section of Extrapyramidal Disorders, Hospital Frances, Buenos Aires, Argentina

ABSTRACT

The most effective therapy for Parkinson's disease (PD) is still levodopa, despite the development of newer drugs and improved surgical techniques. In many patients, however, the beneficial effects of levodopa are eventually compromised by the development of major problems such as motor fluctuations, dyskinesias and psychiatric complications, which appear within five to 10 years of starting treatment. The severity of disease and duration of levodopa therapy are the major factors determining the incidence of complications. However, motor fluctuations, dyskinesias and psychiatric problems have different pathophysiological origins, despite their occurrence in the same patient. An improved understanding of the pathophysiology of the basal ganglia has provided new insights into the mechanisms responsible for the major features present in PD patients with motor complications. Pharmacodynamic mechanisms are of paramount importance, and the mode of dopaminergic stimulation (pulsatile versus continuous) at the receptor level and modifications occurring in the striatopallidal pathways are key factors in the development of complications.

Levodopa plus carbidopa or benserazide remains the most effective therapy for Parkinson's disease (PD) despite the advent of several newer drugs and the development of modern surgical techniques. Levodopa administered three or four times per day markedly ameliorates the motor manifestations of PD and reduces the associated disability. This beneficial effect usually lasts for a variable period of some five to 10 years. Subsequently, the initial success is blurred in at least 50% of patients by the development of motor and cognitive complications (Table 1). Some of these problems (Table 1b) are believed to arise as a consequence of progression and extension of the degenerative process and are therefore independent of any given therapeutic strategy. However, the vast majority of patients suffer treatment-related complications (Table 1a) which form the bulk of day-to-day problems in the clinical management of PD. Since levodopa is the most potent antiparkinsonian drug and because it has been widely utilized in a vast number of patients around the world, a discussion of drug-related complications in PD is necessarily focused on the effect of levodopa.

Table 1: Long-term complications in Parkinson's disease		
A. Levodopa-related		
Motor:	a) Fluctuations:	Simple 'wearing off' phenomenon Complex 'on-off' phenomenon
	b) Dyskinesias:	'On'-period chorea or mobile dystonia Diphasic dyskinesias 'Off'-period dystonic postures
Non-motor phenomenon during 'off' periods:		Sensory: pain, akathisia, restless legs Autonomic: pallor, sweating, tachycardia, dyspnea, etc. Cognitive/psychiatric: depression, anxiety, panic attacks
Psychiatric complications:		Sleep abnormalities (nightmares, vivid dreams), hallucinations, delirium, paranoia, hypersexuality, gambling
B. Treatment-unrelated (usually in late stages of disease)		
Cognitive decline – dementia		
Sensory disturbances: pain, paresthesias, nocturnal akathisia		
Autonomic (mild) disturbances: gastrointestinal, genitourinary, skin, cardiovascular, sweating		
Mood alterations – depression		
Postural and gait disturbances – falls		
Speech disturbance		

The major problems associated with chronic levodopa use are (1) motor fluctuations, (2) dyskinesias, and (3) psychiatric complications. Several authors have addressed the problem of the causative role of levodopa in the origin of these complications.[1-6] All such studies, as well as our own,[7,8] indicate that disease severity and duration of levodopa therapy are the major factors determining the incidence of complications. However, they are intimately interconnected and very difficult to dissociate, making retrospective analysis to assess their relative role as causative factors almost impossible. Accordingly, loss of substantia nigra neurons and the concomitant deficit in striatal dopamine on the one hand and a putative iatrogenic action of levodopa on the other, are the two major issues for discussion.

Motor fluctuations and dyskinesias often occur together in the same patient but their pathophysiological origin is not necessarily identical. Similarly, psychiatric problems are also more frequently seen in patients with motor complications[9] but probably arise by different mechanisms and circumstances. We will therefore discuss each problem separately in this chapter and will attempt to provide a unified conclusion.

CLINICAL PRESENTATION

Motor fluctuations

Oscillations in motor capability in PD are predominantly related to levodopa intake. Episodes of unexpected freezing and the reverse, paradoxic kinesias, are well documented but rare in comparison with the clinical problem of motor fluctuations,[10] which affect some 60% of the general parkinsonian population and nearly 100% of those with PD of onset below 50 years of age.[8,11] Two major types of clinical response to levodopa may be distinguished – (a) the *long-duration* response, which consists of an improvement of parkinsonian signs occurring several days (3–10) after initiation of levodopa and a similar temporal deterioration after cessation, and (b) the *short-duration* response, which consists of a marked improvement of parkinsonian signs lasting for about three hours or less (even minutes). Both responses occur together and cannot be considered independently. In many patients, the short duration response becomes clinically relevant only after many years of showing a 'medium-duration response', that is, when the duration of the improvement lasts for longer than the usual 6–8 hours interval between levodopa doses. At this stage, there is no fluctuation during the day, provided levodopa is taken regularly and without alteration in its absorption from the digestive tract, but parkinsonian features return during the night.

As both disease duration and time under levodopa increase, the short-duration response becomes more overt (Figure 1) and ultimately consists of the following features – (a) abrupt onset, (b) large magnitude (difference between baseline 'off' and 'on' scores), (c) short duration (a few minutes to two hours), and (d) worsening of motor state below baseline scores ('negative response') giving rise to the phenomenon of the 'super-off'.

The 'wearing off' consists of a series of short-duration responses to levodopa administration at regular intervals. The more accentuated the short-duration response becomes, the greater the likelihood that this simple predictable pattern will turn into a complicated 'on-off' pattern. In this state, individual doses may fail completely to provide benefit and the relationship between levodopa ingestion and benefit become ill-defined, leading in some cases to a completely unpredictable pattern. However, this is largely related to the schedule of levodopa.[10] Thus, the motor response of the most complicated parkinsonian patient with motor fluctuations will become quite predictable if levodopa (or apomorphine to avoid absorption problems) is given in sufficiently high doses, separated by long intervals (6–8 hours).

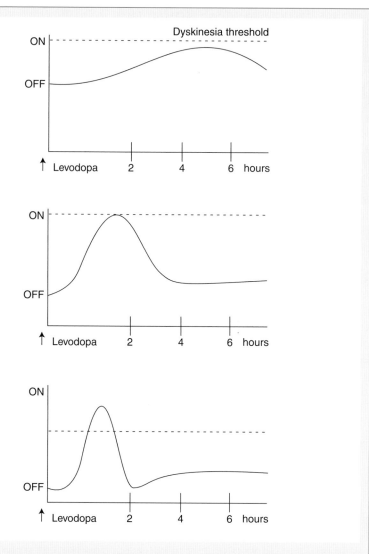

Figure 1: Schematic summary of the changes in pharmacologic responsiveness according to the degree of severity and evolution in Parkinson's disease. In the initial stage (top) the response to acute challenge with levodopa induces a very long-lasting response with a slow onset and offset and reduced magnitude. In more advanced stages (middle), the baseline 'off' severity is greater and the response becomes shorter in duration, brisker and of larger magnitude. The dyskinetic threshold is also decreased. In very advances stages (bottom), the response is extremely fast in onset, very brief and particularly large in magnitude. There is also a deterioration of the motor state in the post-'off' and the dyskinetic threshold is so reduced that there is no 'on' without dyskinesias.

Dyskinesias

Dyskinesia is a very common (40–70%) complication associated with long-term levodopa therapy.[1,5,11,12] Dystonic postures may be the initial manifestation of PD and might therefore occur before starting levodopa. However, in the vast majority of patients dyskinesias are drug-induced. Apomorphine and other dopamine agonists[13] may also induce dyskinesias when given in monotherapy, but in clinical practice dyskinesias are, as a rule, related to levodopa. Patients with a stable response under chronic levodopa therapy may show mild choreiform dyskinesias, particularly when under stress or performing a complicated task. More often, however, dyskinesias are linked with the short-duration response. There are three major patterns:

(a) 'On' dyskinesias taking the form of chorea or dystonic movements and embracing the whole 'on' period or just during the 'peak dose' effect. The neck and proximal arm muscles, the trunk and the mouth are most often involved. 'Severe on'-period chorea of generalized distribution affects some 15–20% of patients.[7]

(b) Diphasic dyskinesias occur in approximately 20–25% of patients and typically appear before levodopa turns the patient 'on', disappear during the 'on' period and emerge again before the end of the effect.[7–10] They are short-lasting (10–30 minutes) but may be extremely severe and associated with great discomfort.[10,11] There are several motor manifestations with a diphasic pattern.[14] The most frequent type consists of repetitive, stereotyped 'kicking' movements of the lower limbs. Electromyographic recording of these movements shows a well-organized alternating pattern of contraction of antagonist muscles in the leg. The movement by itself is therefore well structured, but abnormally released beyond voluntary control coinciding with low dopaminergic stimulation.[14] Dystonic postures and wild ballistic movements may also be seen with a diphasic presentation in a smaller proportion of patients.[7,10,14] During an episode of diphasic dyskinesias, one can observe repetitive involuntary movements of one or both legs coinciding with tremor in the upper limbs and relative immobility. This combination gives rise to the typical clinical picture of stereotyped repetitive movements and reduced motor capacity, particularly reflected as a bizarre gait pattern.[14]

(c) 'Off' period dystonia consists of focal, segmental or generalized postures. The most common presentation is foot dystonia particularly in the early morning before the first dose of levodopa has been taken.[10,12] Generalized 'off' dystonia may be extremely disabling, particularly when accompanied by pain and autonomic symptoms.

Non-motor fluctuations

This refers to symptoms and signs usually occurring during the 'off' period which are not motor in nature. Riley and Lang classified these as autonomic, sensory and cognitive/psychiatric.[15] A recent survey[16] of 130 patients with motor fluctuations detected non-motor complaints in 17% (n=22). The more common manifestations were anxiety (n=4), panic attack (n=4), dyspnea (n=4), depression (n=3), and limb dysesthesia (n=3). This study found the non-motor symptoms coinciding with the motor 'off' state. We have observed sensory symptoms (burning of the feet, abdominal and limb pain) and depression, without obvious changes in the motor state, to be the only indications of low or inadequate dopaminergic stimulation.

Cognitive problems during the 'on' state may be less conspicuous but nevertheless important. It is quite usual to see confusion, reduced alertness and mental cloudiness as a 'peak dose' phenomenon not necessarily accompanied by severe chorea or hallucinations. In a well-controlled study, Kulisevsky et al.[17] assessed the effect of levodopa on a battery of frontal lobe tests in patients with PD showing a stable motor response and in another group with motor fluctuations to levodopa. They observed that levodopa significantly decreased the response time in verbal and visuospatial memory tests and reduced efficacy in performing the Wisconsin card sorting test. The latter was particularly altered in patients with fluctuations at one hour after levodopa intake, this negative effect disappearing four hours later. This report elegantly showed a derangement of frontal executive functions as a 'peak dose' effect. The fact that more severe patients showed the greatest abnormalities suggests that the underlying pathological process also plays a relevant role and makes unlikely the idea of levodopa overdosage leading to 'toxic' levels of dopamine in less denervated areas.

Psychiatric complications

Drug-induced psychiatric problems are a common complication in PD patients chronically treated with levodopa. From the management perspective, the most troublesome problem is drug-induced psychosis. Several studies have suggested that psychiatric side effects are more common in patients with certain clinical features, dementia being the most important predisposing factor. Psychotic disturbances affect up to 80% of patients with concomitant dementia and 20% of patients without dementia. Other important risk factors are advanced age, premorbid psychiatric illness, long disease duration and use of high doses of antiparkinsonian medications.

The most salient clinical features in order of frequency are abnormal dreaming and sleep disruption, nightmares, vivid dreams, delusions and organic confusional psychosis. Since the description of Nausieda et al.,[18] the clinical features of drug-induced psychosis can be viewed in most patients as a continuum from altered dreaming with myoclonus, vivid dreams plus nocturnal hallucinations, to development of a non-confusional organic delusional syndrome and ultimately a psychotic state.

The pathogenesis of drug-induced psychiatric complications in PD is just starting to be studied and is not clearly understood. At present, the most widely accepted concept is that the psychotic effects of antiparkinsonian drugs may related to abnormal stimulation of the mesolimbic–mesocortical dopaminergic system, although the role of other neurotransmitters, such as serotonin, cannot be ruled out.

Since the introduction of the atypical neuroleptic family of drugs, the management of psychiatric complications has undergone considerable change. Under the eponym 'atypical neuroleptic' are a number of drugs with antipsychotic activity similar to that of the typical neuroleptics but with a very low capacity to induce tardive dyskinesia and aggravate parkinsonism. At present, clozapine is the most effective treatment available. In order to avoid some side effects, such as postural hypotension and daytime sedation, it is recommended that patients start with a dose of 6.25 mg at night and increase by this amount every few days to efficacy or toxicity. It is very unusual to require more than 100 mg daily. The long-term efficacy of clozapine in controlling psychiatric complications and sleep problems in parkinsonian patients is now well established.[19] Clozapine has the inconvenience of its capacity to produce agranulocytosis in a proportion of patients (cumulative one-year incidence of 0.8%) and this requires frequent and regular monitoring of blood counts. It is also recommended that concomitant use of other drugs capable of inducing agranulocytosis, such as captopril, carbamazepine or carbimazole, is avoided. This serious side effect of clozapine has propitiated the use of other atypical neuroleptics in parkinsonian patients with dopaminomimetic psychosis. Among these, risperidone and remoxipride have been tested in PD patients. The most important conclusion of these studies is that both drugs are effective against drug-induced psychosis in PD but they increase parkinsonian features. Ondansetron is a serotonin 5-HT$_3$ receptor antagonist utilized successfully as an antiemetic and is well-tolerated and effective in the management of hallucinations in PD.[20]

PATHOPHYSIOLOGICAL ORIGIN OF MOTOR COMPLICATIONS–INITIAL CONCEPTS

In this section we shall review and summarize the data and thoughts which led to the prevailing pathophysiological explanations for motor complications in the last two decades. Standard doses of levodopa do not induce the 'on-off' phenomenon and dyskinesias in monkeys and humans with spared dopaminergic function. The use of a very high dose of levodopa over a prolonged period has recently been associated with chorea in intact monkeys,[21] but this represents an extreme and very unusual situation. In any case, there is agreement that nigrostriatal denervation increases the sensitivity to development of dyskinesias. Loss of the dopaminergic regulatory tone over the striatum and non-physiological replacement therapy with levodopa are the basic factors determining the origin of motor complications in PD.[14,22]

The pathophysiological mechanisms of motor complications have been divided into three categories – (1) peripheral pharmacokinetic mechanisms, (2) central pharmacokinetic mechanisms, and (3) pharmacodynamic mechanisms.[22]

Peripheral pharmacokinetics

The peripheral pharmacokinetics of levodopa, that is, the factors modifying plasma levels of levodopa and its delivery into the brain, do not change with severity of disease or time under levodopa treatment and are identical in patients with a stable response and in those with fluctuations and dyskinesias.[23,24] The clinical change from a stable response to a fluctuating pattern is therefore not due to modifications in the peripheral handling of levodopa but to central factors. In the early stages of the disease, when nigrostriatal denervation is not yet profuse, the pulsatile delivery of levodopa (i.e. tablets given 3–4 times daily) is transformed into a sustained response and there are no overt changes in motor capability. The dyskinesia threshold is high (Figure 1) and involuntary movements are not seen at either peak doses or in-between doses.

Central pharmacokinetics

The central kinetics of levodopa are modified by the extent of nigrostriatal denervation.[25] Thus, peak striatal levels of dopamine are reduced and decline faster in rats with complete 6-hydroxydopamine destruction of the nigrostriatal pathway than in those with a partial lesion. Using the same animal model but inducing partial lesions, Papa et al.[26] found that the larger the lesion, the shorter the duration of the motor response to levodopa, mimicking the 'wearing off' phenomenon. In monkeys with severe dopaminergic depletion induced by MPTP (1-methyl-4-phenyl-1,2,3,6-tetrahydropyridine) administration, the first dose of levodopa is accompanied by a short-duration response and dyskinesias may also be elicited at the beginning of treatment.[13]

A short-lasting motor improvement is therefore the normal pharmacologic response to dopaminergic drugs with a short half-life. The fact that it does not occur, or is not clinically overt, in the early stages of disease evolution and levodopa therapy was explained in the past by the 'storage hypothesis'.[27–30] In its simple formulation, this hypothesis indicates that fluctuations in the form of the 'wearing off' phenomenon start when the capacity of nigrostriatal terminals to store dopamine from exogenously-administered levodopa falls below a critical level, so that the striatal dopamine concentration is governed and dictated by levodopa plasma levels. The lack of presynaptic buffering capacity would also result in greater postsynaptic delivery of newly-synthesized dopamine, thus explaining the reduction in dyskinesia threshold accompanying the more severe stages of PD.[28,29] In keeping with this idea was the observation that duration of the motor response following intravenous administration of levodopa is longer in less advanced patients (untreated and stable) than in those with greater disease severity[28] and that continuous administration of levodopa could abolish 'off' periods in patients with simple, predictable 'wearing off'-type of fluctuations in whom defective storage was mainly implicated.[30,31] It was also postulated that postsynaptic mechanisms played a role in the origin of complex 'on-off' fluctuations in more severe and advanced patients.[28–31]

[18]

The storage hypothesis provided the ground for a vast number of very important pharmacologic observations in PD and had the virtue of being intuitively easy to understand. It is therefore not surprising that it became, and remains, highly popular in the explanation of motor fluctuations in PD. However, the paramount role of presynaptic storing of dopamine in the origin of motor complications has recently been challenged. Several studies have shown that the motor response to apomorphine, which does not depend upon storage mechanisms at all, is qualitatively and quantitatively identical to the one elicited by levodopa.[32] Thus, following apomorphine acute administration, the response duration is longer and the magnitude smaller in the less affected patients[33,34] and *vice versa* (Table 2). In parkinsonian patients with asymmetric degrees of motor signs, the duration of the response to either levodopa or apomorphine was significantly reduced in the most affected side.[35] Moreover, levodopa withdrawal for a period of 7–10 days resulted in prolonged duration of the 'on' condition induced either by an intravenous steady-state infusion of levodopa or by apomorphine infusion (Figure 2), despite deterioration in the 'off' basal motor score. Since levodopa 'drug holidays' are believed not to induce changes in the number of functioning nigrostriatal fibers, these changes have to be attributed to pharmacodynamic modifications.

Table 2: Motor response to intravenous apomorphine in *de novo* and fluctuating patients

	De novo (n = 8)	Fluctuating (n = 20)	P
UPDRS 'off' basal	28 ± 3.6	47.8 ± 17.1	<0.001
Latency to 'on' (min)	94 ± 34	62.8 ± 38.4	<0.1
Total dose to 'on' (mg)	3.3 ± 0.8	2.7 ± 1	<0.1
UPDRS 'on'	14 ± 5.3	19.3 ± 9.3	<0.1
% improvement	50.8 ± 15.4	59.7 ± 11.4	<0.1
Duration of 'on' (min)	141 ± 38.1	50 ± 20	<0.001
UPDRS 'off' post-infusion	27.5 ± 4.1	46.8 ± 18.1	<0.001
Total dose of apomorphine (mg/h)	6.2 ± 2.3	7.8 ± 2.7	<0.1

Pharmacodynamic mechanisms

The first concept to explore regarding pharmacodynamic abnormalities in PD is the logical possibility that chronic levodopa therapy and disease progression induce modifications in the number of dopamine striatal receptors or in their affinity state.[21] In fact, several biochemical studies performed with post-mortem material showed no significant differences in dopamine D_2 receptor binding in the striatum of parkinsonian patients.

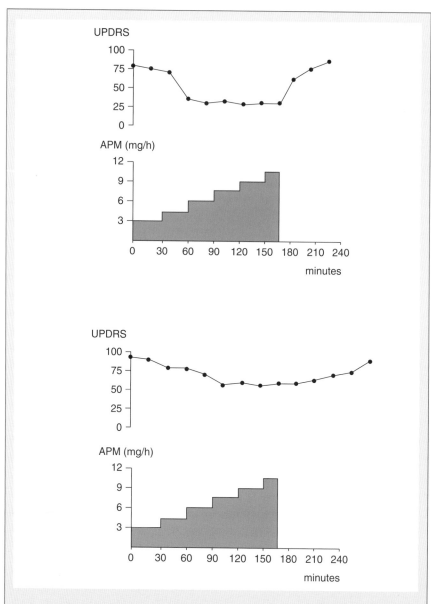

Figure 2: Motor response to intravenous infusion of apomorphine (APM) at increasing rate before (top) and after (bottom) a seven-day period of levodopa 'drug holiday'. There is a noticeable increase in the duration of the 'on' response following cessation of the infusion.

Positron emission tomography studies assessing striatal binding to raclopride in patients with disease severity of different degrees have also failed to detect clear-cut receptor abnormalities associated with chronic treatment.[36] In the model of MPTP-induced parkinsonism in monkeys, expression of D_2 receptor mRNA in the striatum is increased after intoxication and reversed by levodopa to normal levels without modifying the expression of preproenkephalin.[37] The preliminary conclusion is therefore that gross abnormalities of dopaminergic striatal receptors are not the major problem associated with the origin of motor complications.

Two major pharmacodynamic mechanisms are presently recognized as playing a role in the origin of motor complications – (1) those derived from the different behavioral and biochemical effects caused by pulsatile and continuous dopaminergic stimulation, and (2) the changes induced by dopaminergic drugs to striatal GABA output neurons and basal ganglia circuits.

1. *Pulsatile versus continuous dopamine stimulation.* The development of the concept of continuous dopaminergic stimulation greatly contributed to the shift in emphasis from clinicopharmacologic to pharmacodynamic mechanisms. Thus, chronic infusion of dopamine agonists such as lisuride and apomorphine over many months and intravenous levodopa infusions for several days[31] ameliorated 'on-off' fluctuations and dyskinesias[38,39] to a degree not achievable with standard therapy. It was also shown that the motor response to apomorphine boluses separated by a time interval of less than 60 minutes was markedly reduced in fluctuating patients but was unchanged in *de novo* patients with milder disease severity.[40] Such results were also observed in rats with 6-hydroxydopamine lesion of the nigrostriatal pathway[41] and monkeys with MPTP-induced parkinsonism.[42] The development of tolerance to repeated dopaminergic stimulation explained why increased levodopa administration, in the usual pulsatile manner, is often associated with failure of individual doses.[43]

These clinical observations were paralleled by a series of elegant experimental studies showing marked differences in the biochemical effects elicited by pulsatile or continuous administration of levodopa and dopamine agonists.[44] Basically, it was found that reversal of the biochemical abnormalities induced by striatal denervation was not achievable with repeated, pulsatile stimulation. Continuous infusion of the same dopaminergic drugs had a more physiologic impact, partially restoring striatal abnormalities. Interestingly, a combination of pulsatile and continuous administration was found to be the best approach to normalize striatal biochemistry after dopaminergic denervation.[13,44] Exactly the same conclusion had been reached from clinical and pharmacologic observations in patients.[43,45]

Pharmacodynamic abnormalities in the motor response after chronic levodopa utilization are believed to appear mainly as a consequence of its pulsatile, discontinuous delivery,[14,30,45] which is far removed from mimicking the physiologic control of dopamine in the nigrostriatal system.[46] Thus, striatal dopamine release seems to occur *via* two different mechanisms – (a) a spike-dependent *phasic effect*, which is short-lasting (<50–100 ms) and highly restricted to specific striatal regions since the released dopamine is rapidly removed from the synaptic cleft; (b) a *tonic effect* lasting minutes to hours, which is independent of bursting neuronal firing in the substantia nigra compacta and may regulate widespread striatal regions. Tonic dopamine release is mainly regulated by the activity of glutamatergic corticostriatal afferents.[47]

The acute motoric effect of levodopa administration is mediated by the phasic mechanism of dopamine release while continuous treatment increases the number of tonically firing neurons in the substantia nigra compacta (SNc).[48] It is tempting to suggest that the latter mechanism underlies the long-duration response while the former provides the pharmacologic basis for the short-duration response.

The above experimental results indicate that pulsatile administration of levodopa and other dopaminergic drugs is not the ideal option in order to replace striatal dopamine depletion in PD. Treatment with a combination of a long-acting dopamine agonist and small amount of levodopa (25–50 mg 2–3 times daily) might be suggested as the most physiologic treatment to reduce the incidence of complications.[45,48]

2. *Basal ganglia output pathways.* The above reviewed mechanisms were centered on the action of dopaminergic drugs in the striatum. However, we believe that a comprehensive discussion of the problems associated with chronic levodopa therapy presently requires a basic knowledge of basal ganglia physiologic mechanisms. This is suggested in the first instance by a relatively simple clinical observation – patients with PD in advanced stages may get substantial control of their motor problems by surgical treatment.[45] Currently, pallidotomy and deep brain stimulation of the internal pallidum or subthalamic nucleus can provide a marked improvement of the major parkinsonian features and at the same time abolishing drug-induced dyskinesias. This occurs by modifying the characteristics of the dopaminergic pharmacologic response (Table 3) without acting at the level of the

Table 3: Effect of deep brain stimulation of the subthalamic nucleus or internal globus pallidum on the response to apomorphine in Parkinson's disease

n = 14	Pre-operation	Post-operation	P
Latency (min)	11 (5–30)	12 (5–20)	>0.05
Duration (min)	26 (15–70)	46 (22–90)	<0.01
Magnitude	37 ± 16	15 ± 10	<0.001

nigrostriatal system. Thus, surgery shifts the response pattern from a short-duration response towards a long-duration response. This effect of improved parkinsonism and reduced (or even abolished) dyskinesias is difficult to observe with the available drug treatments and requires a revision of the pathophysiological concepts and the origin of motor complications. We shall briefly summarize the most relevant points of a vast body of important advances in the understanding of basal ganglia functional anatomy and pathophysiology which has taken place in recent years.

The basal ganglia can be viewed as components of several larger corticobasal ganglia–thalamocortical circuits that are anatomically and functionally segregated in parallel. The 'motor circuit' is the most relevant in the pathophysiology of the cardinal signs (akinesia/bradykinesia, rigidity and tremor) of PD. This 'motor loop' includes the precentral motor areas (areas 4 and 6, supplementary motor area) and postcentral sensory fields (3a–b, 2, 1), which in a somatotopically-organized fashion project to the putamen. Detailed anatomochemical studies have shown that putaminal output reaches the medial globus pallidum (GPm) and the substantia nigra reticulata (SNr) through two different projections, which arise from separate putaminal neuronal populations. There is a 'direct' monosynaptic pathway from putamen to GPm that is GABAergic and colocalized with substance P (SP) and dynorphin, and an 'indirect' pathway which arises from GABA–enkephalinergic putaminal neurons and projects to the lateral globus pallidus (GPl). The work of Gerfen *et al.* in the rat[44] with 6-hydroxydopamine-induced lesions of the nigrostriatal pathway showed that dopamine inhibits the GABA–enkephalin neurons but excites the GABA–SP–dynorphin neurons. GPl sends a GABAergic inhibitory projection to the sensorimotor region of the STN and also to the GPm. The STN exerts a powerful excitatory drive onto the GPm and SNr, which in turn project to the ventrolateral and anterior thalamus *en route* to the premotor cortices. The output from the GPm (through the ansa lenticularis) and SNr to the thalamus is GABAergic and therefore inhibitory. The GPm also projects to the non-cholinergic portion of the pedunculopontine nucleus and the SNr connects with the superior colliculus and mesopontine tegmentum.[50] The latter brainstem nuclei project back to the basal ganglia predominantly upon the subthalamic nucleus, which receives cholinergic, glutamatergic and GABAergic inputs.[51] Movement facilitation is associated with phasic inhibition of tonic discharges of the GPm/SNr output nuclei. The opposite, that is, excessive discharges of the GPm/SNr, leads to movement inhibition (akinesia/bradykinesia).

Loss of dopaminergic neurons in the SNc reduces the normal inhibition (Figure 3a) of the nigrostriatal pathway on GABA–enkephalin neurons, which increases their activity, thus overinhibiting the GPi (Figure 3b). The inhibitory tone of GPi on the STN is reduced and the STN increases its activity well over the normal to excite the GPm/SNr. Hyperactivity of the STN and overexcitation of its efferent targets can now be considered to be the pathophysiological hallmark of the parkinsonian state (Figure 3b). Increased activity of GPm/SNr leads to excessive inhibition of the thalamus and reduced thalamo-cortical activation. This appears to account for the hypokinetic features of PD. Phasic oscillations and hypersynchrony in neuronal firing is also important and possibly responsible for tremor. It has

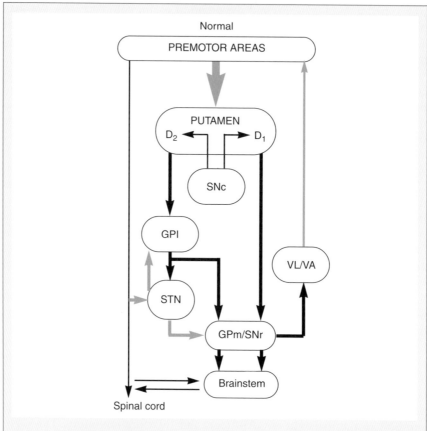

Figure 3a: Summary diagram of basal ganglia main circuits in the normal state. Black arrows = GABA – mediated inhibition; grey arrows = glutamate – mediated excitation.

been classically recognized that tremor cells are mainly recorded in the motor thalamus; however, phasic firing in synchrony with tremor in the limbs can also be recorded from the STN, GPm and even GPl. In parkinsonian monkeys and patients with PD, lesioning the GPm and the STN may completely abolish tremor, suggesting a critical role of the STN–GPm axis in the origin of tremor in PD.

According to the model, dyskinesias appear in association with a reduction in the STN–GPi circuit leading to decrease GPi inhibition of the motor thalamus, which results in excessive stimulation of cortical motor areas (Figure 3c). There are several problems in acceptance of this explanation. Dyskinesia is a global term which embraces several types of movement disorders (chorea, dystonia, tics, myoclonus, etc). It is unlikely that their origin could be explained by an identical pathophysiological mechanism. In particular, levodopa-induced dyskinesias have different clinical presentations.[7] The most common is chorea, which consists of irregular,

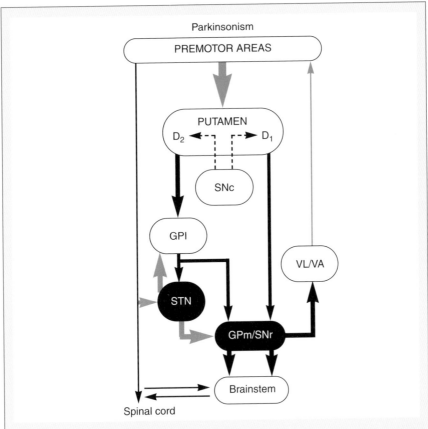

Figure 3b: Summary diagram of basal ganglia main circuits in the parkinsonian state. Hyperactivity in the subthalamic nucleus (STN)-globus pallidus internum (GPi) circuit is the hallmark of parkinsonism.

seemingly unpurposeful, continuous movements without a regular pattern of muscle activation. It has now been shown that functional inactivation or lesion of the STN leading to reduced activity of the GPi provokes choreic and ballistic movements in monkeys which are indistinguishable from those induced in MPTP monkeys treated with levodopa or a dopamine agonist.[52] Administration of apomorphine to parkinsonian monkeys which developed dyskinesias was associated with an increase in the STN 2-deoxyglucose (2-DG) uptake (a marker of synaptic afferent activity) indicating excessive inhibitory activity from the GPe and reduction in the rate of neuronal firing in the GPi.[53,54] It was therefore suggested that dyskinesia induced by levodopa, like chorea–ballism following lesion of the STN, results as a consequence of diminished activity of the STN–GPi pathway.[52] However, the origin of levodopa-induced dyskinesias may not be that simple. If dyskinesias are merely the result of reduced activity in the STN–GPi circuit leading to decreased GPi output, lesion of the GPi in a normal animal or person should

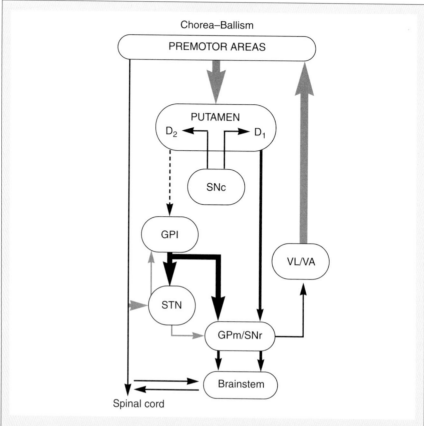

Figure 3c: Summary diagram of basal ganglia main circuits in the dyskinetic state. Lesion of the STN changes the pattern of activity in the GPi to induce chorea-ballism. A similar problem may be occurring in PD patients with levodopa-induced dyskinesias.

produce dyskinesias, and pallidotomy should not alleviate levodopa-induced dyskinesias. In fact, the opposite is the case. Inactivation of the GPi in monkeys by cooling or by muscimol infusion, and small lesions induced by restricted kainic acid injections, have never been associated with choreic–ballic dyskinesias but with mild dystonic posturing.[55] In patients with PD, lesion of the sensorimotor region of the GPi and inactivation by high-frequency electrical stimulation induce marked alleviation of the classic parkinsonian features and usually stop levodopa-induced dyskinesias.[49]

We have studied the effect of levodopa administration (for several months) on the expression of the messenger for glutamic acid decarboxylase (GAD mRNA) in MPTP monkeys who developed dyskinesias and in patients with PD. GAD67 mRNA levels in GPi and SNr were reduced in comparison with the parkinsonian non-treated monkeys but still fell within the normal range,[56] in keeping with the findings with 2-DG.[53] Patients with PD, chronically treated with levodopa and other drugs, showed values similar to those found in controls.[56]

The metabolic studies indicate that hypoactivity of the GPi, as judged with respect to the normal state, is not a feature of levodopa-induced dyskinesias, yet reduction in the STN–GPi/SNr activity with respect to the parkinsonian state is a general finding. This is possibly explained by a recent electrophysiologic study[57] in which choreic dyskinesias were induced in normal monkeys by injecting bicuculline into the GPe and GPi and neuronal activity was recorded during the occurrence of involuntary movements. A large number of neurons (81% in GPe and 79% in GPi) changed their firing characteristics coinciding with dyskinesias. Most neurons in GPe (85%) increased their firing rate and changed their pattern of discharge, thus, the fast spike activity became faster and the typical pauses longer but more regular. The effect of bicuculline on GPi activity was less homogeneous. Fifty nine percent of neurons increased their activity and 41% decreased their firing initially. The firing rate varied throughout the recording period and the total number of neurons showing an elevation in discharge rate during dyskinesias was 85%. An interesting observation was that around the same recording site in GPi, some neurons could decrease and others increase their activity while dyskinesias were present.

We presently believe that levodopa-induced dyskinesias are more likely to be the product of a change in the pattern of GPi output rather than a simple reduction in its firing rate. In other words, the origin of dyskinesias requires the GPi to convey a kind of erroneous signal to the cortex *via* the thalamus. This is precisely why pallidotomy stops levodopa-induced dyskinesias in PD.

THE ORIGIN OF LONG–TERM COMPLICATIONS –NEW IDEAS

Ideas regarding the origin of motor complications in PD have developed under the strong influence of levodopa therapy and its mechanism of action. The recent acquisition of more selective dopaminergic agonists[21] with a longer-lasting action and the upcoming results with surgical techniques will modify the insight into the origin of long-term complications in PD. In this final section, we shall first summarize the prevailing thoughts on the origin of motor complications highlighting their relative importance and will then discuss our new understanding of these problems.

Regarding the classic concepts, we can conclude with the following remarks:

- Peripheral pharmacokinetic factors play a secondary role in the pathophysiology of motor complications. They become of practical importance only after central problems arise.

- Central kinetic mechanisms are relevant in the origin of the 'wearing off' phenomenon as far as levodopa remains the major therapeutic approach, particularly if it continues to be delivered in the standard pulsatile manner. On the other hand, the introduction of slow-release levodopa or the early use of a dopamine agonist alone or in combination with a low dose of levodopa could limit the relative importance of presynaptic mechanisms.

- Pharmacodynamic factors play a paramount role in the pathophysiology of motor complications. The current belief is that the mode of dopaminergic stimulation (pulsatile *versus* continuous) at the receptor level and modifications occurring in the striatopallidal pathways are key factors in the development of complications.

The severity of the parkinsonian syndrome is directly dependent upon the degree of nigrostriatal denervation. The greater the dopamine depletion, the more severe are the parkinsonian features. At the neuronal level this is mediated by increased neuronal firing in the basal ganglia output pathway (GPi and SNr). Reduction in this excessive neuronal activity by pallidotomy or deep brain stimulation of the STN or GPm modifies the pharmacologic response to dopaminergic drugs without inducing changes in the dopaminergic nigrostriatal system. It is conceivable, therefore, that some of the problems associated with nigrostriatal denervation and chronic levodopa therapy are governed by downstream mechanisms, particularly those concerning the characteristics of neuronal activity in the basal ganglia output nuclei.

In conclusion, we propose the following pathophysiological mechanisms for the major features present in patients with motor complications:

- The duration of the motor response to levodopa is inversely correlated with the degree of neuronal hyperactivity in the STN–GPm circuit. Whether or not the level of hyperactivity in this pathway is solely regulated by striatopallidal (GPe) afferents within the 'indirect' circuit is open to question.[58] Dopaminergic fibers projecting directly onto the SNr, STN and GPm could also play a role.

- The magnitude of the response is determined by the severity of the basal 'off' state and therefore depends directly upon the intensity of SNc damage.

- The briskness and abruptness of the response is not explained by pharmacokinetic factors but is related to central changes leading to a steeper concentration-response curve.[59] We believe that modifications in the affinity state of dopamine receptors may explain this problem.

- Dyskinesias depend upon the existence of abnormal neuronal firing in the GPm. Levodopa-induced dyskinesias often consist of fragments of movements which resemble normal patterns that are abnormally released. They are related to non-physiologic and chronic dopaminergic stimulation which sensitizes subgroups of dopamine receptors. This leads to abnormal activity in the striatopallidal projections giving rise to aberrant neuronal signals from the GPm to the cortex *via* motor thalamus. The fact that dyskinesias occur more often in the most severely affected body part suggests that denervation plays an important role in their origin, possibly disinhibiting the glutamatergic corticostriatal projection.

References

1. Cotzias GC, Papavasilious PS, Gellene R. Modification of parkinsonism: chronic treatment with levodopa. N Engl J Med 1969; 280: 337–345.

2. Nutt JG, Woodward WR, Carter JH, Gancher ST. Effect of long-term therapy on the pharmacodynamics of levodopa. Arch Neurol 1992; 49: 1123–1130.

3. De Jong GJ, Meerwaldt JD, Schmitz PIM. Factors that influence the occurrence of response variations in Parkinson's disease. Ann Neurol 1987; 22: 4–7.

4. Muenter MD, Tyce GM. Levodopa therapy of Parkinson's disease; plasma levodopa concentration, therapeutic response and side effects. Mayo Clin Proc 1971; 46: 231–239.

5. Mones RJ, Elizan TS, Siegel GJ. Analysis of levodopa-induced dyskinesia in 51 patients with Parkinson's disease. J Neurol Neurosurg Psychiatr 1971; 34: 668.

6. Peppe A, Dambrosia JM, Chase TN. Risk factors for motor response complications in levodopa-treated parkinsonian patients. In, Narabayashi H, Nagatsu T, Yanagisawa N, Mizuno Y, eds, Advances in Neurology, Vol 60: Parkinson's disease: from basic research to treatment. New York: Raven Press, 1993: 698–702.

7. Luquin MR, Scipioni O, Vaamonde J, Gershanik O, Obeso JA. Levodopa-induced dyskinesias in Parkinson's disease. Clinical and pharmacological classification. Mov Disord 1992; 7: 117–124.

8. Grandas F, Luquin MR, Rodriguez M, Vaamonde J, Lera G, Obeso JA. Fluctuaciones motoras en la enfermedad de Parkinson: Factores de riesgo. Neurologia 1992; 7: 89–93.

9. Mayeux R. Mental state. In, Koller WC, ed, Handbook of Parkinson's disease. New York: Marcel Dekker, 1992: 159–184.

10. Marsden CD, Parkes JD, Quinn N. Fluctuations of disability in Parkinson's disease: clinical aspects. In: Marsden CD, Fahn S, eds, Movement Disorders. London: Butterworths, 1982: 96–119.

11. Quinn N, Critchley P, Marsden CD. Young onset Parkinson's disease. Mov Disord 1987; 2: 73–91.

12. Nutt JG. Levodopa-induced dyskinesias. Neurol 1990; 40: 340–345.

13. Bédard PJ, et al., this volume.

14. Obeso JA, Grandas F, Vaamonde J, Luquin MR, Artieda J, Lera G, Rodriguez ME, Martinez-Lage JM. Motor complications associated with chronic levodopa therapy in Parkinson's disease. Neurol 1989; 39: 11–19.

15. Riley DE, Lang AE. The spectrum of levodopa-related fluctuations in Parkinson's disease. Neurol 1993; 43: 1459–1464.

16. Hillan ME, Sage JI. Non-motor fluctuations in patients with Parkinson's disease. Neurol 1996; 47: 1180–1183.

17. Kulisevsky J, Avila A, Antonijoan R, et al. Acute effects of levodopa on neurological performance in stable and fluctuating Parkinson's disease patients at different levodopa plasma doses. Brain 1996; 119: 2121–2132.

18. Nausieda PA, Weiner WJ, Kaplan LR, Weber S, Klawans HL. Sleep disruption in the course of chronic levodopa therapy: an early feature of levodopa psychosis. Clin Neuropharmacol 1982; 5: 183–194.

19. Friedman JH, Lannon MC. Clozapine in the treatment of psychosis in Parkinson's disease. Neurol 1989; 39: 1219–1221.

20. Zoldan J, Friedberg G, Goldberg-Stern H, Melamed E. Ondansetron for hallucinosis in advanced Parkinson's disease. Lancet 1993; 341: 562–563.

21. Jenner P, Tulloch I, this volume.

22. Fahn S. Fluctuations of disability in Parkinson's disease: pathophysiology. In: Marsden CD, Fahn S, eds, Movement Disorders. London: Butterworths 1982: 119–126.

23. Nutt JG, Fellman JH. Pharmacokinetics of levodopa. Clin Neuropharmacol 1984; 7: 35–49.

24. Fabbrini G, Juncos J, Mouradian MM, Serrati C, Chase TN. Levodopa pharmacokinetic mechanisms and motor fluctuations in Parkinson's disease. Ann Neurol 1987; 21: 370–376.

25. Wooten GF. Pharmacokinetics of levodopa. In: Marsden CD, Fahn S, eds, Movement Disorders 2. London: Butterworth Scientific 1987: 231–248.

26. Papa SM, Engber TM, Kask AM, Chase TN. Motor fluctuations in levodopa-treated parkinsonian rats: relation to lesion extent and treatment duration. Brain Res. 1994, 662: 69–74.

27. Wooten GF. Progress in understanding the pathophysiology of treatment-related fluctuations in Parkinson's disease. Ann Neurol 1988; 24: 366–371.

28. Fabbrini G, Mouradian MM, Juncos JL, Schlegel J, Bartko T, Chase TN. Motor fluctuations in Parkinson's disease: central pathophysiological mechanisms. Part I. Ann Neurol 1988; 24: 366–371.

29. Mouradian MM, Juncos JL, Fabbrini G, Chase TN. Motor fluctuations in Parkinson's disease: pathogenetic and therapeutic studies. Ann Neurol 1987; 22: 475–479.

30. Chase TN, Baronti F, Fabbrini G, Heuser IJ, Juncos JL, Mouradian MM. Rationale for continuous dopaminomimetic therapy of Parkinson's disease. Neurol 1989; 39 (Suppl 2):7–10.

31. Mouradian MM, Heuser IJE, Baronti F, Chase TN. Modification of central dopaminergic mechanisms by continuous levodopa therapy for advanced Parkinson's disease. Ann Neurol 1990; 27: 18–23.

32. Colosimo, Merello M, Hughes AJ, Sieradzan K, Lees AJ. Motor response to acute dopaminergic challenge with apomorphine and levodopa in Parkinson's disease: implications for the pathogenesis of the 'on-off' phenomenon. J Neurol Neurosurg Psychiatr 1996; 60: 634–637.

33. Grandas F, Gancher ST, Rodriguez M, Lera, Nutt JG, Obeso JA. Differences in the motor response to apomorphine between untreated and fluctuating patients with Parkinson's disease. Clin Neuropharmacol 1992; 15: 13–18.

34. Bravi D, Mouradian MM, Roberts JW, Davis TL, Sohn YH, Chase TN. Wearing-off fluctuations in Parkinson's disease: contributions of postsynaptic mechanisms. Ann Neurol 1994; 36: 27–31.

35. Rodriguez M, Lera G, Vaamonde J, Luquin MR, Obeso JA. Motor response to apomorphine in asymmetric Parkinson's disease. J Neurol Neurosurg Psychiatr 1994; 57: 562–6.

36. Brooks DJ, this volume.

37. Herrero MT, Augood SJ, Asensi H, et al. Effects of levodopa therapy on dopamine D_2 receptor mRNA expression in the striatum of MPTP-intoxicated parkinsonian monkeys. Mol Brain Res 1996, 42: 149–155.

38. Vaamonde J, Luquin MR, Obeso JA. Subcutaneous lisuride infusion in Parkinson's disease: response to chronic administration in 34 patients. Brain 1991; 114: 601–614.

39. Kempster PA, Frankel JP, Stern GM, Lees AJ. Comparison of motor response to apomorphine and levodopa in Parkinson's disease. J Neurol Neurosurg Psychiatr 1990; 53: 1004–1007.

40. Grandas F, Obeso JA. Motor response following repeated apomorphine administration is reduced in Parkinson's disease. Clin Neuropharmacol 1989; 12: 14–22.

41. Castro R, Abreu P, Calzadilla CH, Rodríguez M. Increased or decreased locomotor response in rats following

repeated administration of apomorphine depends on dosage interval. Psychopharmacol 1986; 85: 333–339.

42. Luquin MR, Laguna J, Herrero MT, Obeso JA. Behavioral tolerance to repeated apomorphine administration in parkinsonian monkeys. J Neurol Sci 1993; 114: 40–44.

43. Obeso JA, Luquin MR, Grandas F, Vaamonde J, Laguna J, Martinez-Lage JM. Motor response to repeated dopaminergic stimulation in Parkinson's disease. Clin Neuropharmacol 1992; 15: 75–79.

44. Gerfen CR, this volume.

45. Obeso JA, Grandas F, Herrero MT, Horowski R. The role of pulsatile *versus* continuous dopamine receptor stimulation for functional recovery in Parkinson's disease. Eur J Neurosci 1994; 6: 889–897.

46. Grace AA. Phasic *versus* tonic dopamine release and the modulation of dopamine system responsivity: a hypothesis for the etiology of schizophrenia. Neurosci 1991; 41: 1–24.

47. Calabresi P, Mercuri NB, Sancesario G, Bernardi G. Electrophysiology of dopamine-denervated striatal neurons. Brain 1993; 116: 443–452.

48. Harden G, Grace A. Activation of dopamine cell firing by repeated levodopa administration to dopamine-depleted rats: its potential role in mediating the therapeutic response to levodopa treatment. J Neurosci 1995; 15: 6157–6166.

49. Obeso JA, Guridi J, DeLong M. Surgery for Parkinson's disease. J Neurol Neurosurg Psychiatr 1997; 62: 2–8.

50. Scarnati E. The pedunculopontine nucleus and related structures: Functional organization. In, Obeso JA, DeLong MR, Ohye Ch, Marsden CD, eds, The basal ganglia and surgical treatment of Parkinson's disease. Adv Neurol. New York: Raven Press, in press.

51. Bevan MD, Bolam JP. Cholinergic, GABAergic and glutamate-enriched inputs from the mesopontine tegmentum to the subthalamic nucleus in the rat. Neurosci 1995; 15: 7105–7120.

52. Crossman AR. A hypothesis on the pathophysiological mechanisms that underlie levodopa or dopamine agonist-induced dyskinesia in Parkinson's disease. Mov Disord 1990; 5: 100–108.

53. Mitchell JJ, Boyce S, Sambrook MA, Crossman AR. A 2-deoxyglucose study of the effects of dopamine agonists on the parkinsonian primate brain. Implications for the neuronal mechanisms that mediate dopamine agonist-induced dyskinesia. Brain 1992; 115: 809–824.

54. Filion M, Tremblay L, Bédard PJ. Effects of dopamine agonists on the spontaneous activity of globus pallidus neurons in monkeys with MPTP-induced parkinsonism. Brain Res 1991; 547: 152–161.

55. DeLong MR, Georgopoulos AP. Motor functions of the basal ganglia. In, Handbook of Physiology. The nervous system II. Chapter 21: 1017–1061.

56. Herrero MT, Levy R, Ruberg M, Luquin MR, Villares J, Guillen J, Faucheux B, Javoy-Agid F, Guridi J, Agid Y, Obeso JA, Hirsch EC. Consequence of nigrostriatal denervation and levodopa therapy on the expression of glutamic acid decarboxylase messenger RNA in the pallidum. Neurol 1996; 47: 219–224.

57. Matsumura M, Tremblay L, Richard H, Filion M. Activity of pallidal neurons in the monkey during dyskinesia induced by injection of bicuculline in the external pallidum. Neurosci 1994; 73: 59–70.

58. Levy R, Hazrati N, Herrero MT, Vila M, Hassani OK, Mouroux M, Ruberg M, Asensi H, Agid Y, Féger J, Obeso JA, Parent A, Hirsch EC. Re-evaluation of the functional anatomy of the basal ganglia in normal and parkinsonian states. Neurosci 1997, 76: 335–343.

59. Nutt JG, Holford N. The response to levodopa in Parkinson's disease: imposing pharmacological law and order. Ann Neurol 1996; 39: 561–573.

DISCUSSION

Olanow: The benefits of chronic subthalamic nucleus (STN) stimulation in our patients is similar to what you have shown with pharmacologic challenge. We have shown improvement in the 'off' state but not in the 'on' state. When we induced the 'on' state with drug or with stimulation without drug, they were virtually identical, paralleling what you have shown. I think these observations make an interesting argument as to what may be the mechanism of the short-duration motor fluctuations.

Sanchez-Ramos: When you stimulate the STN, do you see any dyskinesias akin to an STN lesion ?

Obeso: You may, but the dyskinesias induced by STN stimulation resemble levodopa-induced dyskinesia and not hemiballism. However, bear in mind that an STN lesion in a normal subject presumably occurs in the setting of normal basal ganglia circuitry which is not the case in PD. The STN is clearly able to induce dyskinesias in normal and parkinsonian patients, but the threshold in the parkinsonian patient is much higher. In other words, a bigger lesion or a more intensive current is required to induce dyskinesia in parkinsonism than in a normal individual. In this regard, it is interesting to speculate that the reduction in dyskinesia seen with pallidotomy may be due to damage to a specific STN-pallidal circuit.

Olanow: However, it is still not clear which fibers are being damaged with GPi pallidotomy.

Obeso: That is correct, but I suspect that within the GPi there are specific regions which are responsible for dyskinesias.

Tolosa: It seems to me that what you have shown is that by stimulating the GPi or STN, the parkinsonian disability is eliminated on the contralateral side. If this is maintained, the patient remains in an 'on' state and no fluctuations are seen. I did not understand your conclusions because I thought that disease fluctuations were related to disease severity, and that you have merely normalized the circuitry so that no fluctuations are possible.

Obeso: I think you did understand the point. With stimulation of these target regions, the severity of the 'off' state is much reduced and therefore the magnitude of the motor fluctuation is diminished or abolished. In other words, if the baseline severity is reduced, so too is the magnitude of the motor fluctuation. With pharmacologic therapies, 'on' responses can be induced but if there is reduced central storage, the duration of benefit is minimal. In contrast, with electrical stimulation, one can maintain benefits for sustained periods of time.

Obeso: The storage hypothesis focused on the duration of the levodopa response but it should be evident that the motor fluctuation itself represents the magnitude of difference between the parkinsonian state when the patient is 'on' and 'off'.

Olanow: Nutt and I did a study in patients where we measured levodopa and its metabolites in the ventricles following an intravenous infusion of levodopa. In severe patients, the factor determining whether they were 'on' or 'off' was the threshold level of dopamine in the ventricle which probably reflects dopamine levels in the brain. The magnitude of 'on' was the same regardless of the degree of increase in levodopa concentration above threshold. The duration of the response depended on the duration of time that levodopa levels remained above threshold. This would argue in favor of the storage hypothesis.

Calne: I am still confused by this issue of the models. On the one hand, stimulation of the STN improves parkinsonism and induces dyskinesia, but on the other hand, there is a clear improvement in both with pallidotomy. The improvement in dyskinesia is even more striking than in the parkinsonism. This is difficult to explain by the model of the direct/indirect pathways. In pallidotomy, one can see where the lesions are on the MRI scan. Everything clinical has a degree of crudity but the issue of dyskinesia and parkinsonism improving together in pallidotomy is a fundamental problem and differs from that seen with all other therapies where improvement in one is associated with worsening in the other.

Olanow: I am not yet convinced that pallidotomy meaningfully improves parkinsonism and certainly it does not do this to the extent that it improves dyskinesia. The magnitude of improvement in parkinsonian features that has been reported to date is subtle and is within the range that can be seen with placebo. No controlled study of pallidotomy has ever been done and I think that we need to prove that the parkinsonism is in fact improved.

Calne: It will be difficult to do a controlled study on pallidotomy because the results are so striking. In our study which is in press, there is not much change in the 'on' phase but the 'off' phase is unequivocally improved.

Olanow: Based strictly on the published data, of which there are sadly very little, that case is not yet proven. In many studies it is far from clear that there has been any improvement. Caution is advised in taking the patient's word for whether they are feeling better, especially if their dyskinesia has gone.

Calne: I agree with what you say but you have the disadvantage of not being able to see our paper which is in press.

Obeso: I agree that the published data are not particularly impressive. We wrote a letter to *The Lancet* following publication of the Lozano paper to say that the changes in UPDRS could be considered within the placebo range, but the UPDRS is relatively insensitive to unilateral effects. We have data to show that several measures of movement time in the upper limb were improved by 70% in comparison to baseline. I do believe that pallidotomy has the capacity to improve both akinesia and dyskinesia.

Miyasaki: I should clarify that the first patients to receive pallidotomy in our center (Toronto) had severe PD and were wheelchair-bound. Thus they may have had a limited capacity to improve. Our later patients had less severe disease. Benefits seen in these later patients may have been inadequately represented in our publication because they were diluted by the less prominent benefit obtained in our original patients.

Calne: I think what I have is a *déjà vu* experience of the early reports of levodopa where people insisted on a controlled study.

Olanow: But they did a controlled study and showed that it worked.

Calne: Yes, but there was a long lag time. What I am trying to say is that if the study is definite enough, you do not need a placebo and you cannot do a placebo study for something like a pallidotomy.

Olanow: I agree, but the history of medicine is full of examples where doctors felt strongly that an intervention was effective but when subjected to critical evaluation, they proved to be of no therapeutic value.

Obeso: We all require more experience. I think that the results of bilateral stimulation of the GPi or STN will be more striking and will convince the unconvinced.

Rajput: Could you comment on the role of the NMDA receptor antagonist in dyskinesia? In a recent paper by Papa *et al.* there was improvement in dyskinesia in levodopa-treated monkeys with the introduction of an NMDA receptor antagonist. In my own studies, 25% of patients who have dyskinesia improve significantly with the addition of amantadine without changing the levodopa dose.

Obeso: NBQX was not particularly effective in our monkey model.

Jenner: Investigators in Manchester are manipulating glutamatergic systems. Amantadine is a very difficult drug to draw any conclusions from because it is a dopa reuptake blocker, a dopa releaser, and an NMDA antagonist.

Olanow: To add to our confusion, Papa's paper reported that the Lilly NMDA receptor antagonist had a U-shaped activity curve in the monkey.

Depending upon the dose, it either had no effect, some improving effect, or a worsening effect on the dyskinesia.

Rajput: Amantadine would not be acting as a dopaminergic or cholinergic agent to relieve dyskinesia. Anticholinergic agents have been used for a long time and they do not relieve dyskinesia. Dopaminergic agents give either no relief or worsening of dyskinesia. It must be NMDA antagonism or a mechanism that we do not yet know of.

Jenner: We have been looking at dopamine reuptake blockers, so we are manipulating endogenous dopamine release in MPTP-treated monkeys. We now have three compounds that are antiparkinsonian but which do not provoke dyskinesia in levodopa-primed animals. Dyskinesia can therefore be avoided depending on the mechanism of dopamine release. We have not yet performed these studies in combination with levodopa but are planning to do so.

CHAPTER TWO

A rationale for using dopamine agonists as primary symptomatic therapy in Parkinson's disease

C. WARREN OLANOW, MD, FRCP(C)

Department of Neurology, Mount Sinai School of Medicine, New York,
New York, USA

ABSTRACT

Levodopa is the gold standard for the treatment of Parkinson's disease (PD), and is the most potent antiparkinsonian agent currently available. Its long-term use is, however, complicated by the development of motor complications in the majority of patients. Moreover, levodopa may accelerate the rate of cell degeneration by promoting oxidant stress. In the search for alternative therapy, dopamine agonists have been shown to offer several advantages over levodopa as initial symptomatic treatment for PD. Dopamine agonists are associated with a reduced incidence of motor complications and recent studies suggest that they are antioxidants capable of inhibiting oxidant stress, and providing neuroprotection. The available clinical information supports an approach in which treatment of PD is started with dopamine agonists, and in which levodopa is reserved until such time as the agonist can no longer control parkinsonian features satisfactorily. While agonists lack the clinical potency of levodopa, comparable benefits with fewer side effects can be attained by using levodopa as an adjunct when the clinical efficacy of the agonist is insufficient. Controlled clinical trials to better evaluate issues such as the benefits of high dose dopamine agonist treatment, and neuroprotection in patients, are currently underway.

Levodopa combined with a decarboxylase inhibitor is the standard symptomatic therapy for Parkinson's disease (PD). However, chronic levodopa treatment is associated with the development of motor complications (motor fluctuations and dyskinesias) in the majority of patients (Table 1).[1] Direct-acting dopamine agonists that stimulate dopamine

Table 1: Problems with levodopa
• Associated with high incidence of motor complications
• Primes for development of motor complications
• Promotes oxidative stress
• May accelerate neurodegeneration

D_2 receptors have long been known to provide antiparkinsonian benefits and have been widely used in the treatment of PD. To date, they have been primarily employed as an adjunct to levodopa in patients with advanced disease who have already developed motor complications. However, there is increasing laboratory and clinical evidence to suggest that dopamine agonists offer advantages over levodopa in the treatment of early PD (Table 2) and should be considered as the initial symptomatic therapy.

Table 2: Advantages of dopamine agonists
• Associated with reduced incidence of motor complications
• Do not prime for development of motor complications
• Have antioxidant effects
• May provide neuroprotection

Firstly, there is substantial preclinical and clinical evidence indicating that dopamine agonists are associated with a reduced incidence of motor complications in comparison with levodopa. Secondly, there is a theoretical concern that levodopa, because of its potential to generate free radicals and other reactive oxidant species (ROS), might accelerate the rate of cell death in PD.[2] This is particularly alarming in view of the growing body of evidence implicating oxidative stress in the pathogenesis of PD.[3] Dopamine agonists permit a delay in the introduction of levodopa therapy. In addition, recent studies suggest that dopamine agonists are themselves antioxidants that can directly inhibit oxidant stress. Taken together, these observations suggest that it may be preferable to initiate symptomatic treatment of PD patients with dopamine agonists and delay the introduction of levodopa. This paper will review the evidence supporting these claims and provide a rationale for using dopamine agonists as primary symptomatic therapy for patients with early PD.

DOPAMINE AGONISTS AND MOTOR COMPLICATIONS

It has long been clear that chronic levodopa administration in PD patients is associated with the development of motor fluctuations and dyskinesias. After approximately five to 10 years of treatment, as many as 80% of PD patients suffer from these motor complications.[1] The precise mechanism responsible for dyskinesia and motor fluctuations is not known, although speculations have focused on both pharmacokinetic and pharmacodynamic mechanisms.[4–6] Current thinking suggests that the progressive degeneration of dopamine terminals that occurs with advancing PD causes a reduction in central dopamine storage and a diminished capacity to buffer fluctuations in the plasma concentration of levodopa.[7] Thus, fluctuations in plasma levodopa associated with the drug's short half-life are translated into fluctuations in striatal dopamine. This in turn causes dopamine receptors to be exposed to alternating high and low concentrations of dopamine, which results in motor fluctuations and postsynaptic changes leading to the development of dyskinesias.[8] In advanced PD, where there is little, if any, dopamine storage, factors such as dietary proteins or alterations in gastrointestinal transit time which interfere with levodopa absorption and its delivery to the brain[4] tend to aggravate motor complications. In contrast, dyskinesia and motor fluctuations can be attenuated by constant infusion of levodopa or other dopaminergic agents.[9–11] These observations suggest that dopamine agonists which have a longer half-life than levodopa may be less prone to induce motor complications.

Animal studies support this hypothesis. Bédard and colleagues were the first to demonstrate that levodopa induces dyskinesia more frequently in MPTP-treated monkeys than does the dopamine agonist, bromocriptine.[11] Both levodopa and bromocriptine provided comparable behavioral benefits in these monkeys. However, all (14) levodopa-treated monkeys rapidly developed dyskinesia while this complication was seen in only one of 10 treated with bromocriptine. Similar observations have been made by Jenner and colleagues.[12] They noted that in MPTP-treated common marmosets, dyskinesias were much less frequent and less severe when the animals were treated with bromocriptine or ropinirole than with levodopa. Dyskinesias developed within one to two days following treatment with levodopa, but were hardly seen at all in animals treated with bromocriptine or ropinirole. Again, motor benefits were comparable in all groups. It is likely that this potential to protect against the development of dyskinesia is, at least to some extent, dependent on half-life, as it is only seen with dopamine agonists having a relatively long half-life, such as bromocriptine and ropinirole, and is not seen with short-acting dopamine agonists such as PHNO or quinpirole.[13,14] Further, this phenomenon is not exclusively related to D_2 receptor stimulation as dyskinesia can be seen with short-acting D_1 agonists such as CY208243 but does not occur with the long-acting D_1 agonists such as SKF38393.

Interestingly, exposure to levodopa appears to prime for the development of motor complications. Thus, while bromocriptine or ropinirole do not induce dyskinesia in the MPTP-treated monkey, they will do so if they are administered following previous levodopa treatment. However, the dyskinesia associated with long-acting agonists in this situation are still less than those seen if levodopa treatment is maintained, despite both treatments providing comparable levels of behavioral control.[15,16] These findings have important implications for the treatment of PD. They suggest that exposure to even a single dose of levodopa may induce a sequence of events leading to motor complications. The precise mechanism whereby levodopa leads to these adverse events is not known but recent studies suggest that it may result from levodopa-related effects on preproenkephalin message in dopamine-lesioned animals. Dopamine lesions are associated with upregulation of preproenkephalin and downregulation of preprotachykinin. Levodopa normalizes levels of preprotachykinin but not of preproenkephalin, which remains elevated in animals experiencing dyskinesia. This contrasts with ropinirole treatment which normalizes levels of both and induces much less dyskinesia than levodopa.[12] Similarly, Gerfen *et al.* showed that D_2 agonists reverse the increased expression of enkephalin associated with dopamine lesions.[17] Interestingly, Jenner and his colleagues have recently shown that high doses of levodopa (80 mg/kg) can induce dyskinesia in some normal monkeys (unpublished observations). Preproenkephalin levels were increased in animals who developed dyskinesia but not in those who did not. These findings suggest that an increase in the message for the enkephalin peptide underlies the development of dyskinesia and may account for the fact that pulsatile administration of levodopa induces dyskinesia.

The severity of dopamine depletion and the manner in which levodopa is replaced may also influence whether the drug causes motor complications. As discussed above, patients with severe PD may no longer have sufficient numbers of striatal dopamine terminals to buffer fluctuations in the peripheral levodopa concentration. Thus, oral doses of levodopa can cause striatal dopamine receptors to be exposed to alternating high and low concentrations of dopamine with the risk of developing motor complications. In support of this concept, continuous infusion of levodopa or short-acting dopamine agonists causes fewer motor complications than pulsatile administration of these agents in both animals models and PD patients.[10,18] Continuous and pulsatile levodopa administration have been shown to differentially affect basal ganglia function,[9,19] with dyskinesia being more likely to occur with pulsatile than with continuous delivery. In contrast, dyskinesia rarely develops with long-acting agonists such as cabergoline.[20] The basis for this effect is not completely understood, but it appears that intermittent stimulation of dopamine receptors induces changes in early genes and peptides which lead to the development of dyskinesia. Dopamine agonists such as bromocriptine or ropinirole may be less likely to induce this phenomenon because, in comparison to levodopa, they have a longer half-life, more stable pharmacokinetics, and less dependence on central storage to buffer fluctuations in plasma concentration. Thus, in the denervated state, long-acting dopamine agonists or continuous administration of a dopaminergic agent may provide more physiologic stimulation of dopamine receptors than occurs with oral doses of levodopa.

These laboratory observations suggest that dopamine agonists may be less likely to induce motor complications in PD patients. Indeed, such clinical information as is available suggests that this is the case. Retrospective trials in

PD patients demonstrate that dopamine agonist monotherapy is associated with a lower incidence of motor fluctuations and dyskinesia than is seen with levodopa.[21,22] However, few patients can be sustained on dopamine agonists alone for more than one or two years. In the majority, efficacy wanes and additional treatment is required. Rinne popularized the view of utilizing combined therapy in which early PD patients receive treatment with both a dopamine agonist and levodopa.[23] Using this combined therapy, he reported that patients had comparable clinical benefit and fewer adverse events than patients treated with levodopa alone. Unfortunately, these studies were retrospective and open-label, and it has been argued that the case had not yet been made for recommending dopamine agonists as early therapy for PD.[24] More recently, Montastruc *et al.* performed a five-year, prospective, open-label study, and demonstrated that motor complications were indeed less frequent and occurred after a longer latency in patients randomized to receive bromocriptine plus supplemental levodopa compared to levodopa alone.[25] We had similar results in our five-year prospective, blinded study in which early PD patients were randomized to treatment with bromocriptine plus supplemental levodopa *versus* levodopa alone.[26] Clinical benefits were comparable in the two groups but adverse events were much less frequent in the dopamine agonist-treated group.

Thus, existing clinical and laboratory information suggests that dopamine agonists are less likely to induce motor complications than levodopa. As initial treatment with a dopamine agonist and subsequent supplementation with levodopa appears to be able to provide comparable clinical benefit and a reduced incidence of adverse events compared to treatment with levodopa alone, this would appear to be the preferred form of treatment. Furthermore, as laboratory studies suggest that exposure to even a single dose of levodopa may prime for the development of motor complications with subsequent administration of agonists, it may be preferable to utilize maximally-tolerated doses of a dopamine agonist before starting levodopa so as to delay the introduction of levodopa for as long as possible. Long-term prospective double-blind studies are required to confirm these hypotheses.

NEUROPROTECTION

A delay in the introduction of levodopa and the early use of dopamine agonists may also provide neuroprotective benefits. A body of evidence suggests that oxidant stress is involved in the pathogenesis of PD.[3] In this regard, there is concern that levodopa, through its conversion to dopamine, might accelerate neuronal damage in PD based on the capacity of dopamine to generate oxidative metabolites and oxidative stress.[2,27] In addition, levodopa can undergo auto-oxidation to form reactive oxidant species including semiquinones which can combine with glutathione to further reduce the already compromised levels of this important brain antioxidant.[28] Numerous *in vitro* studies have demonstrated that both levodopa and dopamine can be toxic to cultured dopaminergic neurons.[29–33] In particular, levodopa can induce oxidant stress as determined by a reduction in reduced glutathione (GSH),[34] and increases in oxidized glutathione (GSSG),[35] hydroxyl radical formation,[36] mitochondrial damage,[37] markers of lipid peroxidation[38] and oxidative DNA damage.[39] Indeed, levodopa might account for the widespread oxidative damage to DNA that is found in the brains of PD patients.[40] Levodopa does not appear to cause degeneration of dopamine neurons in normal rodents or humans,[41–43] but this may not be the case in PD where the SNc is in a state of oxidant stress and oxidant defense mechanisms are compromised. Indeed, levodopa has been shown to enhance dopamine cell loss in animals treated with MPTP or 6-OHDA.[44,45] Furthermore, Jenner and colleagues have shown recently that very large doses of levodopa can induce upregulation of glial fibrillary acidic protein (GFAP) in the SNc of normal monkeys, suggestive of levodopa-induced tissue injury (unpublished observations).

The possibility that dopamine agonists might be neuroprotective might thus be considered, based on their capacity to provide a levodopa-sparing effect by delaying the introduction of this medication (Table 3). In addition, however, a D_2 receptor agonist might also provide protective effects by stimulating D_2 autoreceptors on dopamine neurons that inhibit dopamine release and turnover. Recent studies indicate that this is in fact the case. There is reduced dopamine release and electrical firing when cultured dopaminergic cells are treated with the dopamine agonist pramipexole.[46,47] In addition, dopamine agonists have now been shown to have antioxidant properties and to be capable of directly scavenging the hydroxyl, superoxide, and nitric oxide radicals (Table 4).[46,48–51]

Table 3: Possible mechanisms of neuroprotection by dopamine agonists

- Levodopa-sparing effect
- Decreased dopamine release and turnover
- Direct antioxidant effects

Taken together, these findings suggest that dopamine agonists have the potential to provide neuroprotective benefits for PD patients. In tissue culture models, the dopamine agonists bromocriptine, pramipexole and pergolide have been shown to protect dopaminergic neurons from a variety of toxic stimuli including levodopa (unpublished observations).[52] *In vivo* studies also support a neuroprotective role for dopamine agonists (Table 4). In the rodent, bromocriptine protects SNc dopamine neurons from intraventricular 6-OHDA administration.[48] Further, Fischer rats fed a diet enriched with pergolide are protected from the age-related reduction of nigral dopaminergic neurons and have reduced byproducts of oxidative metabolism such as lipofuscin.[53]

There is very little clinical information bearing on the issue of neuroprotection in PD patients. In the Sindepar study, after one year of

Table 4: Evidence that dopamine agonists have antioxidant properties

In vitro

- Agonists scavenge hydroxyl, superoxide and nitric oxide radicals
- Agonists protect cultured dopamine neurons

In vivo

- Agonists protect SNc neurons from 6-hydroxydopamine
- Agonists protect against age-related degeneration of nigrostriatal neurons

treatment there was no difference in the rate of progression of the signs and symptoms of PD in patients randomized to receive Sinemet® *versus* bromocriptine.[54] In the Prado study, there was a higher mortality rate in patients treated with levodopa alone compared to those treated with bromocriptine plus lower doses of levodopa.[55] However, this study was not specifically designed to address the issue of agonist-related neuroprotection and long-term studies remain to be performed before it can be established that dopamine agonists alter the natural course of PD.

CONCLUSION

Levodopa is the gold standard for the treatment of PD but long-term management is less than optimal. While the drug is the most potent of the antiparkinsonian agents currently available, its long-term use is complicated by the development of motor complications in the majority of patients. Furthermore, there is concern that levodopa may promote oxidant stress and thereby accelerate the rate of cell degeneration. For these reasons, alternate strategies have been sought. One such approach is the use of dopamine agonists as primary symptomatic therapy. Dopamine agonists offer a number of advantages over conventional levodopa treatment as the initial symptomatic treatment for PD. Preclinical studies indicate that dopamine agonists with a relatively long half-life have a reduced propensity to induce motor complications in comparison to levodopa. Furthermore, it appears that exposure to even a single dose of levodopa may prime for the development of dyskinesia regardless of which drug is subsequently employed. This suggests that it might even be best to push dopamine agonists to maximal tolerated benefit before considering the introduction of levodopa. Additionally, there are now numerous laboratory studies demonstrating the potential of levodopa to induce neurodegeneration and of dopamine agonists to provide neuroprotection. For all of these reasons, using dopamine agonists as the initial symptomatic therapy and delaying levodopa until the agonist can no longer provide satisfactory clinical control is a rational approach to the treatment of patients with early PD. Indeed, on theoretical grounds, an argument could be made for maximizing the use of dopamine agonists and delaying the introduction of levodopa for as long as possible.

Clinical information is relatively lacking. Nevertheless, the available studies support an approach in which treatment is started with dopamine agonists and levodopa is reserved until such time as the agonist can no longer satisfactorily control parkinsonian features. Numerous trials have demonstrated reduced motor complications when treatment is initiated with a dopamine agonist. While agonists lack the clinical potency of levodopa, comparable benefits with fewer side effects can be attained by using levodopa as an adjunct when agonist treatment alone does not provide satisfactory clinical control. Trials of high dose dopamine agonists are few, but suggest that they are well-tolerated in many and can provide additional benefits in comparison to the low doses that are traditionally employed. There is little information on the potential of dopamine agonists to provide neuroprotection in patients. Controlled clinical trials to better evaluate each of these issues are either underway or anticipated in the near future. For the present, based on existing information, a treatment strategy employing dopamine agonists as primary symptomatic therapy and levodopa as an adjunct appears to be the best way of treating PD. Indeed, based on the potential of pulsatile administration of levodopa to induce motor complications, it might be preferable to introduce levodopa in a long-acting formulation coupled with a COMT inhibitor in order to try and simulate the benefits associated with continuous infusion of levodopa. This approach, starting with a dopamine agonist, has the advantage of (1) reducing the incidence of levodopa-related motor complications; (2) avoiding the priming effect of levodopa for as long as possible; (3) reducing the cumulative exposure to levodopa with its potential to generate oxidative metabolites over the course of the disease; and (4) providing putative neuroprotective effects.

REFERENCES

1. Fahn S. Adverse effects of levodopa. In, Olanow CW, Lieberman AN, eds, The scientific basis for the treatment of Parkinson's disease. Lancashire: Parthenon Publishing Group 1992: 89–112.

2. Olanow CW. A rationale for dopamine agonists as primary therapy for Parkinson's disease. Can J Neurosci 1992; 19: 108–112.

3. Jenner P, Olanow CW. Oxidative stress and the pathogenesis of Parkinson's disease. Neurol 1996; 47: 161–170.

4. Nutt JG, Woodward WR, Hammerstad JP, Carter JH, Anderson JL. The 'on-off' phenomenon in Parkinson's disease: relation to levodopa absorption and transport. N Engl J Med 1984; 310: 483–488.

5. Fabbrini G, Mouradian M, Juncos JL, Schlegel J, Bartko T, Chase TN. Motor fluctuations in Parkinson's disease: central pathophysiological mechanisms Part I. Ann Neurol 1988; 24: 366–371.

6. Nutt JG, Holford NHG. The response to levodopa in Parkinson's disease: imposing pharmacologic law and order. Ann Neurol 1996; 39: 561–573.

7. Woodward WR, Olanow CW, Beckner RM, Hauser RA, Gauger LL, Cedarbaum JM, Nutt JG. The effect of levodopa infusions with and without phenylalanine challenges in parkinsonian patients: plasma and ventricular CSF levodopa levels and clinical responses. Neurol 1993; 43: 1704–1708.

8. Chase TN, Baronti F, Fabbrini G, Heuser IJ, Juncos JL, Mouradian MM. Rationale for continuous dopaminomimetic therapy of Parkinson's disease. Neurol 1989; 39 (Suppl 2): 7–10.

9. Juncos JL, Engber TM, Raisman R, Chase TN. Continuous and intermittent levodopa differentially affect basal ganglia function. Ann Neurol 1989; 25: 473–478.

10. Blanchet PJ, Calon F, Martel JC, Bédard PJ, Di Paolo T, Walters RR, Piercey MF. Continuous administration decreases and pulsatile administration increases behavioral sensitivity to a novel dopamine D_2 agonist (U-91356A) in MPTP monkeys. J Pharmacol Exp Ther 1995; 272: 854–859.

11. Bédard PJ, Di Paolo T, Falardeau P, Boucher R. Chronic treatment with levodopa but not bromocriptine induces dyskinesia in MPTP-parkinsonian monkeys. Correlation with ^3H spiperone binding. Brain Res 1986; 379: 294–299.

12. Pearce RKB, Banerji T, Jenner P, Marsden CD. Effects of repeated treatment with levodopa, bromocriptine and ropinirole in drug-naïve MPTP-treated common marmosets. Br J Pharmacol 1996; 118 (Suppl): 37P.

13. Falardeau P, Bouchard S, Bédard PJ, Boucher R, Di Paolo T. Behavioural and biochemical effect of chronic treatment with D_1 and/or D_2 dopamine agonists in MPTP monkeys. Eur J Pharmacol 1988; 150: 59–66.

14. Gagnon C, Bédard PJ, Di Paolo T. Effect of chronic treatment of MPTP monkeys with dopamine D_1 and/or D_2 receptor agonists. Eur J Pharmacol 1990; 178: 115–120.

15. Gomez-Mancilla B, Bédard PJ. Effects of D_1 and D_2 agonists and antagonists on dyskinesia produced by levodopa in 1-methyl-4-phenyl-1,2,3,6-tetrahydropyridine-treated monkeys. J Pharmacol Exp Ther 1991; 259: 409–413.

16. Blanchet PJ, Bédard PJ, Britton DR, Kebabian JW. Differential effect of selective D_1 and D_2 dopamine receptor agonists on levodopa-induced dyskinesia in MPTP monkeys. J Pharmacol Exp Ther 1993; 267: 275–279.

17. Gerfen CR, Engber TM, Mahan LC, Susel Z, Chase TN, Monsma FJ Jr, Sibley DR. D_1 and D_2 dopamine receptor-regulated gene expression of

striatonigral and striatopallidal neurons. Science 1009; 250:1429.

18. Blanchet PJ, Grondin R, Bédard PJ. Dyskinesia and wearing off following dopamine D_1 agonist treatment in drug-naïve and MPTP-lesioned primates. Mov Disord 1995; 11: 91–94.

19. Engber TM, Susel Z, Juncos J, Chase TN. Continuous and intermittent levodopa differentially affect rotation induced by D_1 and D_2 dopamine agonists. Eur J Pharmacol 1989; 168: 291–298.

20. Grondin R, Goulet M, Di Paolo T, Bédard PJ. Cabergoline, a long-acting D_2 receptor agonist, produces a sustained antiparkinsonian effect with transient dyskinesias. Brain Res 1996; 735: 298–306.

21. Montastruc JL, Rascol O, Rascol A. A randomised controlled study of bromo-criptine versus levodopa in previously untreated parkinsonian patients: a three-year follow-up. J Neurol Neurosurg Psychiatr 1989; 52: 773–775.

22. Lees AJ, Stern GM. Sustained bromo-criptine therapy in previously untreated patients with Parkinson's disease. J Neurol Neurosurg Psychiatr 1981; 44: 1021–1023.

23. Rinne UK. Brief communications: early combination of bromocriptine and levodopa in the treatment of Parkinson's disease: a five-year follow-up. Neurol 1987; 37: 826–828.

24. Factor SA, Weiner WJ. Viewpoint: early combination therapy with bromo-criptine and levodopa in Parkinson's disease. Mov Disord 1993; 8: 257–262.

25. Montastruc JL, Rascol O, Senard JM, Rascol A. A randomised controlled study comparing bromocriptine to which levodopa was later added, with levodopa alone in previously untreated patients with Parkinson's disease: a five-year follow-up. J Neurol Neurosurg Psychiatr 1994; 57: 1034–1038.

26. Olanow CW, Alberts M, Stajich J, Burch G. A randomized blinded study of low dose bromocriptine versus low dose carbidopa/levodopa in untreated Parkinson patients. In, Fahn S, Marsden CD, Calne D, Goldstein M, eds, Recent developments in Parkinson's disease, vol. 2. Macmillan Health Care 1987: 201–208.

27. Spina MB, Cohen G. Dopamine turn-over and glutathione oxidation: implications for Parkinson's disease. Proc Nat Acad Sci USA 1989; 86: 1398–1400.

28. Ogawa N, Edamatsu R, Mizukawa K, et al. Degeneration of dopaminergic neurons and free radicals: possible participation of levodopa. Adv Neurol 1993; 60: 242–250.

29. Tanaka M, Sotomatsu A, Kanai H, Hirai S. Dopa and dopamine cause cultured neuronal death in the presence of iron. J Neurosci 1991; 101: 198–203.

30. Ziv I, Melamed E, Nardi N, Offen D, Barzilai A. Dopamine induces apoptosis-like cell death in cultured chick sympa-thetic neurons – a possible novel patho-genetic mechanism in Parkinson's disease? Neurosci Lett 1994; 170: 136–140.

31. Mytileneou C, Han S-K, Cohen G. Toxic and protective effects of levodopa on mesencephalic cell cultures. J Neurochem 1993; 61: 1470–1478.

32. Walkinshaw G, Waters CM. Induction of apoptosis in catecholaminergic PC 12 cells by levodopa. Implications for the treatment of Parkinson's disease. J Clin Invest 1995; 95: 2458–2464.

33. Michel PP, Hefti F. Toxicity of 6-hydroxydopamine and dopamine for dopaminergic neurons in culture. J Neurosci Res 1990; 26: 428–435.

34. Spencer JPE, Jenner P, Halliwell B. Superoxide-dependent depletion of reduced glutathione by levodopa and dopamine. Relevance to Parkinson's disease. Neuro Report 1995; 6: 1480–1484.

35. Spina MB, Cohen G. Exposure of striatal synaptosomes to levodopa elevates levels of oxidized glutathione. J Pharmacol Exp Ther 1988; 247: 502–507.

36. Spencer Smith T, Parker WD Jr, Bennett JP. Levodopa increases nigral production of hydroxyl radicals *in vivo:* potential levodopa toxicity? Neuro Report 1994; 5: 1009–1011.

37. Przedborski S, Jackson-Lewis V, Muthane U, Jiang H, Ferreira M, Naini AB, Fahn S. Chronic levodopa administration alters cerebral mitochondrial respiratory chain activity. Ann Neurol 1993; 34: 715–723.

38. Tanaka M, Sotomatsu A, Kanai H, Hirai S. Combined histochemical and biochemical demonstration of nigral vulnerability to lipid peroxidation induced by dopa and iron. Neurosci Lett 1992; 140: 42–46.

39. Spencer JPE, Jenner A, Aruoma OI, Evans PJ, Kaur H, Dexter DT, Jenner P, Lees AJ, Marsden CD, Halliwell B. Intense oxidative DNA damage promoted by levodopa and its metabolites: implications for neurodegenerative disease. FEBS Lett 1994; 353: 246–250.

40. Sanchez-Ramos JR, Overvik E, Ames BN. A marker of oxyradical-mediated DNA damage (8-hydroxy-2'deoxyguanosine) is increased in nigrostriatum of Parkinson's disease brain. Neurodegen 1994; 3: 197–204.

41. Hefti F, Melamed E, Bhawan J, Wurtman R. Long-term administration of levodopa does not damage dopaminergic neurons in the mouse. Neurol 1981; 31: 1194–1195.

42. Perry TL, Yong VW, Ito M, Foulks JG, Wall RA, Godin DV, Clavier RM. Nigrostriatal dopaminergic neurons remain undamaged in rats given high doses of levodopa and carbidopa chronically. J Neurochem 1984; 43: 990–993.

43. Quinn N, Parkes JD, Janoto I, Marsden CD. Preservation of substantia nigra neurons and locus coeruleus in patients receiving levodopa (2 gm) plus decarboxylase inhibitor over a four-year period. Mov Disord 1986; 1: 65–68.

44. Blunt SB, Jenner P, Marsden CD. Suppressive effect of levodopa on dopamine cells remaining in the ventral tegmental area of rats previously exposed to the neurotoxin 6-hydroxydopamine. Mov Disord 1993; 8: 129–133.

45. Ogawa N, Asanuma M, Kondo Y, Yamamoto M, Mori A. Differential effects of chronic levodopa treatment on lipid peroxidation in the mouse brain with or without pretreatment with 6-hydroxydopamine. Neurosci Lett 1994; 171: 55–58.

46. Carter AJ, Muller RE. Pramipexole, a dopamine D_2 receptor agonist, decreases the extracellular concentration of dopamine in vivo. Eur J Pharmacol 1991; 200: 65–72.

47. Piercey MF, Camacho-Ochoa M, Smith MW. Functional roles for dopamine receptor subtypes. Clin Neuropharmacol 1995; 18: 34–42.

48. Ogawa N, Tanaka K, Asanuma M, et al. Bromocriptine protects mice against 6-hydroxydopamine and scavenges hydroxyl free radical in vitro. Brain Res 1994; 657: 207–213.

49. Yoshikawa T, Minamiyama Y, Naito Y, et al. Antioxidant properties of bromocriptine, a dopamine agonist. J Neurochem 1994; 62: 1034–1038.

50. Clow A, Freestone C, Lewis E, Dexter D, Sandler M, Glover V. The effect of pergolide and MDL 72974 on rat brain CuZn superoxide dismutase. Neurosci Lett 1993; 164: 41–43.

51. Ogawa N, this volume

52. Carvey PM, Ling Z-D. The effects of pramipexole on mesencephalic-derived neurotrophic activity. Neurol, in press.

53. Felten DL, Felten SY, Fuller RW, Romano TD, Smalstig EB, Wong DT, Clemens JA. Chronic dietary pergolide preserves nigrostriatal neuronal integrity in aged Fischer 344 rats. Neurobiol Ageing 1992; 13: 339–351.

54. Olanow CW, Hauser RA, Gauger L, et al. The effect of deprenyl and levodopa on the progression of signs and symptoms in Parkinson's disease. Ann Neurol 1995; 38: 771–777.

55. Przuntek H, Welzel D, Blümner E, Danielczyk W, Letzel H, Kaiser HJ, Kraus PH, Riederer P, Schwarzmann D, Wolf H. Bromocriptine lessens the incidence of mortality in levodopa-treated parkinsonian patients: Prado study discontinued. Eur J Clin Pharmacol 1992; 43: 357–363.

DISCUSSION

Scarlato: Does levodopa normally produce free radicals ?

Olanow: Levodopa can undergo auto-oxidation to generate reactive oxidant species including semiquinones. These in turn can react with glutathione to further compromise levels of this critical antioxidant. In addition, levodopa can generate hydrogen peroxide and the cytotoxic hydroxyl radical by way of its decarboxylation to dopamine. So there is no doubt that levodopa can generate free radicals – the question is if it causes radical-mediated damage. In normal animals it does not, presumably because defense mechanisms are adequate and oxidant-mediated damage is avoided. However, this may not be the case in PD where there is increased iron, decreased defenses, and the substantia nigra is in a state of oxidant stress. The problem is even more confusing. In tissue culture, levodopa can induce degeneration of dopaminergic neurons if administered in high doses, but in low doses it causes upregulation of 'survival molecules' such as glutathione and renders these cells relatively resistant to otherwise toxic stimuli. The question is, what is happening in the substantia nigra of humans and, more specifically, PD patients? In normal animals, levodopa has not been shown to induce damage or degeneration to dopaminergic neurons. However, in animals deficient in glutathione or with 6-OHDA lesions, levodopa promotes degeneration of dopamine neurons. Furthermore, Jenner *et al.* have shown recently that monkeys receiving large doses of levodopa can develop dyskinesia and show upregulation of GFAP in the striatum and SNc, indicative of local damage. So, levodopa can generate free radicals and this is of particular concern in PD patients, but there is as yet no definitive evidence that levodopa adversely affects the course of PD.

Melamed: Levodopa is known to damage dopamine cells in tissue culture. In contrast, we have also found that low doses protect cells against exposure to otherwise toxic stimuli such as higher concentrations of dopamine. We do not know what concentration of levodopa is present at the level of the cell membrane but it might be that low doses of levodopa are protective rather than harmful in PD patients, and there is as yet no evidence that it accelerates the natural course of disease progression.

Olanow: You are right, of course. However, dopamine agonists can provide satisfactory clinical control in most patients with early disease and they have a reduced potential to induce motor complications. In addition, as I discussed in my paper, there is no evidence that dopamine agonists induce degeneration of dopaminergic neurons and there is evidence to suggest that they are neuroprotective in both tissue culture and animal models. Furthermore, the protective effects that are seen with low doses of levodopa appear to be a response to tissue injury as they can be eliminated by blocking its oxidative metabolism. For these reasons, it does not seem rational to introduce levodopa because of its putative neuroprotective effect. On the other hand, I would not be hesitant to introduce levodopa when dopamine agonists can no longer provide satisfactory clinical control.

Melamed: Is there any proof of accelerated degeneration of the substantia nigra neurons when a certain level of loss has occurred due to compensatory excessive firing of the remaining neurons, and increased dopamine turnover and free radical formation?

Calne: No such evidence is available and, in fact, I think the opposite occurs. Our PET studies demonstrate that with advancing disease, there is a deceleration in the rate of disease progression suggestive of a decline in the rate of cell loss. It is noteworthy that this slowing occurs in the face of continued administration of levodopa. Dr. Olanow's own transplant work also argues against ongoing oxidative stress or an adverse effect of levodopa. Here, nigral neurons are degenerating, but newly-transplanted cells survive and do not show features of oxidative damage despite continued treatment with levodopa and their residence within a parkinsonian brain. I think these observations support the notion that PD is due to a single event in which cells drop out over a prolonged period of time, rather than to an ongoing process such as oxidative stress or levodopa-mediated adversity.

Olanow: This is a fascinating area of debate and obviously the answers are not known. Still, there is a body of evidence suggesting that the nigra is in a state of oxidative stress[3] and if you can obtain comparable clinical control with reduced side effects by starting with an agonist and delaying the introduction of levodopa, this would appear to be the most logical strategy to pursue. The fact that this approach decreases the theoretical risk of enhancing oxidative stress with levodopa supports this approach, even if it ultimately turns out that levodopa is not directly toxic to dopaminergic neurons.

Rascol: In the Montastruc study, high doses of bromocriptine were given followed by low doses of levodopa. This approach was associated with a reduction in the frequency of motor fluctuations and dyskinesias. However, even in high doses, bromocriptine does not control symptomatic progression and levodopa is eventually required.

Bédard: The Montastruc study introduced a D_2 dopamine agonist early. When symptoms worsened, they supplemented treatment with levodopa. Using this approach, there was a reduced frequency and delay in the emergence of levodopa-related side effects. Still, many did occur. Why not introduce another D_2 agonist or a D_1 agonist after the initial agonist has ceased providing satisfactory benefit, thereby further delaying the introduction of levodopa?

Olanow: You raise a good point. If levodopa primes for the development of motor complications, then it may be best to exercise all possibilities before resorting to initiating levodopa. It is clear that agonists act differently in different individuals and may provide different levels of clinical benefit. The role of D_1 *versus* D_2 has not yet been worked out but the notion of trying different agonists before resorting to levodopa seems rational. By the same token, when levodopa is introduced, it may make sense to employ a long-acting formulation of levodopa coupled with a COMT inhibitor in an attempt to provide continuous dopaminergic stimulation of dopamine receptors based on preclinical evidence that pulsatile stimulation contributes to the development of motor complications.

Ogawa: I use multiple dopamine agonists in my practice. I have swapped from bromocriptine to cabergoline with very good effect. Then, when the patient got worse, I changed back to bromocriptine, again with good effect. Using this approach, the need for levodopa can be delayed for much longer in some patients.

Tolosa: Is it really worth going to all that trouble, rather than just giving patients levodopa from the onset of disability?

Olanow: In my opinion it is. As patients advance, disability is frequently the result of levodopa-related adverse events rather than an inability to respond to dopaminergic medications. If adverse events could be avoided or minimized, this would be of enormous value to many patients and they would have markedly diminished functional disability.

Stocchi: I also use dopamine agonists first and supplement with levodopa. But, in my experience, the waning effect is not due to the development of motor fluctuations or dyskinesia, in contrast to levodopa, but to a general decline in efficacy.

Melamed: The efficacy of bromocriptine may depend on the number of surviving dopamine neurons and their capacity to manufacture dopamine so as to provide necessary D_1 receptor stimulation. Preclinical studies indicate that both D_1 and D_2 receptors must be stimulated in order to have maximal dopaminergic effect. It is possible that the use of one or more dopamine agonists with D_1 and D_2 receptor stimulation profiles might provide an enhanced clinical response in the more advanced stages of the disease.

Rascol: It is noteworthy that if high dose bromocriptine has to be withdrawn because of adverse events such as psychosis, treatment with levodopa immediately causes 'on-off' fluctuations and dyskinesias. This suggests that it is the combination of disease severity and specific characteristics of levodopa that result in the development of these motor complications.

Sanchez-Ramos: In our studies, we have been able to substitute large doses of pergolide for levodopa in patients with advanced disease complicated by severe motor fluctuations and dyskinesias. These patients have enjoyed comparable clinical benefits with reduced motor complications. This suggests that levodopa plays a critical role in both the generation and sustenance of dyskinesias and motor fluctuations.

Leenders: Are dopamine agonists less well-tolerated in depression? What about the mortality issue?

Olanow: I know of no evidence to suggest that dopamine agonists are less well-tolerated in depression and some studies suggest that these drugs may have antidepressant effects. In my practice, if a patient has parkinsonism plus depression, I treat the parkinsonism first and the depression afterwards if it is necessary. In choosing the antiparkinsonian medication, I use whatever agent I would have used in the patient if they were not depressed and am not influenced by the depression. In contrast, if the patient has hallucinations or confusion, I prefer to use levodopa/carbidopa. With respect to the mortality issue, one study by Przuntek and his colleagues noted increased mortality in patients treated with levodopa compared to those receiving bromocriptine plus a lower dose of levodopa. They speculated that the increased deaths were due to cardiovascular effects but the specific mechanism responsible for the difference in the two groups was not elucidated. This issue has not been reported in other studies and requires further evaluation.

Obeso: If it is established that dopamine agonists are well-tolerated and do not induce motor complications, would there be an advantage in starting dopamine agonists at the time of diagnosis, not waiting until patients develop functional disability? In this way, one could maintain constant dopaminergic tone and possibly avoid downstream changes that occur as a result of chronic dopamine deficiency.

Olanow: That is an interesting comment. Dopamine deficiency is associated with disinhibition of the excitatory neurons originating in the subthalamic nucleus. They provide glutamatergic innervation to the GPi, SNr, brain stem and the SNc and could lead to excitatory damage in these structures. Benabid and his colleagues have recently shown that lesions of the STN protect against neuronal loss in the SNc secondary to MPTP administration. The early use of a dopamine replacement strategy would be expected to decrease firing in the STN and thereby possibly protect neurons in the GPi and STN. Because levodopa is associated with a high incidence of motor side effects which relates to the time of their introduction, most neurologists would be reluctant to consider such a strategy. However, if dopamine agonists can be safely administered and do not increase the risk of motor complications, then I think that the early introduction of these agents at the time of diagnosis is a strategy that should be considered and tested.

Basic Science Issues

Dopamine function in the striatum: implications for dopamine receptor agonist treatment of Parkinson's disease

CHARLES R. GERFEN, PhD

Laboratory of Systems Neuroscience, National Institute of Mental Health,
Bethesda, Maryland, USA

ABSTRACT

The loss of dopamine innervation of the striatum is a critical element of the movement dysfunction observed in Parkinson's disease (PD). Dopamine receptor activation results in altered gene regulation in subsets of striatal neural populations and the selective pharmacologic manipulation of dopamine receptor subtypes results in patterns of altered gene regulation reflecting the functional organization of the basal ganglia. The results of such studies demonstrate that (1) D_1 agonist treatment alone results in D_1 receptor-mediated increased gene expression in the entire population of direct projecting striatal neurons; (2) combined D_1 and D_2 agonists produce opposite effects on gene regulation in the 'direct' and 'indirect' neuron populations and (3) the potentiated response of 'direct' striatal projection neurons to combined D_1 and D_2 agonists compares with D_1 agonist alone. These results suggest that an effective pharmacologic treatment for PD would include a continuous D_2 agonist, supplemented with intermittent D_1 agonist (or levodopa) treatment.

The severity of movement dysfunction that results from the loss of dopamine innervation of the striatum in Parkinson's disease (PD) attests to the critical function of this neurotransmitter to basal ganglia function.[1] Recent advances in molecular biology have enabled studies that provide new insights into the dynamic modulatory role that dopamine plays in affecting basal ganglia function. The basis of such studies is that dopamine receptor activation results in altered gene regulation in subsets of striatal neuron populations identified on the basis of their connections and/or receptor subtype phenotype.[2] Selective pharmacologic manipulation of dopamine receptor subtypes results in patterns of altered gene regulation that reflect the functional organization of the basal ganglia. Altered levels of mRNAs encoding a variety of proteins and peptides within striatal neurons secondary to pharmacologic treatments may be measured with *in situ* hybridization histochemical techniques. Several fundamental features of striatal organization and dopamine's related role have emerged. First, the connectional organization of the basal ganglia displays the existence of separate striatal output systems, which themselves have antagonistic effects on basal ganglia output.[1,2] The two major families of dopamine receptors, the D_1 and D_2 subtypes, are differentially expressed by the two striatal output systems.[2,4] Second, the neuropeptides that co-segregate in neurons with the D_1 and D_2 receptor subtypes are oppositely affected by activation of these receptors.[4] Third, immediate early gene transcription factors in striatal neurons display rapid responses to dopamine receptor activation that provide further demonstration of the opposite effects of D_1 and D_2 receptor activation on striatal output systems.[5–7] Moreover, they also demonstrate intercellular interactions between striatal neurons in response to dopamine receptor manipulation, which underlie synergistic responses to D_1 and D_2 receptor co-stimulation.[7] Together, these findings suggest that dopamine modulates the relative activity of the two striatal output systems which in turn determines the output of the basal ganglia, which influences the frontal cortical areas involved in the preparatory functions of behavior.

Other experimental paradigms reveal the existence of adaptive mechanisms in the striatum that serve to modulate dopamine receptor-mediated function. For example, repeated administration of cocaine alters striatal dynorphin levels which results in diminished D_1 dopamine-mediated immediate early gene induction in the striatum in response to cocaine.[8–10] These results suggest that opioid mechanisms in the striatum normally function to blunt the response of striatal neurons to excessive dopamine receptor stimulation. Significantly, such mechanisms appear to be absent in the animals in which the nigrostriatal dopamine system is lesioned. A comparison of dopamine-mediated gene regulation in normal animals and animal models of PD provide several potential pharmacologic strategies to reverse or prevent the abnormal response of striatal neurons that result from dopamine depletion.

FUNCTIONAL ORGANIZATION OF THE BASAL GANGLIA

Dopamine function in the striatum needs to be considered in the context of the functional organization of the basal ganglia and its major nuclear complex, the striatum (Figure 1).[2,11] The striatum, which is composed of the caudate, putamen and nucleus accumbens, receives excitatory input from

Editors' note. This paper describes the anatomy of the basal ganglia system in the rodent. Note that in the primate, globus pallidus pars externa is equivalent to globus pallidus, and globus pallidus pars interna and substantia nigra pars reticularis are equivalent to the entopeduncular nucleus and substantia nigra in the rodent.

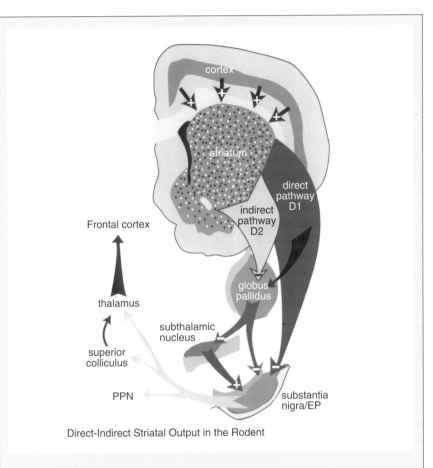

Direct-Indirect Striatal Output in the Rodent

Figure 1: Summary diagram of the 'direct' and 'indirect' striatal output pathways. Layer 5 cortical neurons provide excitatory input (+) to the striatum. The direct striatal projection is provided by D_1/substance P/dynorphin-containing neurons to the substantia nigra and entopeduncular nucleus, and to a lesser degree to the globus pallidus. The indirect striatal projection is provided by D_2/enkephalin-containing neurons that project to the globus pallidus (externa in primate). The globus pallidus in turn provides an inhibitory projection to the substantia nigra pars reticularis and to the subthalamic nucleus. The subthalamic nucleus provides an excitatory input to the substantia nigra reticulata. Thus, the 'direct' and 'indirect' pathways provide antagonistic input to the substantia nigra (the basal ganglia output). The GABA neurons in the substantia nigra reticulata provide an inhibitory projection to the superior colliculus, pedunculopontine nucleus (not shown) and thalamus. The thalamic nuclei receiving this output project to the frontal cortex. The entopeduncular (EP) nucleus in the rodent and the globus pallidus pars interna (GPi) in the primate are connected in a manner similar to the substantia nigra reticulata but are not shown.

[57]

most of the cerebral cortex. This input is organized both topographically and convergently, such that there is an overlap of projections into the striatum from cortical areas that are interconnected. Cortical input targets the major neuronal cell type in the striatum, the spiny projection neuron,[12] which constitute over 90% of the neurons in the striatum. Spiny projection neurons are composed of two main types,[13] those which project directly and those which project indirectly, to the GABAergic output neurons of the basal ganglia in the entopeduncular nucleus in the rodent or the internal segment of the globus pallidus in primates. The output neurons of the basal ganglia provide tonic inhibition to thalamic nuclei that project to frontal cortical areas, and to the superior colliculus and pedunculopontine nucleus. Striatal regulation of basal ganglia output is determined by the relative activity of the 'direct' and 'indirect' striatal output pathways. The 'direct' pathway provides inhibitory input to the SN/EP, which serves to disinhibit and thus facilitates activity in the thalamocortical connections.[14] The 'indirect' pathway, by way of connections through the globus pallidus and subthalamic nucleus, provides excitatory input[15,16] and thus increases inhibition of thalamocortical connections. While this summary of the functional organization of the striatum is oversimplified, it serves as a model for examining dopamine function in the striatum. Moreover, despite its oversimplification, the model appears to provide a reasonable explanation of the clinical akinesia of PD. According to the model, dopamine depletion leads to increased output of the 'indirect' striatal output system, increased pallidal output, consequent inhibition of thalamocortical connections, and ultimately parkinsonian akinesia.[1] Reversal of parkinsonian akinesia in both animal models and human clinical cases with lesions that target the 'indirect' striatal output system provide support for the model.[17]

The medium spiny projection neurons of the striatum may be subdivided into two types based on their projection targets.[13] One type, referred to as the 'direct' neurons, extends axons to the entopeduncular nucleus in rodents and the globus pallidus/substantia nigra pars reticularis complex in primates. The designation of these neurons is based on their direct projection to the output nuclei of the basal ganglia. The second type of neuron, referred to as the 'indirect' projecting neurons, provides an axon that projects to and arborizes extensively within the globus pallidus. The designation of these neurons is based on their multisynaptic connections. These include connections which run from the striatum to the globus pallidus externa, subthalamic nucleus, and globus pallidus interna/substantia nigra pars reticularis (entopeduncular nucleus in the rodent). Direct and indirect striatal projecting neurons are thus distinct neuronal populations. Estimates of the percentage of these two types of projection in the striatum approximate 50 % for each.[18]

Both 'direct' and 'indirect' spiny projection neurons utilize GABA as their primary neurotransmitter,[19] and thus provide inhibitory inputs to their targets.[14] However, these two neuron populations are distinct in their differential expression of a number of other neurochemical markers (Figure 2). Direct projecting neurons express the D_1 dopamine receptor

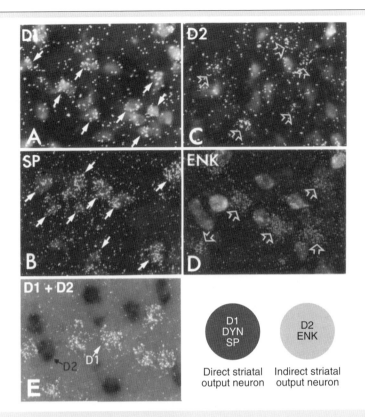

Figure 2: *In situ* hybridization histochemical localization of mRNAs to identify peptides and dopamine receptor subtypes in striatal spiny projection neurons. Neurons in the 'direct' pathway contain both D_1 and substance P mRNAs, whereas neurons in the 'indirect' pathway contain both D_2 and enkephalin mRNAs (A–D). In the rodent, neurons that project to the substantia nigra are retrogradely labeled with the fluorescent dye fluorogold (black-labeled cell bodies). *In situ* hybridization labeling of mRNA is shown by white grains. (A) D_1 dopamine receptor mRNA is localized in labeled striatonigral neurons (arrows). (B) Substance P mRNA is also localized in labeled striatonigral neurons (arrows). (C) D_2 dopamine receptor mRNA is not contained in labeled striatonigral neurons but in unlabeled striatopallidal neurons (open arrows). (D) Enkephalin mRNA is also contained in unlabeled striatopallidal neurons (open arrows). (E) Both D_1 and D_2 mRNAs are labeled in the same section, D_1 mRNA with an ^{35}S-riboprobe that is marked by white silver grains over neurons and D_2 mRNA with a digoxigenin-riboprobe that is labeled with a dark immunoreactive reaction. D_1 and D_2 mRNAs are segregated in separate neurons, with less than 5% of the entire population of striatal spiny projection neurons containing appreciable amounts of both receptor subtypes. Data from Gerfen *et al.*[4].

subtype and the peptides substance P and dynorphin.[18] Indirect projecting neurons express the D_2 dopamine receptor subtype, and the peptide enkephalin.[18] Although these relationships are certainly not absolute, they are remarkably accurate approximations. For example, it has been reported that more than 95% of D_1-containing neurons co-localize substance P mRNA, whereas over 95% of D_2-containing neurons co-express enkephalin mRNA.[20]

DOPAMINE-MEDIATED GENE REGULATION

Dopamine-mediated changes in gene regulation in striatal neurons reflect a range of cellular responses, from those that occur relatively immediately after receptor activation to those with a longer time course. The former are typified by the rapid induction of so-called immediate early genes, such as *c-fos*, which are often transcription factors responsible for the secondary induction of other genes.[21–23] The latter are typified by neuropeptides, which are themselves under transcriptional regulation.[24–26] Induction of immediate early genes is presumed to reflect, in some manner, synaptic-mediated change in the physiologic response of the neuron.[23] While this presumption is not always correct, as a working principle, changes in immediate early gene levels generally reflect an alteration in the physiologic activity of a neuron. In most cases, induction of immediate early genes requires relatively excessive receptor stimulation or an aberrant receptor response. Thus, while extremely useful, immediate early gene responses are necessarily interpreted in the context of the limitations of understanding cellular mechanisms responsible for their expression.

Longer term changes through gene regulation of other neurochemical markers also occur as a consequence of receptor-mediated mechanisms. Among these are changes in the level of expression of neurotransmitter receptors, signal transduction proteins, and neurotransmitter or neuropeptide levels. Such changes generally occur as a secondary consequence of transcription factor function, and as such often follow temporally the induction of immediate early genes. In many cases, these longer time course gene regulation effects are persistent, and may function as an adaptive response to excessive or aberrant synaptic neurotransmission.

Immediate early genes

Among the markers of rapidly-occurring gene regulation responses, the most commonly used is the induction of *c-fos*, which can be demonstrated with either immunohistochemical localization of the protein or *in situ* hybridization localization of the mRNA. These can be induced in the striatum with a number of dopaminergic pharmacologic treatments.[5–7,27–29] The basal level of expression of *c-fos* is relatively low and undetectable in most striatal neurons. Thus, induction of *c-fos* is a useful way to demonstrate an increase in the response of a striatal neuron. Pharmacologic treatments that result in *c-fos* induction include various psychostimulant drugs such as cocaine and amphetamine, D_1-receptor agonists, and D_2-receptor antagonists. In such treatment paradigms, the striatal neuron population in which c-fos induction occurs corresponds to the dopamine receptor subtype expressed by the neuron.[5,7,28] For example, D_1 receptor agonist treatment, in the dopamine-depleted striatum, results in c-fos induction in striatonigral projection neurons[5] which express the D_1 receptor subtype.[7] Conversely, blockade of D_2 receptors with neuroleptic agents results in the induction of c-fos selectively in striatopallidal neurons[27] which are part of the indirect pathway and express the D_2 receptor subtype.[7] Psychostimulants such as cocaine induce immediate early genes in striatonigral projection neurons through D_1-mediated mechanisms.[8,9,29,30]

Most studies of dopamine receptor-mediated induction of early genes in the striatum demonstrate D_1 agonist induction of c-fos in direct striatal projection neurons[5] and D_2 antagonist induction of c-fos in indirect striatal projection neurons.[27] Results with combined D_1 and D_2 agonist treatments are less straightforward. Several studies have demonstrated that when D_1 and D_2 agonist treatments are combined, there is a synergistic response with a greater number of c-fos positive striatal neurons than with D_1 agonist treatment alone.[31,32] One interpretation of these results is that D_2 receptor activation is necessary for a full D_1 agonist effect to be obtained.[31,32] Such synergistic responses are often described to involve mechanisms in which D_1 and D_2 receptors are co-expressed in the same neuron population.[33-35] It is also possible that the synergistic response involves extrastriatal sites of action as the drugs are administered systemically.[31]

We examined the question of D_1–D_2 dopamine receptor synergy in a two-part study.[7] In the first experiment, the level of mRNAs encoding two immediate early genes c-fos and zif268 were measured at the cellular level in a dose-response paradigm (Figure 3). In comparison to controls, results demonstrated that the number of striatal neurons displaying increased levels of c-fos mRNA to a given dose of the D_1 agonist SKF38393 (0.5–1.5 mg/kg) was increased when this treatment was combined with the D_2 agonist quinpirole (1 mg/kg). This result is consistent with those obtained with studies of the immunohistochemical localization of c-fos protein. In contrast, there was no change in the number of neurons expressing zif268 mRNA levels when treated with the D_1 agonist administered either alone or in combination with D_2 agonist treatment. However, the amount of labeling per cell was significantly increased with the combined D_1 and D_2 agonist treatment. The number of zif268-labeled striatal neurons showing increased levels was roughly half of the striatal neuron population. This finding suggests that D_1 agonist treatment alone (at doses of 0.5–1.5 mg/kg) results in an increase in the D_1-mediated immediate early gene zif268 in most of the striatal neurons that express the D_1 receptor, and that combined D_1 and D_2 agonist treatment further elevates immediate early gene mRNA levels in this same neuronal population.

A direct examination of the striatal neuron populations in which altered zif268 mRNA levels occurs was examined using combined localization of the mRNA encoding enkephalin (ENK), (a marker of the D_2-containing 'indirect' striatal projection population), and the mRNA encoding the immediate early gene *zif268*.[7] Enkephalin mRNA was labeled immunohistochemically and *zif268* mRNA was localized with a radioactive (^{35}S-UTP) ribonucleotide probe (Figure 3). The level of *zif268* mRNA expression was examined in the dopamine-depleted striatum and compared with the unlesioned striatum. In the unlesioned striatum, *zif268* mRNA was expressed in both ENK+ and ENK– neurons. Levels were slightly higher in ENK– neurons. In the dopamine-depleted striatum, ENK+ neurons displayed a significant increase in *zif268* mRNA levels while levels were significantly decreased in ENK– neurons. This result is consistent with the effects of dopamine depletion on peptides in these neurons.[4,36] We also examined the level of *zif268* mRNA in the dopamine-depleted striatum of animals treated with the D_1 agonist (SKF38393, 1 mg/kg). *zif268* mRNA levels were significantly elevated in ENK– neurons but unchanged in ENK+ neurons. This result is consistent with the notion that D_1 agonists selectively activate D_1 (ENK–) neurons. Notably, the entire population of ENK– neurons showed elevated *zif268* mRNA levels. Finally, the effects of combined D_1 (SKF38393, 1 mg/kg) and D_2 (quinpirole, 1 mg/kg) agonists was compared to that of D_1 agonist alone. In this case, the entire population of ENK– neurons displayed a further significant increase in *zif268* mRNA levels, whereas the entire population of ENK+ neurons displayed a significant decrease in *zif268* mRNA levels. This result suggests that the addition of D_2 agonist treatment causes a decrease in the *zif268* mRNA levels in ENK+, D_2-containing neurons. These experiments raise the possibility that the D_2 (ENK+) neurons exert an inhibitory influence on D_1 (ENK–) neurons. To date, no direct physiologic evidence of such inhibitory interactions has been demonstrated,[37] but axonal collaterals and synaptic contacts are well established.[12]

The following conclusions may be drawn from these studies in the dopamine-depleted striatum. First, D_1 agonist treatment alone results in D_1 receptor-mediated increased gene expression in the entire population of direct projecting striatal neurons. Second, combined D_1 and D_2 agonist treatment results in opposite effects on gene regulation in the 'direct' and 'indirect' neuron populations. Third, the potentiated response of 'direct' striatal projection neurons to combined D_1 and D_2 agonist treatment compares with D_1 agonist treatment alone, and might reflect interneuronal interactions rather than interactions between receptors located on the same neurons. This finding suggests that the effects of D_2 agonist treatment involves disinhibition of D_1-'direct' projecting neurons, such that the behavioral effects of such treatment may be mediated through the 'direct' striatal projection pathway.

Neuropeptide regulation

In addition to the rapid induction of transcription factors such as *c-fos* and *zif268*, manipulation of dopaminergic systems also induces robust changes in other gene expression that may be secondary to the immediate early gene

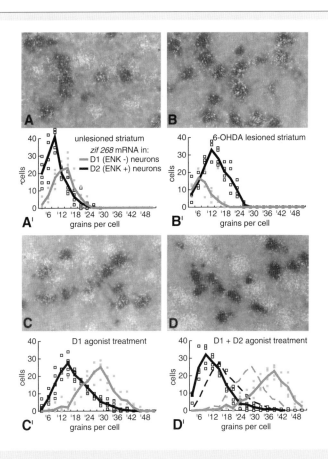

Figure 3: Photomicrographs and frequency distribution of the amount of *zif268* mRNA labeling in the striatum of animals with 6-OHDA depletion of dopamine in the striatum on one side and treated with D_1 and D_2 agonists. (A) Unlesioned and vehicle-treated striatum; (B) dopamine-depleted striatum, vehicle-treated; (C) dopamine-depleted striatum, D_1 agonist (SKF38393, 1 mg/kg); (D) dopamine-depleted striatum, D_1 agonist (SKF38393, 1 mg/kg) and D_2 agonist (quinpirole, 1 mg/kg). All drugs were administered intraperitoneally, and the animals killed 60 min following drug injection. Photomicrographs (A–D) show *zif268* mRNA labeling (^{35}S-generated silver grains, white) in sections labeled for enkephalin mRNA (black cells labeled with alkaline phosphatase reaction product). Frequency distribution graphs (A'–D') provide data on the average amount of *zif268* mRNA label per cell for enkephalin-positive cells, which are putative D_2-containing neurons (ENK+, individual cases marked as black squares, average marked as a black line), and enkephalin-negative, putative D_1-containing cells (ENK-, individual cases marked as gray boxes, average marked as a gray line). Data from Gerfen et al.[7]

responses. For example, mRNAs encoding the various neuropeptides display patterns that reflect the segregation of D_1 receptors to 'direct' and D_2 receptors to 'indirect' striatal projection neurons (Figure 4). Striatal dopamine depletion results in a characteristic elevation of enkephalin in D_2-containing striatopallidal neurons and a decrease in expression of dynorphin and substance P which are co-localized in D_1-containing striatonigral neurons. This lesion-induced elevation of enkephalin in D_2-containing neurons is selectively reversed by treating the animals with a D_2-selective agonist (quinpirole, 1 mg/kg/day). This same agonist has no effect on peptide levels in D_1-containing neurons. Treatment with a D_1-selective agonist (SKF38393) normalizes substance P and greatly elevates dynorphin mRNA levels in 'direct' projecting neurons without affecting peptide levels in 'indirect' projecting neurons. These results demonstrate that it is the segregation of D_1 and D_2 receptors on the 'direct' and 'indirect' striatal projection neurons which underlie the effects of dopamine depletion on peptide gene regulation in these neurons.

Several aspects of dopamine-mediated regulation of striatal peptides in the dopamine-depleted striatum are significant.[4,36] First, the manner in which a given dopamine agonist is administered is critical to the observed effect. Continuous treatment with a selective D_2-agonist (quinpirole 1 mg/kg/day) reversed elevated enkephalin mRNA levels whereas repeated acute treatment had no effect. On the other hand, selective D_1-agonist treatment (SKF38393 10 mg/kg once a day for 21 days) only altered peptide levels in 'direct' striatonigral neurons when administered as repeated acute treatments. These results suggest that D_2-mediated gene regulation requires ongoing occupation of the receptor, whereas D_1-mediated gene regulation is effective with acute receptor activation. Such effects may also have implications for the pharmacologic treatment of PD. Second, the regulation of the two peptides that are co-expressed in D_1 neurons, dynorphin and substance P, show substantially different dopamine-mediated regulation profiles. This demonstrates the existence of multiple gene regulatory pathways linked to the activation of a single receptor subtype. Of interest is the very large increase in dynorphin mRNA levels that occurs following repeated D_1 agonist treatment.

Adaptive responses: dopamine–opiate interactions

The robust increase in dynorphin mRNA levels following repeated D_1 agonist treatment is one of the most distinctive responses to dopamine agonist treatment in the dopamine–depleted striatum. The functional significance of this response is suggested from a comparison of the effects of D_1 receptor activation in the dopamine-innervated striatum. Whereas the D_1 agonist SKF38393 at doses of 1–10 mg/kg results in significant induction of immediate early genes and elevated dynorphin mRNA levels in the dopamine-depleted striatum, such treatment has little effect in the dopamine-innervated striatum. However, high doses of the indirect dopamine agonist cocaine (25 mg/kg), which prolongs the efficacy of released

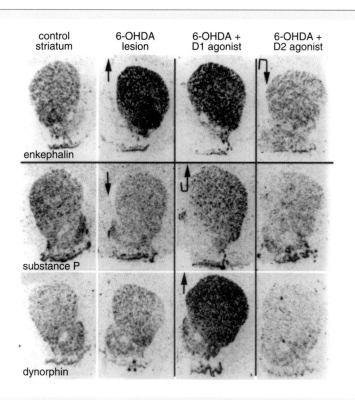

| | control striatum | 6-OHDA lesion | 6-OHDA + D1 agonist | 6-OHDA + D2 agonist |

enkephalin

substance P

dynorphin

Figure 4: Data from an experiment demonstrating D_1- and D_2-receptor selective gene regulation in 'direct' and 'indirect' striatal projection neurons. Images are of coronal sections of film autoradiographs labeled with *in situ* hybridization histochemical localization of enkephalin mRNA (top row), substance P mRNA (middle row) and dynorphin mRNA (bottom row) from an intact rat striatum (control striatum: first column), from a striatum depleted of dopamine (6-OHDA lesion: second column), from a dopamine-depleted striatum of an animal treated with the D_1 agonist SKF38393 (single daily injections of 5 mg/kg for 21 days), and from a dopamine-depleted striatum of an animal treated with a D_2 agonist quinpirole (continuous treatment with 1 mg/kg for 21 days). Dopamine depletion elevates enkephalin, decreases substance P and has little effect on dynorphin. Subsequent D_1 agonist treatment has no effect on enkephalin (contained in D_2-bearing neurons) but reverses the lesion-induced decrease in substance P and causes a large increase in dynorphin mRNA both of which are contained in D_1-bearing neurons. On the other hand, subsequent to dopamine depletion of the striatum, D_2 agonist treatment reverses the lesion-induced elevation of enkephalin mRNA in neurons bearing D_2 receptors, but has no effect on substance P or dynorphin in D_1-bearing neurons. Adapted from Gerfen *et al.*[4]

dopamine by blocking its reuptake via the dopamine transporter, elicits the induction of immediate early genes in the striatum of normal rats through a D_1-mediated mechanism.[8–10] This experimental paradigm provides some insight into the adaptive mechanisms that function in the normal striatum to modulate the response of striatal neurons to excessive dopamine receptor activation.

In a dose-response experiment, cocaine was administered at a dose of 20 mg/kg once a day for four days. Levels of *c-fos* and peptide mRNA were analyzed in the striatum on each of those days, 45 minutes after the drug administration.[8] Results demonstrated that after the first injection of cocaine there was a significant induction of *c-fos* mRNA in the dorsal striatum (Figure 5). A similar pattern and level of induction was also observed on the second day of treatment, but the level of induction decreased after the third and fourth days. The regional pattern of cocaine-induced *c-fos* induction after the first injection was complementary to the pattern of dynorphin mRNA expression in the striatum. That is, dynorphin mRNA, which is expressed in direct projecting neurons, has a higher basal level of expression on a per cell basis in the ventral striatum (including the nucleus accumbens) than in the dorsal striatal region in which *c-fos* mRNA levels were elevated. None of the other peptide mRNA levels measured, including enkephalin and substance P, displayed this complementary pattern. With successive cocaine injections, levels of dynorphin mRNA in the dorsal striatal region became elevated coincident with a decrease in *c-fos* mRNA.

These results led to the proposal that dynorphin functions to 'blunt' the cocaine-induction of *c-fos* and that repeated cocaine administration results in an adaptive response to increased dynorphin expression. As a test of this, spiradoline, an agonist of the kappa opiate receptor on which dynorphin is thought to act, was co-administered systemically with cocaine in drug-naïve animals. In this case, cocaine-induced *c-fos* in the dorsal striatum was markedly reduced. This result substantiated our proposed action of dynorphin in blunting the responses of striatal projection neurons to excessive dopamine receptor activation.

In a second study, we further clarified the role of dynorphin in modulating the response to cocaine.[9] Firstly, we characterized the *c-fos* response to cocaine. When the D_1 antagonist SCH23390 was infused directly into the striatum prior to a systemic administration of cocaine, the induction of *c-fos* and *zif268* mRNA was blocked. This demonstrated that the cocaine induction of immediate early genes in the dorsal striatum is a D_1 receptor-mediated response. This is expected, as cocaine treatment results in elevated dynorphin and substance P mRNA levels in neurons which express the D_1 dopamine receptor.[38] Secondly, whereas in the prior study, systemically administered spiradoline blocked cocaine-induced *c-fos* mRNA in the dorsal striatum, it could not be determined whether the action of the dynorphin agonist was occurring within the striatum. To examine this question directly, spiradoline was infused directly into the striatum. When administered in this fashion, it also blocked cocaine induction of immediate early genes in the dorsal striatum.

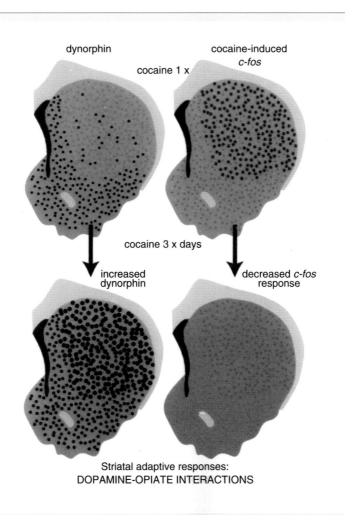

dynorphin

cocaine-induced
c-fos

cocaine 1 x

cocaine 3 x days

increased
dynorphin

decreased *c-fos*
response

Striatal adaptive responses:
DOPAMINE-OPIATE INTERACTIONS

Figure 5: Diagram of the regional response within the striatum to the indirect dopamine agonist cocaine demonstrating the functional role of dynorphin in modulating this response. The basal level of dynorphin expression shows a higher level in ventral and medial striatal regions. A single injection of cocaine induces the immediate early gene *c-fos* by a D_1-mediated mechanism in the dorsal lateral striatal region, complementary to the area showing high levels of dynorphin. Repeated treatment with cocaine (single daily injections of 30 mg/kg for three days) results in an increase in dynorphin levels in the dorsal striatal region, which has low basal expression, and a marked reduction of *c-fos* induction in this area, in which *c-fos* had previously been induced. These data suggest that dynorphin blunts the response of neurons to D_1 receptor stimulation. Further studies have shown that this effect is mediated through kappa opiate receptors. Data from Steiner and Gerfen.[8]

These results suggest a functional role for dynorphin in the striatum to modify the response of 'direct' striatal projection neurons to excessive D_1 receptor stimulation. Evidence in support of such a function comes first from the finding that the D_1-mediated cocaine induction of immediate early genes in the striatum occurs in the dorsal striatal region in which dynorphin is normally at a relatively low level, and does not occur in regions with constitutively high levels of dynorphin. Secondly, repeated cocaine treatment results in an adaptive response in the dorsal region that involves induction of dynorphin levels coincident with a decreased D_1-mediated cocaine induction of immediate early genes. Thirdly, pharmacologic treatment with a dynorphin agonist can mimic the adaptive response of elevated dynorphin levels by blocking D_1-mediated immediate early gene induction in the dorsal striatum.

Among the questions that remain is the mechanism by which dynorphin effects the D_1 receptor-mediated response. Dynorphin is thought to act primarily at kappa opiate receptor sites. *In situ* hybridization histochemical studies have identified kappa receptor mRNA at very low levels in striatal neurons, with the highest levels occurring in the ventral striatum.[37] The most abundant level of expression appears to be in dopamine neurons in the substantia nigra pars compacta. Thus, one possibility is that dynorphin acts presynaptically to limit the release of dopamine in the striatum. To address this, we conducted a study using D_1 agonist induction of immediate early genes in the dopamine-depleted striatum.[10] In this case, the intrastriatal injection of the kappa receptor agonist spiradoline was ineffective at decreasing the response to D_1 agonist induction of striatal immediate early genes. Moreover, repeated daily injections of the D_1 agonist SKF38393 (5 mg/kg) for four days did not reduce the level of induction of immediate early genes, although the level of dynorphin mRNA resulting from such treatments was considerably elevated. Thus, the adaptive response to excessive D_1 receptor stimulation that results in elevated dynorphin expression in the dopamine-depleted striatum does not produce the same attenuation of response as occurs to cocaine treatment in the normal striatum. There are several explanations for this difference. One is that in the normal striatum, dynorphin acts presynaptically to reduce dopamine release and thus blunt the response of D_1 receptor stimulation. This is consistent with the localization of kappa receptors on dopamine terminals. However, the situation is different in the dopamine-denervated striatum. It is possible that the supersensitive D_1 receptor response that results in the induction of immediate early genes is unaffected by dynorphin. What is apparent is that in the dopamine-depleted striatum the mechanisms that are normally in place to provide for adaptive attenuation of neuronal response to repeated D_1 receptor stimulation are ineffective.

IMPLICATIONS FOR PHARMACOLOGIC TREATMENT OF PD

A number of results from the studies of dopamine-mediated gene regulation have relevance to the pharmacologic use of dopamine agonists for the treatment of PD. Perhaps the most critical is the finding that dopamine oppositely regulates the 'direct' and 'indirect' striatal projection neurons through their respective expression of the D_1 and D_2 dopamine receptor subtypes. As this appears to be so fundamental to striatal function, it is worthwhile to summarize supportive experimental evidence.

First, the D_1 and D_2 dopamine receptor subtypes are segregated to the 'direct' and 'indirect' striatal projection neurons as indicated by both *in situ* hybridization localization of the mRNAs encoding these receptor subtypes[4,38,39] and from immunohistochemical localization of the receptor proteins.[40,41] Such expression patterns appear across species from rats to primates and in both the normal and the dopamine-depleted striatum. Given the estimate that the D_1 and D_2 dopamine receptor subtypes together account for over 95% of the dopamine receptor binding in the striatum,[41] it is reasonable to presume that most of the physiologic effects of dopamine in the striatum are a consequence of activation of these two main receptor subtypes.

Second, in the dopamine-depleted striatum D_1- and D_2-selective agonist treatments result in opposite effects on immediate early genes in 'direct' and 'indirect' striatal neurons.[7] In 'direct' projection neurons, D_1 agonists result in the induction of immediate early genes, whereas in 'indirect' projection neurons, D_2 agonist treatment results in a decrease in the expression of immediate early genes. While the primary effects of each receptor-selective agonist occur on the neurons expressing the appropriate receptor, secondary effects may also occur in neurons not expressing the activated receptor. For example, activation of the D_2 receptor results in an effect on D_1-expressing neurons, exhibited as a potentiated response to D_1 receptor stimulation. Such indirect effects suggest interactions between neuronal types, presumably through local axon collaterals.

Third, similar to the rapid response of striatal neurons to agonist treatment, longer term gene regulation effects are seen. These indicate that dopamine has opposite effects on D_1- and D_2-expressing neurons.[4,26,36] Among such effects are changes in neuropeptides expressed by striatal neurons. Substance P and dynorphin co-localize with the D_1 subtype and enkephalin with the D_2 subtype. Dopamine deafferentation of the striatum results in decreased substance P and dynorphin, which is selectively reversed with D_1 agonist treatment, whereas enkephalin is decreased by the lesion and reversed selectively with D_2 agonist treatment.

One of the more interesting results of dopamine agonist-mediated gene regulation is that the time course of administration of the drugs not only is critical to the effect obtained, but that the efficacy depends on the dopamine receptor subtype targeted.[4] This is evident from the finding that continuous treatment with the D_2 agonist quinpirole reversed elevated enkephalin mRNA levels resulting from dopamine depletion, whereas repeated daily injections were ineffective. The opposite was the case with D_1 agonist reversal of dopamine depletion effects on substance P and dynorphin. These findings have several potentially important consequences for the treatment of PD. According to the 'direct–indirect' pathway model, akinesia in PD is caused

[69]

by increased activity through the 'indirect' pathway. Such increased function in this D_2-expressing pathway is consistent with the elevation of a number of markers, including enkephalin, in 'indirect' striatal neurons following dopamine depletion. The finding that optimal normalization of such markers occurs with a continuous D_2 agonist treatment but not with either intermittent D_2 agonist treatment or with any schedule of D_1 agonist treatment suggests that a pharmacologic treatment involving continuous D_2 agonist administration should be considered as a therapy for PD. In the experimental study which led to this conclusion, the D_2 agonist quinpirole was employed. D_2 agonists which have a longer time course of action might be equally effective using a repeated administration injection schedule, provided that the D_2 receptors are continuously occupied. Gene regulation paradigms using the normalization of enkephalin mRNA levels in 'indirect' D_2 neurons would provide a means of measuring the effectiveness of the various D_2 agonists. Of interest is the finding that continuous levodopa treatment does not mimic continuous D_2 agonist treatment in reversing gene regulation in 'indirect' striatal neurons (Gerfen and Engber, unpublished results).

While continuous D_2 agonist treatment normalizes function in the 'indirect' striatal projection neurons, it is unlikely that such effects would be sufficient to fully restore normal striatal function, due in part to the 'direct' striatal neuron population. Intermittent repeated, and not continuous, treatment with D_1 agonists is required to reverse decreases in neuropeptide and D_1 receptor mRNA levels in 'direct' striatal projection neurons. Similar results are obtained with levodopa (Gerfen and Engber, unpublished results). Such treatments result in behavioral activation, measured as contraversive turning in unilateral dopamine-depleted animals. These results suggest that an effective pharmacologic treatment would include a continuous D_2 agonist treatment supplemented with intermittent D_1 agonist (or levodopa) treatment.

However, there are some additional issues regarding D_1 agonist activation of 'direct' striatal neurons in the dopamine-depleted striatum concerning the 'supersensitive' D_1 receptor response. D_1 agonist treatment normalizes substance P in 'direct' striatal projecting neurons, but it induces abnormally high dynorphin levels. Such long-term changes indicate that repeated activation of D_1 receptors in the denervated striatum might result in aberrant neuronal responses leading to motor complications such as dyskinesia.

Although there is currently no consensus as to the mechanism underlying dyskinesia, there is some evidence that it results from long-term effects of levodopa use. Gene regulation studies raise the possibility that dyskinesia is the consequence of repeated activation of D_1 receptors in 'direct' striatal neurons. Recognizing that a conclusive linkage between D_1 supersensitivity and dyskinesias has not been completely forged, there is sufficient evidence to at least consider this possibility. First, while D_1 supersensitivity might be defined in a number of ways, including increased behavioral responding or increased D_1 receptor number, a measure that appears to provide some indication of the cellular functional response is the induction of immediate early genes following acute treatment with a D_1 agonist. Second, in the dopamine-depleted striatum, D_1 agonist induction of immediate early genes is distinguished from that which occurs in the normal striatum. In the normal striatum, repeated excessive D_1 receptor activation results in adaptive responses that severely reduce the effect of acute D_1 receptor activation, as measured by the immediate early gene response. As discussed, such adaptation appears to involve dynorphin production as an adaptive response of 'direct' striatal neurons to excessive D_1 receptor activation. In the dopamine-depleted striatum this adaptive response appears to occur, but without effect, such that the level of dynorphin production continues to rise but the D_1 response of the neurons remains undiminished. This persistence of D_1 supersensitivity, or a lack of desensitization in the dopamine-depleted striatum to repeated D_1 agonist treatment, suggests that the normal adaptive mechanisms by which striatal neurons regulate excessive response to D_1 receptor stimulation are not operative. Thus it appears that once D_1 supersensitivity has developed, the striatum lacks the capacity to reverse these changes. From the perspective of developing dopamine agonist therapies for the treatment of PD, strategies should therefore be pursued that minimize the development of D_1 receptor supersensitivity. Based on this hypothesis, a suggested treatment regimen might be the use of a continuous D_2 agonist supplemented with a low dose of either levodopa or a D_1 agonist.

In conclusion, studies of dopamine receptor-mediated gene regulation have provided some insights relevant to the development of dopamine agonist therapy for the treatment of PD. First, dopamine oppositely regulates the 'direct' and 'indirect' striatal projection neurons through their respective expression of the D_1 and D_2 dopamine receptor subtypes. Second, the time course of administration of the dopamine agonists is not only critical to the effect obtained, but the efficacy depends on the dopamine receptor subtype targeted. Thus, optimal effects on 'indirect' striatal projection neurons require continuous D_2 receptor occupancy, whereas acute intermittent D_1 receptor activation is required for restoration of function of the 'direct' striatal projection pathway. Finally, the development and persistence of D_1 receptor supersensitivity is suggested to underlie the development of behavioral side effects that occur with long-term dopamine replacement therapy. This phenomenon appears to reflect the loss of normal adaptive mechanisms within the striatum, involving opioid peptide systems, that serve to regulate the response of striatal neurons to excessive dopamine receptor stimulation.

References

1. Albin RL, Young AB, Penney JB. The functional anatomy of basal ganglia disorders. Trends Neurosci 1989; 12: 366.

2. Gerfen CR. The neostriatal mosaic: multiple levels of compartmental organization. Trends Neurosci 1992; 15:133.

3. Kebabian JW, Calne DB. Multiple receptors for dopamine. Nature 1979; 277: 93.

4. Gerfen CR, Engber TM, Mahan LC, Susel Z, Chase TN, Monsma FJ Jr, Sibley DR. D_1 and D_2 dopamine receptor-regulated gene expression of striatonigral and striatopallidal neurons. Science 1990; 250:1429.

5. Robertson GS, Vincent SR, Fibiger HC. D_1 and D_2 dopamine receptors differentially regulate c-fos expression in striatonigral and striatopallidal neurons. Neurosci 1992; 49: 285.

6. Keefe K, Gerfen CR. Synergistic response to combined D_1- and D_2-dopamine receptor stimulation in striatum: immediate early gene response to intrastriatal drug administration. Neurosci 1995; 66: 903.

7. Gerfen CR, Keefe KA, Gauda EB. D_1 and D_2 dopamine receptor function in the striatum: co-activation of D_1- and D_2-dopamine receptors on separate populations of neurons results in potentiated immediate early gene response in D_1-containing neurons. J Neurosci 1995; 15: 8167.

8. Steiner H, Gerfen CR. Cocaine-induced c-fos messenger RNA is inversely related to dynorphin expression in striatum. J Neurosci 1993; 13: 5066.

9. Steiner H, Gerfen CR. Kappa opioid receptor inhibition of D_1 dopamine receptor-mediated induction of immediate early genes in striatum. J Comp Neurol 1994; 353: 200.

10. Steiner H, Gerfen CR. Dynorphin regulates D_1 dopamine receptor-mediated responsesin the striatum: relative contributions of pre- and postsynaptic mechanisms in dorsal and ventral striatum demonstrated by altered immediate-early gene induction. J Comp Neurol, in press.

11. Gerfen CR, Wilson CJ. The basal ganglia. In, Hokfelt T, Bjorklund A, Swanson LW, eds, Handbook of Chemical Neuroanatomy. Amsterdam: Elsevier, 1996: 381.

12. Wilson CJ, Groves PM. Fine structure and synaptic connections of the common spiny neuron of the rat neostriatum: a study employing intracellular injection of horseradish peroxidase. J Comp Neurol 1980; 194: 599.

13. Kawaguchi Y, Wilson CJ, Emson PC. Projection subtypes of rat neostriatal matrix cells revealed by intracellular injection of biocytin. J Neurosci 1990; 10: 3421.

14. Deniau JM, Chevalier G. Disinhibition as a basic process in the expression of striatal functions. II. The striato-nigral influence on thalamocortical cells of the ventromedial thalamic nucleus. Brain Res 1985; 334: 227.

15. Kita H, Chang HT, Kitai ST. Pallidal inputs to subthalamus: intracellular analysis. Brain Res 1983; 264: 255.

16. Kita H, Kitai ST. Efferent projections of the subthalamic nucleus in the rat: light and electron microscopic analysis with the PHA-L method. J Comp Neurol 1987; 260: 435.

17. Bergman H, Wichmann T, DeLong MR. Reversal of experimental parkinsonism by lesions of the subthalamic nucleus. Science 1990; 249: 1436.

18. Gerfen CR, Young WS. Distribution of striatonigral and striatopallidal peptidergic neurons in both patch and matrix compartments: an *in situ* hybridization histochemistry and fluorescent retrograde tracing study. Brain Res 1988; 460: 161.

19. Kita H, Kitai ST. Glutamate decarboxylase immunoreactive neurons in rat neostriatum: their morphological types and populations. Brain Res 1988; 447: 346.

20. Le Moine C, Bloch B. D$_1$ and D$_2$ dopamine receptor gene expression in the rat striatum: sensitive cRNA probes demonstrate prominent segregation of D$_1$ and D$_2$ mRNAs in distinct neuronal populations of the dorsal and ventral striatum. J Comp Neurol 1995; 355: 418.

21. Curran T, Gordon MB, Rubino KL, Sambucetti LC. Isolation and characterization of the c-fos(rat) cDNA and analysis of post-translational modification in vitro. Oncogene 1987; 2: 79.

22. Milbrandt J. A nerve growth factor-induced gene encodes a possible transcriptional regulatory factor. Science 1987; 238: 797.

23. Morgan JI, Curran, T. Stimulus-transcription coupling in neurons: role of cellular immediate-early genes. Trends Neurosci 1989;12: 459.

24. Hong JS, Yang H-YT, Fratta W, Costa E. Rat striatal methionine-enkephalin content after chronic treatment with cataleptogenic and noncataleptogenic drugs. J Pharmacol Exp Ther 1978; 205: 141.

25. Hanson GR, Merchant KM, Letter AA, Bush L, Gibb JW. Methamphetamine-induced changes in the striato-nigral dynorphin system: role of D$_1$ and D$_2$ receptors. Eur J Pharmacol 1987; 144: 245.

26. Young WS III, Bonner TI, Brann MR. Mesencephalic dopaminergic neurons regulate the expression of neuropeptide mRNAs in the rat forebrain. Proc Nat Acad Sci USA 1986; 83: 9827.

27. Dragunow M, Robertson GS, Faull RLM, Robertson HA, Jansen K. D2 dopamine receptor antagonists induce Fos and related proteins in rat striatal neurons. Neurosci 1990; 37: 287.

28. Robertson GS, Herrera DG, Dragunow M, Robertson HA. Levodopa activates c-fos in the striatum ipsilateral to a 6-hydroxydopamine lesion of the substantia nigra. Eur J Pharmacol 1989; 159: 99.

29. Graybiel AM, Moratalla R, Robertson HA. Amphetamine and cocaine induce drug-specific activation of the c-fos gene in striosome-matrix compartments and limbic subdivisions of the striatum. Proc Nat Acad Sci USA 1990; 87: 6912.

30. Cenci MA, Campbell K, Wictorin K, Björklund A. Striatal c-fos induction by cocaine or apomorphine occurs preferentially in output neurons projecting to the substantia nigra in the rat. Eur J Neurosci 1992; 4: 376.

31. Paul ML, Graybiel AM, David J-C, Robertson HA. D$_1$-like and D$_2$-like dopamine receptors synergistically activate rotation and c-fos expression in the dopamine-depleted striatum in a rat model of Parkinson's disease. J Neurosci 1992; 12: 3729.

32. LaHoste GJ, Yu J, Marshall JF. Striatal Fos expression is indicative of dopamine D$_1$/D$_2$ synergism and receptor supersensitivity. Proc Nat Acad Sci USA 1993; 90: 7451.

33. Bertorello AM, Hopfield JF, Aperia A, Greengard P. Inhibition by dopamine of (Na$^+$ + K$^+$) ATPase activity in neostriatal neurons through D$_1$ and D$_2$ dopamine receptor synergism. Nature 1990; 347: 386.

34. Piomelli D, Pilon C, Giros B, Sokoloff P, Martres M-P, Schwartz J-C. Dopamine activation of the arachidonic acid cascade as a basis for D$_1$/D$_2$ receptor synergism. Nature 1991; 353: 164.

35. Surmeier DJ, Eberwine J, Wilson CJ, Cao Y, Stefani A, Kitai ST. Dopamine receptor subtypes co-localize in rat striatonigral neurons. Proc Nat Acad Sci USA 1992; 89: 10178.

36. Jaeger D, Kita H, Wilson CJ. Surround inhibition among projection neurons is weakor nonexistent in the rat neostriatum. J Neurophysiol 1994; 72: 2555.

37. Mansour A, Fox CA, Meng F, Akil H, Watson SJ. k1 receptor mRNA

distribution in the rat CNS: comparison to k receptor binding and prodynorphin mRNA. Mol Cell Neurosci 1994; 5: 124.

38. Le Moine C, Normand E, Guitteny AF, Fouque B, Teoule R, Bloch B. Dopamine receptor gene expression by enkephalin neurons in rat forebrain. Proc Nat Acad Sci USA 1990; 87: 230.

39. Le Moine C, Normand E, Bloch B. Phenotypical characterization of the rat striatal neurons expressing the D_1 dopamine receptor gene. Proc Nat Acad Sci USA 1991; 88: 4205.

40. Levey AI, Hersch SM, Rye DB, Sunahara RK, Niznik HB, Kitt CA, Price DL, Maggio R, Brann MR. Localization of D_1 and D_2 dopamine receptors in brain with subtype-specific antibodies. Proc Nat Acad Sci USA 1993; 90: 8861.

41. Hersch SM, Ciliax BJ, Gutekunst C-Y, Rees HD, Heilman CJ, Uung KKL, Bolam JP, Ince E, Yi H, Levey AI. Electron microscopic analysis of D_1 and D_2 dopamine receptor proteins in the dorsal striatum and their synaptic relationships with motor corticostriatal afferents. J Neurosci 1995; 15: 5222.

DISCUSSION

Olanow: You indicate that the current model is not completely established to be accurate. Which components of the model do you consider to be factual and which elements are still open to question ?

Gerfen: A number of research groups have contributed to the development of the direct and indirect pathway model in its current form. Drs. Young, Penney and Albin[1] suggested that an imbalance in the output of these two pathways was responsible for movement disorders, based on the disinhibitory process in which pauses in activity in the output neurons result in bursts of activity that are related to movement. There is no doubt about the circuitry. However, the relationship of the output of the substantia nigra and the internal segment of the globus pallidus to actual movement is not so clear-cut. This is based on Hikosaka's work on eye movement,[2] in which pauses in activity in GABA neurons in the reticulata result in bursts of activity in the superior colliculus which correlate directly with saccades. However, when attempts have been made to look at similar activity in the generation of arm movements, the picture is not so clear and, in fact, some reports suggest increased activity in the output of the internal segment of the globus pallidus, rather than pauses in activity. Drs. Mink and Thach have suggested that the relationship of this model of basal ganglia outputs to the generation of most movements is unclear.[3]

Obeso: I think we have to get away from the simplistic concept that movement disorders are simply the consequence of too much (i.e. parkinsonism) or too little (i.e. dyskinesia) activity in the basal ganglia output system. The 'pattern' of neuronal activity may be a critical component. I have a question concerning the role of D_1 receptor stimulation in the primate model and in patients. I have never been convinced that the evidence supports its involvement in dyskinesia and I perceive a disparity between your work in the rat model and results in the primate model.

Gerfen: I would maintain that in terms of basic structure and function, there is almost no difference between the rodent and primate. There are differences, however, in terms of some of the more subtle responses, and this must be separated from the view that there are fundamental differences in organization. For example, patterns of D_1 and D_2 receptor expression are similar in the rat and the primate. I agree with you that the model is overly simplistic. It is important to emphasize, though, that dopamine appears to have different effects on these two separate populations of neurons. One pathway may not be dominant over the other; the pattern of activity and interactions between these cells may be more significant. That is why we are trying to generate paradigms to look at the interactions between D_1- and D_2-expressing cells. We find that local interactions within the striatum give rise to patterns of activity that are very complex in the normal animal. When dopamine is removed, much of the heterogeneity in the striatum is lost. It is possible that there are a number of mechanisms in the normal striatum that limit interactions locally. In the lesioned condition, the D_1 supersensitive response of these cells' local interactions that provide for greater heterogeneity may be lost.

Aquilonius: Why are the cholinergic interneurons always left out of your model and what are the effects of cholinergic agonists and antagonists in these models?

Gerfen: I have left the cholinergic interneurons out of the diagrams for clarity, but I agree they are very important. We have tried a number of experiments to examine the interactions involving cholinergic mechanisms and have found that these are very important for striatal function. The problem is that cholinergic drugs cause quick adaptation in these cells, so it has been difficult to isolate the cholinergic components in our gene regulation studies.

Jenner: We have just completed a behavioral study in MPTP-treated animals primed to show dyskinesia. Using a range of cholinergic and anti-cholinergic drugs, we can turn chorea into dystonia, and vice versa, so we can certainly manipulate these abnormal movements. Whether this is via striatal interneurons or through a cholinergic input from the pedunculopontine nucleus is another question. I also have problems with the monkey models in that the pre-protachykinin mRNA and substance P mRNA decrease and enkephalin mRNA increases after MPTP. Pre-protachykinin but not pre-proenkephalin can be normalized by treatment with levodopa.

Gerfen: We have obtained the same result in rats. Originally, we started with levodopa instead of a D_1 and D_2 selective agonist and found that in this model levodopa behaved like a D_1 agonist. In other words, continuous levodopa had no effect on levels of enkephalin or substance P, but discontinuous levodopa normalized substance P in the same way as did D_1 agonists.

Jenner: We have some normal monkeys which have been treated with very high doses of levodopa for three months and which have developed dyskinesias. In these dyskinetic animals, we cannot find any abnormality in pre-protachykinin mRNA but the pre-proenkephalin mRNA is elevated. In non-dyskinetic monkeys treated with levodopa, there is no change in either. I do not understand why both lesions and levodopa increase pre-proenkephalin. Do you know how this works ?

Gerfen: No. Cholinergic mechanisms are always a potential target for these drugs, so they could be a factor. Tachykinin receptors are expressed selectively by the cholinergic neurons, which is one potential pathway involving or invoking cholinergic mechanisms. Also, there are a lot of collaterals and synapses from one spiny neuron to another, and Bolam and others have shown that there are direct interactions between D_1 and D_2 cells.[4] Levodopa could, therefore, be having an effect on neighbouring neurons through either a cholinergic interneuron, other interneurons, or axon collaterals. It would be very interesting to look at changes in the levels of peptides, and also changes in response to expression of immediate early genes. Cocaine is useful in this regard because, using peptides as markers of altered levels of function in these cells, we found very high levels of dynorphin when cells were becoming decreasingly responsive. This was one of the first indications of a dissociation between gene regulation effects and probable physiologic activity in these cells.

Olanow: To what extent do you think that exogenous administration of levodopa influences what you see in contrast to normal receptor stimulation by endogenous dopamine? Studies in the rodent show that endogenous dopamine levels are increased by inhibition of MAO-A but not MAO-B while dopamine derived from exogenous levodopa is increased by inhibition of MAO-B. This suggests that they are metabolized and compartmentalized differently and therefore may have different affects on early genes.

Gerfen: Indeed. In trying to develop paradigms to look at D_1 supersensitivity, we have used reserpine and found that, while animals become behaviorally supersensitive, they do not show the supersensitivity in terms of responsiveness that we have seen. Likewise, when using levodopa, there appear to be confounding aspects to these paradigms.

Obeso: A problem we have with enkephalin *in situ* hybridization studies is that the monkeys remained parkinsonian for most of the time. They are given levodopa just once or twice, so there may be a lag in expression. Recent data show that D_2 expression is reduced by levodopa while enkephalin is not, which supports your findings and shows the dissociation between the behavior of the receptor protein and the peptide.

Gerfen: In a number of experimental paradigms we see a clear dissociation between an increase in peptides and physiologic alterations. Recently, we infused tetradoxin directly into the striatum of animals and continued to see marked receptor-mediated gene regulation effects when the cells were almost certainly not physiologically active. The cocaine paradigm is another indication of altered gene regulation in which there is dissociation of activity in cells from changes in particular gene levels. We should remember that gene regulation studies are not a good substitute for studies on physiologic activity. Both need to be done together.

Olanow: Your studies suggest that D_1 receptor stimulation in the dopamine-lesioned striatum of the rodent may induce dyskinesia. On the other hand, in MPTP monkeys dyskinesias appear to be primarily related to D_2 receptor stimulation. Would you comment?

[77]

Jenner: In levodopa-primed dyskinetic monkeys, repeated administration of a long-acting D_1 agonist (A77636) causes dyskinesias initially but these disappear with repeated stimulation. This does not occur with short-acting agonists.

1. Albin RL, Young AB, Penney JB. The functional anatomy of basal ganglia disorders. Trends Neurosci 1989; 12: 366–375.

2. Hikosaka O. Role of the forebrain in oculomotor function. Prog Brain Res 1991; 87: 101–107.

3. Mink JW, Thach WT. Basal ganglia motor control. II. Late pallidal timing relative to movement onset and inconsistent pallidal coding of movement parameters. J Neurophysiol 1991; 65: 301–329.

4. Yung KK, Smith AD, Levey AI, Bolam JP. Synaptic connections between spiny neurons of the direct and indirect pathways in the neostriatum of the rat: evidence from dopamine receptor and neuropeptide immunostaining. Eur J Neurosci 1996; 8: 861–869.

CHAPTER FOUR

PET studies on basal ganglia and cortical function in Parkinson's disease

DAVID J. BROOKS, MA, MD, FRCP

MRC Cyclotron Unit, Hammersmith Hospital,
London, UK

ABSTRACT

Three-dimensional ^{18}F-dopa positron emission tomography (PET) coupled with statistical parametric mapping now provides a sensitive means of quantitating not only the loss of nigrostriatal dopaminergic fibers in Parkinson's disease (PD) but also dysfunction of nigral and frontal dopaminergic terminals. In early PD, while nigrostriatal dopamine storage is impaired, anterior cingulate dopaminergic activity appears to be increased, subsequently normalizing. ^{18}F-dopa PET is able to detect the presence of bilateral dopaminergic dysfunction in hemiparkinsonian patients and preclinical disease in 30% of asymptomatic at-risk adult relatives in parkinsonian kindreds. This provides strong support for a role of inheritance in this disorder. Additionally, ^{18}F-dopa PET can be used to objectively follow the rate of disease progression and monitor the viability of transplants of fetal tissue. This opens the way for the use of functional imaging to determine the efficacy of putative neuroprotective agents, such as dopamine agonists. Finally, PET has been used to throw light on the in vivo pharmacologic changes underlying the development of treatment complications (fluctuations, dyskinesias) following exposure of PD patients to levodopa and has implicated abnormalities of opioid transmission.

Positron emission tomography (PET) provides a sensitive means of detecting and quantitating *in vivo* regional changes in dopaminergic and non-dopaminergic function in Parkinson's disease (PD). Current tomographs have a reconstructed resolution of approximately 4 mm and so are able to examine the function of individual brainstem nuclei and cortical areas. Conventionally, datasets of regional brain tracer uptake have been collected in 2D mode, that is, only activity in a given transaxial slice has been registered. Software is now available allowing PET data to be acquired in a 3D mode, so that all the activity in the brain volume can be detected simultaneously. Although this leads to increased levels of scatter, the pay-off is a six-fold increase in signal-to-noise allowing regions with low tracer uptake to be sampled far more sensitively with increased resolution. Additionally, the increased sensitivity allows scans to be converted from crude images of tracer activity to parametric maps of either ^{18}F-dopa influx constants (K_i) or ligand volumes of distribution (V_d) on a voxel-by-voxel basis.

Traditionally, region of interest (ROI) analysis has been used to determine regional brain levels of tracer uptake in PD and to compare these with normal controls. There are, however, a number of problems that arise when the ROI approach is employed. First, *a priori* assumptions have to be made about the shape and size of ROIs used to sample brain activity. In most studies concerning PD, circular or elliptical regions have been placed over or around the caudate and putamen. This difficulty can, in part, be overcome by co-aligning all functional images to MRI and using the latter to define ROI shapes. Brain orientation relative to the scanning plane may, however, vary from subject to subject and the co-alignment procedure inevitably introduces error. Second, *a priori* selection of the locations of ROIs has to be made – the striatum in the case of PD – as it is not feasible to analyze every cortical and subcortical area with an ROI approach. This means changes in dopaminergic function in extrastriatal regions may not be detected. Third, brain shape can vary significantly between subjects. Standardized ROI templates do not allow for this while the use of individually tailored ROIs results in non-uniform analyses.

An alternative way of analyzing the changes in dopaminergic and non-dopaminergic function associated with PD and its treatment is to use statistical parametric mapping (SPM).[1] Here, the whole 3D brain volume is considered without any requirement for *a priori* definition of ROIs. In essence, parametric images describing ^{18}F-dopa influx (K_i) or ligand volume of distribution (V_d) on a voxel-by-voxel basis are transformed into standard stereotactic space. Images of group mean tracer uptake with associated standard deviations are then generated. Such statistical datasets can then be used to compare mean tracer uptake in groups of PD patients and control subjects on a voxel-by-voxel basis. Alternatively, individual patient datasets can be compared with a control group dataset. The location of volumes of significantly altered K_i or V_d at preassigned thresholds (generally $p<0.001$ to avoid spurious changes arising from the multiple comparisons performed) is then displayed and the magnitude of these changes can be measured sampling the transformed or untransformed datasets. The SPM approach has the clear advantage that changes in regional function can be detected in brain areas that might not have been predicted. Its disadvantage is the requirement for stereotactic transformation of 3D datasets which reduces resolution and introduces variance.

THE PRESYNAPTIC DOPAMINERGIC SYSTEM IN PD

After its intravenous administration, ^{18}F-dopa is taken up by the terminals of dopaminergic projections over 90 minutes and converted first to ^{18}F-dopamine and then more slowly to the dopamine metabolites DOPAC and HVA.[2] The rate of striatal ^{18}F accumulation, measured with PET, reflects both transport of ^{18}F-dopa into striatal vesicles and its subsequent decarboxylation by aromatic amino acid decarboxylase (AADC). ^{18}F-dopa PET, acquired in conventional 2D mode, has shown that contralateral putaminal dopamine storage is reduced in early cases of PD when only one side is affected while caudate function is preserved.[3-9] In a number of these hemiparkinsonian patients, ^{18}F-dopa uptake is also reduced in the ipsilateral asymptomatic putamen[9] suggesting that PET is capable of demonstrating subclinical involvement of the nigrostriatal dopaminergic system.

It is well known that there is a strong dopaminergic projection from the midbrain tegmentum to prefrontal areas and that the substantia nigra is also rich in dopamine terminals. To date, however, ^{18}F-dopa PET used in 2D mode has failed to identify abnormal ^{18}F-dopa uptake in these extrastriatal areas in PD. Three-dimensional ^{18}F-dopa PET coupled with SPM has now been used to study early hemiparkinsonian patients.[10] SPM detected a significant reduction in mean ^{18}F-dopa uptake in the contralateral right putamen of seven hemiparkinsonian patients with left limb involvement compared to seven age-matched normal controls. In addition, reduced dopamine storage was also found in the head of the right caudate and in the asymptomatic ipsilateral left putamen (Figure 1a). Dorsal striatum was more affected than ventral striatum, emphasizing the selectivity of PD pathology. Surprisingly, increased levels of ^{18}F-dopa uptake were detected in the anterior cingulate cortex (Figure 1b). It is known that lesioning mesofrontal dopaminergic fibers with 6-hydroxydopamine in monkeys leads to a reciprocal increase in potassium-evoked dopamine release from the caudate.[11] It is, therefore, conceivable that as the nigrostriatal dopaminergic system degenerates in early PD there is an adaptive upregulation of mesofrontal dopaminergic activity. This upregulation may not necessarily be of functional significance as it is well established that early PD patients show impairment on cognitive tasks (sorting, planning, fluency) thought to be subserved by prefrontal structures.[12]

Three-dimensional ^{18}F-dopa PET coupled with SPM has also been applied to patients with established bilateral PD.[10] Figure 2 shows an SPM of reduced ^{18}F-dopa uptake in seven patients with established PD compared to 12 controls. It can be seen that statistically significant reductions in mean K_i are revealed not only bilaterally in the caudate and putamen but also in the substantia nigra and midbrain tegmentum where the uptake is reduced to 40% of normal. The increased cingulate ^{18}F-dopa uptake seen in early disease has now normalized.

On average, with the conventional 2D PET approach, PD patients show a mean reduction of 50% in putaminal ^{18}F-dopa signal.[6,13,14] Autopsy studies demonstrate a 60–80% loss of ventrolateral nigra compacta cells and a 95% loss of putaminal dopamine.[15-18] This emphasizes the likelihood that striatal uptake of ^{18}F-dopa reflects the capacity of nigrostriatal terminals to decarboxylate dopa rather than reflecting the number of nigral neurons or the ability of the striatum to manufacture endogenous dopamine from tyrosine.

(a) SPM ANALYSIS – REDUCED ^{18}F-DOPA UPTAKE IN EARLY PD

STATISTICAL ANALYSIS OF PARAMETRIC ^{18}F-DOPA Ki-MAP IMAGES IN 7 PATIENTS WITH EARLY LEFT HEMI-PARKINSON'S DISEASE COMPARED WITH A GROUP OF 7 NORMALS

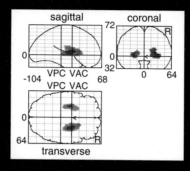

REGION	SIZE (k)	P(n^{max}>k)	Z SCORE	P(Z^{max}>u)	X,	Y,	Z
R-PUTAMEN	574	0.003	5.72	0.000	26	-6	4
L-PUTAMEN	263	0.050	4.34	0.017	-26	-8	4
R-CAUDATE	574	0.003	3.98	0.063	16	16	0
L-CAUDATE	3	0.961	2.35	0.980	-14	14	0

(b) SPM ANALYSIS – INCREASED ^{18}F-DOPA UPTAKE IN EARLY PD

STATISTICAL ANALYSIS OF PARAMETRIC ^{18}F-DOPA Ki-MAP IMAGES IN 7 PATIENTS WITH EARLY LEFT HEMI-PARKINSON'S DISEASE COMPARED WITH A GROUP OF 7 NORMALS

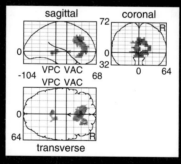

REGION	SIZE (k)	P(n^{max}>k)	Z SCORE	P(Z^{max}>u)	X,	Y,	Z
ANTERIOR CINGULATE	711	0.001	4.52	0.008	-2	32	24
ANTERIOR CINGULATE	241	0.063	3.49	0.267	-6	32	-4

Figure 1: Statistical parametric mapping (SPM) comparing ^{18}F-dopa uptake in groups of seven PD patients with early disease and only left limb involvement and seven age-matched normal controls. It can be seen that ^{18}F-dopa uptake is reduced in right putamen, right caudate, and left putamen, particularly dorsally. At the same time ^{18}F-dopa uptake is increased in the anterior cingulate gyrus (courtesy of J Rakshi).

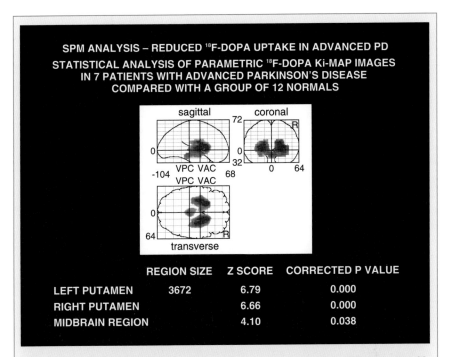

Figure 2: An SPM comparing ^{18}F-dopa uptake in groups of seven PD patients with established bilateral disease compared with 12 age-matched controls. It can be seen that statistically significant reductions in mean K_i are revealed not only bilaterally in caudate and putamen but also in the substantia nigra and midbrain tegmentum (courtesy of J Rakshi).

We have estimated that there is about a 30% loss of specific putamen ^{18}F-dopa uptake at the time of symptom onset in PD.[9] This loss appears to be greater if 3D PET acquisition is employed. ^{18}F-dopa PET therefore provides a potential means of detecting subclinical nigral dysfunction in subjects at risk for PD, such as relatives of affected patients.

DETECTION OF PRECLINICAL DISEASE IN PD

It has been estimated from post-mortem studies that for every patient with brainstem Lewy body disease who presents with clinical PD there may be 15 cases with incidental Lewy body disease who do not have parkinsonian symptoms.[19] It is likely, therefore, that in familial surveys of the prevalence of PD, a significant number of cases of subclinical pathology will be missed. We have used ^{18}F-dopa PET to study 32 asymptomatic adult relatives in seven kindreds with familial PD. Each of these kindreds contained at least two affected individuals with levodopa-responsive parkinsonism clinically indistinguishable from sporadic PD. Six of these kindreds had unknown pathology; the index cases had disease onset between the fourth and seventh decades.[20] The seventh kindred was known to have diffuse Lewy body disease and was characterized by young onset parkinsonism.[21] Affected individuals from these seven kindreds all showed the pattern of reduced striatal ^{18}F-dopa uptake associated with sporadic PD; putamen tracer uptake was more affected than caudate. Eleven of the 32 asymptomatic relatives studied showed levels of putaminal ^{18}F-dopa uptake reduced by more than 2.5 SD below the normal mean.[20] Figure 3 shows striatal ^{18}F-dopa uptake for a normal control, a clinically affected member of one of these seven kindreds, and a sibling with presumed preclinical disease. Formal discriminant analysis assigned nine of these 11 asymptomatic relatives a 100% probability and the other two a 60–70% probability of having PD on the basis of the pattern of their putamen and caudate ^{18}F-dopa uptake. Five of these 11 asymptomatic relatives had an isolated mild postural tremor and four of these were assigned to a PD category by discriminant analysis. Three years after PET, three of the 11 asymptomatic relatives with reduced putamen ^{18}F-dopa uptake have gone on to develop clinical parkinsonism.

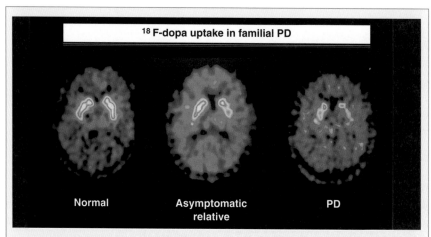

[18] F-dopa uptake in familial PD

Normal   Asymptomatic relative   PD

Figure 3: PET images of striatal ^{18}F-dopa uptake in a normal control, a clinically affected PD patient with familial disease, and his asymptomatic sibling with presumed preclinical disease. Note that ^{18}F-dopa uptake is markedly reduced in the PD patient and is intermediate in the asymptomatic family member as described in the text (courtesy of P Piccini).

The ^{18}F-dopa PET findings in these kindreds have, to date, shown a 34% prevalence of dopaminergic dysfunction in asymptomatic relatives of index cases with familial parkinsonism. This is significantly higher than the 15% prevalence normally quoted for the presence of a positive family history in PD. Our results are most consistent with a dominant pattern of inheritance in these seven kindreds. Our results could also be explained by nigral dysfunction arising from exposure to a common environmental toxin in early life with variable susceptibility to this agent.

Twenty-seven asymptomatic co-twins of affected PD patients have now been studied with 18F-dopa PET, extending the original reported series of 17.[22] Eighteen were monozygotic (MZ) co-twins aged 54–81 years and eight of these showed putamen 18F-dopa uptake reduced more than 2.5 SD below the normal mean. All of these were assigned to a PD category by discriminant analysis. Of these eight asymptomatic co-twins, two had isolated postural tremor on examination and in one of these there was an orthostatic component. This last co-twin developed levodopa-responsive parkinsonism three years after PET. A third co-twin had occasional tremor of the left arm while lying on the PET scanner while a fourth had borderline bradykinesia of finger movements. None of these co-twins were aware of any problem at the time of PET. Nine dizygotic (DZ) asymptomatic co-twins aged 23–67 years also underwent 18F-dopa PET. Two of these had reduced putamen 18F-dopa uptake in the absence of any clinical signs and one of these was assigned to a PD category by discriminant analysis.

In summary, when discriminant analysis is applied to the 18F-dopa PET findings for PD co-twins, it suggests concordance rates of 44% and 11% for nigral dysfunction in MZ and DZ co-twins, respectively. The MZ concordance is much higher than the clinical concordances reported in previous clinical surveys (2–12%) and there is a trend towards a significantly greater prevalence of nigral dysfunction in MZ compared with DZ co-twin cohorts ($p=0.08$). After four years of follow-up, two of the nine asymptomatic co-twins assigned to a PD category by discriminant analysis on the basis of the pattern of their 18F-dopa uptake have developed clear signs of parkinsonism.

The finding of a higher concordance (44% vs. 11%) for dopaminergic dysfunction in MZ compared with DZ co-twins could be interpreted as being more in favor of a genetic etiology than an environmental etiology for PD. The 18F-dopa PET data also do not exclude the possibility of a mitochondrial mode of inheritance in PD. However, mitochondrial DNA is maternally transmitted and such a pattern of inheritance would be predicted to show equal concordance in MZ and DZ twins. An equal concordance has been reported in a study from Cologne where all five DZ and two MZ PD co-twins studied were said to have abnormal 18F-dopa PET findings.[23] Reduced mitochondrial complex I activity has been reported in PD nigra and platelets [24,25] but no excess maternal transmission in PD has been detected. Thus, it seems unlikely that PD arises as a consequence of a mitochondrial gene defect and no specific mitochondrial defect has been identified to date.

While isolated postural tremor appears to be a phenotype of familial parkinsonism, when discriminant analysis was applied to the striatal 18F-dopa uptake data of co-twins and asymptomatic relatives in PD kindreds, those with postural tremor were not assigned to a PD category any more frequently than those without tremor. It would seem likely, therefore, that postural tremor in PD does not arise as a primary consequence of dopaminergic dysfunction though it may be a marker of the presence of familial disease.

There is still debate over whether PD represents an ongoing active degenerative process or is initiated by a subclinical toxic or infective insult in early life and only becomes clinically apparent when additional nigral loss due to natural attrition causes the cell population to fall below a critical threshold.[26] Functional imaging provides a potential means of objectively monitoring disease progression *in vivo* in PD. It has been reported that striatal ^{18}F-dopa influx constants correlate with subsequent post-mortem dopaminergic cell densities in the substantia nigra and striatal dopamine levels. These studies were performed in a group of six patients consisting of single cases of PD, amyotrophic lateral sclerosis and Alzheimer's disease, and three cases of progressive supranuclear palsy.[27] An ^{18}F-dopa PET study in MPTP-exposed monkeys has demonstrated a similar correlation.[28] Consequently, ^{18}F-dopa PET can be used as an indirect measure of nigrostriatal dopaminergic cell counts in PD.

The first reported progression study measured striatal ^{18}F-dopa uptake on two occasions over three years in groups of nine PD and seven normal subjects.[29] The PD patients studied had established disease (mean clinical duration of four years). Both the PD and normal groups showed a similar mean 5% fall in their striatal/cerebellar ^{18}F-dopa uptake ratios measured 60–90 minutes after tracer administration.[30] These workers concluded that the decline in nigral function in PD was slow and similar to that associated with natural aging. In a follow-up study, a significantly more rapid decline of striatal ^{18}F-dopa uptake was demonstrated in this PD group compared with controls over a seven-year period measuring (striatum–occipital):occipital ratios 60–90 minutes after tracer administration. The annual decline in the striatal:cortical uptake ratio was still, however, relatively slow in PD (0.78% of the normal mean value). Based on these studies, the authors estimated that PD must have a long preclinical period (at least 40 years).

A problem with the above studies is that whole striatal ROIs were employed to analyze disease progression whereas the pathology of PD primarily targets dorsal putamen dopamine storage. Using a more sensitive approach, which directly measured putamen ^{18}F-dopa influx constants (K_i), a mean 12% annual decline in baseline putamen K_i value was reported for a group of 17 PD patients with a mean clinical disease duration of 40 months.[31] Figure 4 shows striatal ^{18}F-dopa scans one year apart for one of these 17 patients. In contrast, whole striatal ^{18}F-dopa uptake only declined by 4% per annum, though still faster than the rate of decline reported previously.[30] Ten controls showed no significant change in putamen ^{18}F-dopa uptake over three years. By extrapolating their progression data, these authors estimated that the preclinical period from disease onset to appearance of symptoms was approximately 3±3 years. When the striatum:occipital ratio approach was used to analyze ^{18}F-dopa uptake, a far slower apparent rate of progression was computed.

Subsequently the dataset was extended to a cohort of 32 PD patients with an average clinical disease duration of 3.5 years. Patients were rescanned after

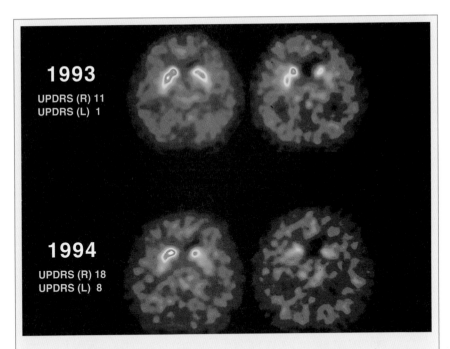

Figure 4: Serial PET images of striatal ^{18}F-dopa uptake collected one year apart in a PD patient. It can be seen that there has been clear progression in the loss of dopamine storage capacity (courtesy of PK Morrish).

a mean of 18 months. The annual decline of the baseline specific putamen ^{18}F-dopa uptake was 9%. Caudate K_i declined by 3% per annum. Interestingly, the earliest cases with a clinical disease duration of less than 26 months appeared to progress most rapidly in this series. Extrapolation based on the level of putamen ^{18}F-dopa uptake at 3.5 and 5 years of clinical disease duration suggested a preclinical window of 6±3 years. It further suggested that symptoms begin when there is a 30% fall in putamen K_i from normal levels (Figure 5). The mean annual rate of increase (worsening) of the motor UPDRS in this group of patients was four points but there was no correlation between change in UPDRS motor scores and putamen K_i value for individual patients. This may reflect the fact that (a) the UPDRS is not determined by loss of dopaminergic function alone, and (b) the patients were receiving varying daily doses of levodopa and, although studied after cessation of medication for 12 hours, were not necessarily fully 'off'.

These findings fit well with a recent pathological study which correlated its cross-sectional post-mortem cell count data with clinical disease duration.[15] This study suggested that nigral cell loss in PD is exponential and occurs at about 10 times the rate of loss associated with aging. Additionally, it estimated a mean preclinical disease period in PD of 4.7 years and symptom onset after a 30% loss of nigral dopamine neurons. There was a six-fold

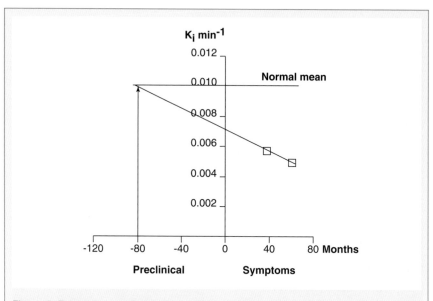

Figure 5: Extrapolation of putaminal ^{18}F-dopa uptake obtained 3.5 and 5 years after symptomatic onset in 32 PD patients. These data suggest a preclinical window of about six years and symptom onset after a 30% fall from normal in putamen K_i .

greater prevalence of degenerating nigral dopamine neurons in PD compared with age-matched controls. Interestingly, there was also a 16-fold higher prevalence of activated microglia suggestive of active neurodegeneration rather than an aging process.[32]

As functional imaging can objectively follow disease progression, it provides a potential means of monitoring the efficacy of putative neuroprotective agents such as dopamine agonists and MAO-B inhibitors. The above-mentioned findings for 32 PD patients suggest that the mean annual rate of decrease of putamen ^{18}F-dopa K_i in PD is 9%. A within-PD patient scan-to-scan error of 13% has been measured for ^{18}F-dopa K_i values measured with PET in 2D mode.[33] From these figures, the number of PD patients required to demonstrate a predetermined degree of neuroprotection with ^{18}F-dopa PET can be computed (Table 1). With the improved sensitivity and reproducibility of ^{18}F-dopa PET acquired in 3D mode and a state-of-the-art-camera, even smaller numbers of patients may be required.

The most dramatic examples of the use of ^{18}F-dopa PET to follow progression of PD are those studies involving patients treated with implants of fetal mesencephalic tissue. Approximately 200 PD patients have now been treated with such striatal implants in European and North American centers. Most have been reported to show clinical improvements but, as implantation techniques and methods of assessment have varied, it is difficult to compare findings from the different centers. Serial ^{18}F-dopa PET provides an objective

Table 1: Scanning interval and number of patients per group (cohort sizes) required to demonstrate 25–100% neuroprotection with ^{18}F-dopa PET in 2D mode with 80% power and $p < 0.05$.

Protection	No. of patients per group at time interval between PET scans			
	1 year	2 year	3 year	5 year
100%	34	10	5	3
50%	130	34	16	7
25%	517	130	59	22

means of examining graft function post-transplantation. Sixteen of 21 PD patients reported to date have shown convincing PET evidence of graft function with a follow-up of six months to six years.[34–39] In general, ^{18}F-dopa uptake in the grafted putamen correlates with timed tests of upper limb function and diminution of time in the 'off' phase.[35,38] One of the transplanted PD patients in the Florida series has subsequently died from an unrelated cause and at post-mortem viable TH-staining graft tissue forming connections with host neurons was seen.[40] No host-derived sprouting was detected. These findings confirm that ^{18}F-dopa PET measures graft function rather than simply reflecting host neuronal sprouting as a reaction to foreign tissue or the presence of blood–brain barrier breakdown.

MECHANISMS OF DYSKINESIAS IN PD

Dyskinesias appear in approximately 80% of PD patients after five years of exposure to levodopa. It has been suggested that their onset requires both a loss of dopamine terminal function and changes in the binding properties of striatal dopamine receptors. At least five different subtypes of dopamine receptors have now been described, but broadly they fall into two classes: D_1-type (D_1, D_5) which are adenyl cyclase-dependent, and D_2-type (D_2, D_3, D_4) which are not. The striatum contains mainly D_1 and D_2 receptors and these play a primary role in modulating locomotor function. It is known that lesioning the nigrostriatal system leads to an upregulation of D_2 receptor binding and it was hypothesized that D_2 receptor supersensitivity might underlie dyskinesia onset. This, however, seems unlikely as initial upregulation of striatal D_2 binding following nigral lesioning tends to normalize either spontaneously or after exposure to levodopa or D_2 agonists in rodent and non-human primate models of PD.[41–43] Chronic exposure to bromocriptine monotherapy rarely induces dyskinesias in PD patients.[44] As this agent is a weak D_1 antagonist as well as a D_2 agonist, this led to the suggestion that dyskinesias may be a consequence of D_1 supersensitivity.[45,46] Both D_1 and D_2 selective agonist monotherapy can, however, induce dyskinesias in MPTP-lesioned monkeys, so it seems unlikely that dyskinesias arise as a consequence of changes in binding properties of a specific dopamine receptor subtype.[47–50]

A large number of PET and SPECT ligands have been used to study striatal D_2 receptor binding in PD. PET studies with spiperone-based tracers and ^{123}I-IBZM SPECT studies have generally reported normal levels of striatal binding in untreated PD patients later shown to be responsive to levodopa or apomorphine.[51–53] ^{11}C-raclopride PET studies have shown 10–20% increases in putamen D_2 binding contralateral to the more affected limbs in *de novo* PD.[54–57] These combined findings suggest that in the untreated PD putamen, D_2 binding is mildly upregulated while caudate D_2 binding remains normal. ^{11}C-SCH23390 is a reversible antagonist at D_1 and D_5 sites. In untreated hemiparkinsonian patients, later shown to be levodopa-responsive, ^{11}C-SCH23390 PET showed no relative upregulation of putamen binding contralateral to the affected limbs, suggesting that D_1 binding is at a normal level.[58]

Striatal D_2 binding in chronically-treated PD cases has been reported to be either normal or decreased. Studies with ^{11}C-methylspiperone PET have reported normal[59,60] and reduced[51] tracer uptake while striatal ^{123}I-IBZM uptake is decreased.[52] ^{11}C-raclopride PET studies suggest that *de novo* PD patients with initially increased putamen D_2 binding show a tendency for this to normalize after several months of exposure to levodopa.[57,61] Chronically-treated PD cases continue to have normal putamen D_2 binding but caudate D_2 binding becomes mildly reduced.[54] To date, no studies have specifically addressed whether levels of striatal D_2 binding vary depending on whether the response to levodopa is sustained or fluctuating with dyskinesias.

Using ^{11}C-SCH23390 and ^{11}C-raclopride PET, striatal D_1 and D_2 binding has been measured in levodopa-treated PD patients divided into groups with and without dyskinesias (N. Turjanski, unpublished observations). The treated groups were matched for duration of clinical disease (3–10 years) and levodopa exposure (0.5–8 years). Table 2 shows the levels of striatal D_1 and D_2 binding (expressed as percentage of normal levels) that were present in the two cohorts of treated PD patients. Levels of D_1 and D_2 binding were similar whether dyskinesias were present or not, suggesting that onset of dyskinesias is not primarily due to changes in dopamine receptor availability.

Table 2: Percentage of normal levels of striatal D_1 and D_2 binding in levodopa-treated PD

	Caudate D_1	Caudate D_2	Putamen D_1	Putamen D_2
Non-dyskinetic PD	89	84*	91	94
Dyskinetic PD	85	84*	90	104

*$p < 0.05$ (Bonferroni corrected)

If dyskinesias do not arise as a primary consequence of altered dopamine receptor binding, what then is their etiology? Non-human primate studies suggest that lesions of the indirect basal ganglia pathway (striatum–external pallidum–subthalamus–internal pallidum) are responsible for chorea.[62,63] Additionally, selective degeneration of striatal–external pallidal projections has been reported in the choreic phenotype of Huntington's disease.[64] Opioid peptides are present in high concentration in the basal ganglia. Striatal–external pallidal projections are enkephalinergic while striatal–internal pallidal projections transmit dynorphin. It might, therefore, be predicted that PD patients with a dyskinetic response to levodopa would have altered levels of basal ganglia enkephalin and dynorphin – and hence altered opioid binding – compared with those patients who show a sustained non-dyskinetic response.

Animal models of PD have also implicated derangement of opioid transmission in the development of dyskinesias (Gerfen, this volume). Following lesioning of dopamine projections, levels of enkephalin increase in the striatum while dynorphin levels are reduced.[65–68] Chronic pulsatile levodopa exposure leads to a further increase in enkephalin levels while dynorphin levels become normalized or elevated.[67–70] It has been suggested that the net effect of a rise in enkephalin and dynorphin levels, following exposure of animals with dopaminergic lesions to chronic levodopa, is to decrease the levels of inhibitory internal pallidal output.[69] This will result in disinhibition of the thalamus and frontal cortex, leading to involuntary movements. In contrast, exposure of dopamine-depleted animals to bromocriptine normalizes preproenkephalin levels and does not elevate dynorphin expression.[70] This differential effect may explain why bromocriptine therapy is associated with a very low incidence of dyskinesias compared with levodopa.

Initial reports suggested that basal ganglia binding of ^{11}C-diprenorphine, a non-selective opioid antagonist, was normal in PD patients without dyskinesias.[71] More recent work has now established that striatal, thalamic, and cingulate ^{11}C-diprenorphine binding is selectively reduced in dyskinetic PD patients.[72] Figure 6 shows an SPM overlaid on an MRI template indicating the areas of significantly decreased ^{11}C-diprenorphine binding in dyskinetic compared with non-dyskinetic PD patients with equivalent disease duration. This finding is of interest because (a) a loss of striatal ^{11}C-diprenorphine binding is also seen in choreic Huntington's disease patients[73] suggesting that disruption of basal ganglia opioid transmission in both these disorders may underlie the onset of chorea, and (b) reduced basal ganglia ^{11}C-diprenorphine binding would be compatible with the presence of raised levels of enkephalin and dynorphin. Perhaps more interestingly, the PET findings combined with animal studies suggest that the role of opioid antagonists in the treatment of dyskinesias needs to be re-examined. There is some evidence that intravenous naloxone can suppress dyskinesias[74] but, to date, trials of opioid antagonists administered orally have probably not used sufficiently high doses to achieve therapeutic brain levels.

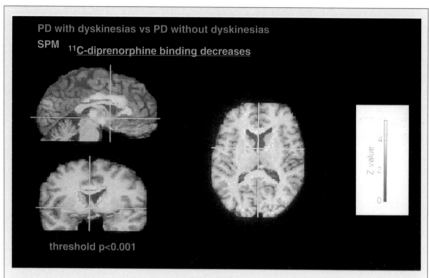

Figure 6: An SPM overlaid on an MRI template showing areas of significantly decreased ¹¹C-diprenorphine binding in dyskinetic compared with non-dyskinetic PD patients with equivalent disease duration (courtesy of P Piccini).

CONCLUSION

Development of software to allow 3D data acquisition and statistical parametric mapping now enables the use of ¹⁸F-dopa PET to localize and quantitate dopaminergic changes in PD, not only in the striatum, but also in the midbrain and frontal regions. ¹⁸F-dopa PET can also be used to detect subclinical abnormalities in dopaminergic function in asymptomatic adult at-risk relatives of patients with familial disease. Perhaps most excitingly, ¹⁸F-dopa PET provides an objective means of monitoring PD progression. In the future, PET is likely to become increasingly important in establishing the role of putative neuroprotective agents and nerve growth factors in the treatment of PD. Finally, PET is helping to throw light on the pharmacologic mechanisms underlying levodopa-associated dyskinesias and has implicated abnormal opioid transmission as an important factor.

REFERENCES

1. Friston KJ, Frith CD, Liddle PF, Dolan RJ, Lammertsma AA, Frackowiak RSJ. The relationship between global and local changes in PET scans. J Cereb Blood Flow Metab 1990; 10: 458–466.

2. Firnau G, Sood S, Chirakal R, Nahmias C, Garnett ES. Cerebral metabolism of 6-18 Fluoro-L-3,4 dihydroxyphenyl-alanine in the primate. J Neurochem 1987; 48: 1077–1082.

3. Garnett ES, Nahmias C, Firmau G. Central dopaminergic pathways in hemiparkinsonism examined by positron emission tomography. Can J Neurol Sci 1984; 11: 174–179.

4. Nahmias C, Garnett ES, Firnau G, Lang A. Striatal dopamine distribution in parkinsonian patients during life. J Neurol Sci 1985; 69: 223–230.

5. Leenders KL, Palmer A, Turton D, et al. Dopa uptake and dopamine receptor binding visualized in the human brain in vivo. In, Fahn S, Marsden CD, Jenner P, Teychenne P, eds, Recent developments in Parkinson's disease. New York: Raven Press, 1986: 103–113.

6. Brooks DJ, Ibanez V, Sawle GV, et al. Differing patterns of striatal 18F-dopa uptake in Parkinson's disease, multiple system atrophy and progressive supranuclear palsy. Ann Neurol 1990; 28: 547–555.

7. Leenders KL, Palmer AJ, Quinn N, et al. Brain dopamine metabolism in patients with Parkinson's disease measured with positron emission tomography. J Neurol Neurosurg Psychiatr 1986; 49: 853–860.

8. Martin WRW, Stoessl AJ, Adam MJ, et al. Positron emission tomography in Parkinson's disease: glucose and dopa metabolism. Adv Neurol 1986; 45: 95–98.

9. Morrish PK, Sawle GV, Brooks DJ. Clinical and 18F-dopa PET findings in early Parkinson's disease. J Neurol Neurosurg Psychiatr 1995; 59: 597–600.

10. Rakshi JS, Uema T, Ito K, et al. Statistical parametric mapping of three dimensional 18F-dopa PET in early and advanced Parkinson's disease. Mov Disord 1996; 11(Suppl 1): 147.

11. Roberts AC, Desalvia MA, Wilkinson LS, et al. 6-hydroxydopamine lesions of the prefrontal cortex in monkeys enhance performance on an analog of the Wisconsin card sort test – possible interactions with subcortical dopamine. J Neurosci 1994; 14: 2531–2544.

12. Owen AM, Sahakian BJ, Hodges JR, Summers BA, Polkey CE, Robbins TW. Dopamine-dependent frontostriatal planning deficits in early Parkinson's disease. Neuropsychol 1995; 9: 126–140.

13. Salmon EP, Brooks DJ, Leenders KL, et al. A two-compartment description and kinetic procedure for measuring regional cerebral 11C-nomifensine uptake using positron emission tomography. J Cereb Blood Flow Metab 1990; 10: 307–316.

14. Leenders KL, Salmon EP, Tyrrell P, et al. The nigrostriatal dopaminergic system assessed in vivo by positron emission tomography in healthy volunteer subjects and patients with Parkinson's disease. Arch Neurol 1990; 47: 1290–1298.

15. Fearnley JM, Lees AJ. Aging and Parkinson's disease: Substantia nigra regional selectivity. Brain 1991; 114: 2283–2301.

16. Rinne IO, Rummukainen J, Lic M, Paljarvi L, Rinne UK. Dementia in Parkinson's disease is related to neuronal loss in the medial substantia nigra. Ann Neurol 1989; 26: 47–50.

17. Kish SJ, Shannak K, Hornykiewicz O. Uneven pattern of dopamine loss in the striatum of patients with idiopathic Parkinson's disease. N Engl J Med 1988; 318: 876–880.

18. Bernheimer H, Birkmayer W, Hornykiewicz O, Jellinger K, Seitelberger F. Brain dopamine and the syndromes of Parkinson and Huntington. Clinical, morphological, and neurochemical correlations. J Neurol Sci 1973; 20: 415–455.

19. Golbe LI. The genetics of Parkinson's disease: a reconsideration. Neurol 1990: 40 (Suppl 3): 7–16.

20. Piccini P, Morrish PK, Turjanski N, et al. Dopaminergic function in familial Parkinson's disease. A clinical and ^{18}F-dopa PET study. Ann Neurol, in press.

21. Mark MH, Burn DJ, Bergen M, Duvoisin RC, Brooks DJ. Familial diffuse Lewy body disease: an ^{18}F-dopa PET study. Mov Disord 1992; 7 (Suppl 1): 142.

22. Burn DJ, Mark MH, Playford ED, et al. Parkinson's disease in twins studied with ^{18}F-dopa and positron emission tomography. Neurol 1992; 42: 1894–1900.

23. Holthoff VA, Vieregge P, Kessler J, et al. Discordant twins with Parkinson's disease – positron emission tomography and early signs of impaired cognitive circuits. Ann Neurol 1994; 36: 176–182.

24. Schapira AHV, Cooper JM, Dexter D, Clark JB, Jenner P, Marsden CD. Mitochondrial complex I deficiency in Parkinson's disease. Ann Neurol 1989; 26: 17–18.

25. Parker WD, Boyson SJ, Parks KJ. Abnormalities of the electron transport chain in idiopathic Parkinson's disease. Ann Neurol 1989; 26: 719–723.

26. Calne DB, Eisen A, McGeer EG, Spencer P. Alzheimer's disease, Parkinson's disease and motor neuron disease: a biotrophic interaction between aging and environment. Lancet 1986; i: 1067–1070.

27. Snow BJ, Tooyama I, McGeer EG, et al. Human positron emission tomographic ^{18}F fluorodopa studies correlate with dopamine cell counts and levels. Ann Neurol 1993; 34: 324–330.

28. Pate BD, Kawamata T, Yamada T, et al. Correlation of striatal fluorodopa uptake in the MPTP monkey with dopaminergic indices. Ann Neurol 1993; 34: 331–338.

29. Bhatt MH, Snow BJ, Martin WRW, Pate BD, Ruth TJ, Calne DB. Positron emission tomography suggests that the rate of progression of idiopathic parkinsonism is slow. Ann Neurol 1991; 29: 673–677.

30. Vingerhoets FJG, Snow BJ, Lee CS, Schulzer M, Mak E, Calne DB. Longitudinal fluorodopa positron emission tomographic studies of the evolution of idiopathic parkinsonism. Ann Neurol 1994; 36: 759–764.

31. Morrish PK, Sawle GV, Brooks DJ. An ^{18}F-dopa PET and clinical study of the rate of progression in Parkinson's disease. Brain 1996; 119: 585–591.

32. McGeer PL, Itagaki S, Boyes BE, McGeer EG. Reactive microglia are positive for HLA-DR in the substantia nigra of Parkinson's and Alzheimer's disease brains. Neurol 1988; 38: 1285–1291.

33. Vingerhoets FJG, Snow BJ, Schulzer M.Reproducibility and discriminating ability of ^{18}F-6-fluoro-L-dopa PET in Parkinson's disease. J Nucl Med 1996; 37: 421–426.

34. Sawle GV, Bloomfield PM, Bjorklund A. Transplantation of fetal dopamine neurons in Parkinson's disease: PET ^{18}F-6-L-Fluorodopa studies in two patients with putaminal implants. Ann Neurol 1992; 31: 166–173.

35. Lindvall O, Sawle G, Widner H, et al. Evidence for long term survival and function of dopaminergic grafts in progressive Parkinson's disease. Ann Neurol 1994; 35: 172–180.

36. Widner H, Tetrud J, Rehncrona S, et al. Bilateral fetal mesencephalic grafting in two patients with parkinsonism induced by 1-methyl-4-phenyl-1,2,3,6-tetrahydropyridine (MPTP). N Engl J Med 1992; 327: 1556–1563.

37. Freeman TB, Olanow CW, Hauser RA, *et al.* Bilateral fetal nigral transplantation into the post-commisural putamen as a treatment of Parkinson's disease: six months follow-up. Ann Neurol 1995; 38: 379–388.

38. Remy P, Samson Y, Hantraye P, *et al.* Clinical correlates of ^{18}F-fluorodopa uptake in five grafted parkinsonian patients. Ann Neurol 1995; 38: 580–588.

39. Wenning GK, Odin P, Morrish PK, *et al.* Short- and long-term survival and function of unilateral intrastriatal dopaminergic grafts in Parkinson's disease. Ann Neurol, in press.

40. Kordower JH, Freeman TB, Snow BJ, *et al.* Neuropathological evidence of graft survival and striatal reinnervation after the transplantation of fetal mesencephalic tissue in a patient with Parkinson's disease. N Engl J Med 1995; 332: 1118–1124.

41. Fuxe K, Agnati LF, Kohler C. Characterization of normal and supersensitive dopamine receptors: effects of ergot drugs and neuropeptides. J Neural Transm 1981; 51: 3–37.

42. Reches A, Wagner HR, Jackson-Lewis V, Yablonski-Alter E, Fahn S. Chronic levodopa or pergolide administration induces downregulation of dopamine receptors in denervated striatum. Neurol 1984; 34: 1208–1212.

43. Murata M, Kanazawa I. Repeated L-dopa administration reduces the ability of dopamine storage and abolishes the supersensitivity of dopamine receptors in the striatum of intact rat. Neurosci Res 1993; 16: 15–23.

44. Lees AJ, Stern GM. Sustained bromocriptine therapy in previously untreated patients with Parkinson's disease. J Neurol Neurosurg Psychiatr 1981; 44: 1020–1023.

45. Mouradian MM, Heuser UE, Baronti F, Fabbrini G, Juncos JL, Chase TN. Pathogenesis of dyskinesias in Parkinson's disease. Ann Neurol 1989; 25: 523–526.

46. Boyce S, Rupniak NMJ, Steventon MJ, Iversen SD. Differential effects of D_1 and D_2 agonists in MPTP-treated primates: functional implications for Parkinson's disease. Neurol 1990; 40: 927–933.

47. Bédard PJ, Gomez-Mancilla B, Blanchette P, Gagnon C, Di Paolo T. Levodopa-induced dyskinesia: facts and fantasy. What does the MPTP monkey tell us? Can J Neurol Sci 1992; 19: 134–137.

48. Blanchet P, Bédard PJ, Britton DR, Kebabian JW. Differential effects of selective D_1 and D_2 dopamine agonists on levodopa-induced dyskinesia in 1-methyl-4-phenyl-1,2,3,6-tetrahydropyridine-exposed monkeys. J Pharmacol Exp Therap 1993; 267: 275–279.

49. Luquin MR, Guillen J, Martinez-Vila E, Laguna J, Martinez Lage JM. Functional interaction between dopamine D_1 and D_2 receptors in MPTP monkeys. Eur J Pharmacol 1994; 253: 215–224.

50. Bédard P, this volume.

51; Leenders KL, Herold S, Palmer AJ, *et al.* Human cerebral dopamine system measured *in vivo* using PET. J Cereb Blood Flow Metab 1985; 5 (Suppl): S157–S158.

52. Brücke T, Podreka I, Angelberger P, *et al.* Dopamine D_2 receptor imaging with SPECT: studies in different neuropsychiatric disorders. J Cereb Blood Flow Metab 1991; 11: 220–228.

53. Schwarz J, Tatsch K, Arnold G, *et al.* ^{123}I-iodobenzamide-SPECT predicts dopaminergic responsiveness in patients with *de novo* parkinsonism. Neurol 1992; 42: 556–561.

54. Brooks DJ, Ibanez V, Sawle GV, *et al.* Striatal D_2 receptor status in Parkinson's disease, striatonigral degeneration, and progressive supranuclear palsy, measured with ^{11}C-raclopride and PET. Ann Neurol 1992; 31: 184–192.

55. Leenders KL, Antonini A, Schwarz J, Hess K, Weindl A, Oertel W. Brain

dopamine D_2 in *de novo* drug-naïve parkinsonian patients measured using PET and ^{11}C-raclopride. Mov Disord 1992; 7 (Suppl 1): 141.

56. Rinne UK, Laitinen A, Rinne JO, Nagren K, Bergman J, Ruotsalainen U. Positron emission tomography demonstrates dopamine D_2 receptor supersensitivity in the striatum of patients with early Parkinson's disease. Mov Disord 1990; 5: 55–59.

57. Antonini A, Schwarz J, Oertel WH, Beer HF, Madeja UK, Leenders KL. ^{11}C-raclopride and positron emission tomography in previously untreated patients with Parkinson's disease: Influence of L-dopa and lisuride therapy on striatal dopamine D_2 receptors. Neurol 1994; 44: 1325–1329.

58. Rinne JO, Laihinen A, Nagren K, *et al.* PET demonstrates different behavior of striatal dopamine D_1 and D_2 receptors in early Parkinson's disease. J Neurosci Res 1990; 27: 494–499.

59. Shinotoh H, Aotsuka A, Yonezawa H, *et al.* Striatal dopamine D_2 receptors in Parkinson's disease and striato-nigral degeneration determined by positron emission tomography. In, Nagatsu T, *et al.*, eds, Basic, clinical and therapeutic advances of Alzheimer's and Parkinson's diseases vol 2. New York: Plenum Press, 1990; 107–110.

60. Hagglund J, Aquilonius SM, Eckernas SA, *et al.* Dopamine receptor properties in Parkinson's disease and Huntington's chorea evaluated by positron emission tomography using ^{11}C-N-methyl-spiperone. Acta Neurol Scand 1987; 75: 87–94.

61. Rinne JO, Laitinen A, Rinne UK, Nagren K, Bergman J, Ruotsalainen U. PET study on striatal dopamine D_2 receptor changes during the progression of early Parkinson's disease. Mov Disord 1993; 8: 134–138.

62. Augood SJ, Emson PC, Mitchell IJ, Boyce S, Clarke CE, Crossman AR. Cellular localization of enkephalin gene expression of MPTP-treated cynomolgus monkeys. Mol Brain Res 1989; 6: 85–92.

63. Boyce S, Clarke CE, Luqin R, *et al.* Induction of chorea and dystonia in Parkinsonian primates. Mov Disord 1990; 5: 3–7.

64. Albin RL, Reiner A, Anderson KD, Penney JB, Young AB. Striatal and nigral neuron subpopulations in rigid Huntington's disease: implications for the functional anatomy of chorea and rigidity-akinesia. Ann Neurol 1990; 27: 357–365.

65. Gerfen CR, McGinty JF, Young III WS. Dopamine differentially regulates dynorphin, substance P and enkephalin expression in striatal neurons: *in vivo* hybridization histochemical analysis. J Neurosci 1991; 11: 1016–1031.

66. Engber TM, Susel Z, Kuo S, *et al.* Levodopa replacement therapy alters enzyme activities in striatum and neuropeptide content in striatal output neurons of 6-hydroxydopamine lesioned rats. Brain Res 1991; 552: 113–118.

67. Mocchetti I, Naranjo J, Costa E. Regulation of striatal enkephalin turnover in rats receiving antagonists of specific dopamine subtypes. J Pharmacol Exp Ther 1987; 241: 1120–1124.

68. Henry B, Brotchie JM. Potential of opioid antagonists in the treatment of levodopa-induced dyskinesias in Parkinson's disease. Drugs Aging 1996; 9: 149–158.

69. Young III WS, Bonner TI, Brann MR. Mesencephalic dopamine neurons regulate the expression of neuropeptide mRNAs in the rat forebrain. Proc Nat Acad Sci USA 1986; 83: 9827–9831.

70. Li SJ, Jiang HK, Satchowiak MS, *et al.* Influence of nigrostriatal dopaminergic tone of the biosynthesis of dynorphin and enkephalin in rat striatum. Brain Res Mol Brain Res 1990; 8: 219–225.

71. Burn DJ, Rinne JO, Quinn NP, Lees AJ, Marsden CD, Brooks DJ. Striatal opioid receptor binding in Parkinson's disease, striatonigral degeneration, and Steel-Richardson-Olszewski syndrome: an ^{11}C-diprenorphine PET study. Brain 1995; 118: 951–958.

72. Piccini P, Weeks RA, Burn DJ, Brooks DJ. PET studies on opioid receptor binding in Parkinson's disease patients with and without levodopa-induced dyskinesias. Neurol 1996: 46 (Suppl): A454.

73. Weeks RA, Cunningham V, Waters S, Harding AE, Brooks DJ. A comparison of region of interest and statistical parametric mapping analysis in PET ligand work: ^{11}C-diprenorphine in Huntington's disease and Tourett's syndrome. J Cereb Blood Flow Metab 1995; 15 (Suppl): S41.

74. Trabucchi M, Bassi S, Frattola L. Effect of naloxone on the 'on-off' syndrome in patients receiving long-term levodopa therapy. Arch Neurol 1982; 39: 120–121.

DISCUSSION

Olanow: There is new information indicating that when an agonist or ligand interacts with a receptor, it induces a conformational change reflecting activation which may not be detected by conventional binding studies. Consequently, it may be misleading to estimate functionality by simply measuring the number of receptors determined by binding.

Brooks: I agree. We cannot be sure whether there is a difference in levels of high and low affinity conformation in these dyskinetic patients because we are only looking at total bioavailability. Likewise, we do not know about the G proteins. Functional imaging is very much limited to those tracers that are available.

Scarlato: Do you have any data supporting or excluding the possibility that maternal transmission is involved in the disease, as is the case for several mitochondrial disorders ?

Brooks: There is no hard evidence for maternal transmission, and our data fit best with an autosomal dominant transmission with reduced penetrance (30–40%). One cannot exclude the possibility that a particular kindred was exposed to some toxin, and had variable susceptibility. The most likely explanation in kindreds with familial PD is that they do carry some sort of dominant genetic susceptibility.

Melamed: The increase in uptake of ^{18}F-dopa in the cingulum is particularly fascinating, as this implies that there may be disinhibition between dopamine zones at the level of the substantia nigra. This may also explain why neurons fire more rapidly when there is partial destruction of the substantia nigra, because dopamine molecules released from the dendrites in the substantia nigra have further to travel. That may be why there is disinhibition between neighboring dopaminergic neurons in the nigra and why the cingulum has an increased uptake of levodopa. The question is whether there is disinhibition between the substantia nigra pars compacta, the A10 and A9 regions.

Brooks: We did see some increased uptake in the midbrain initially but it seemed to be above the level of the nigra, in the upper midbrain, so it is not clear what this represents. This was an unexpected finding and needs to be reproduced.

Rajput: In the general population, how many normal subjects have abnormal fluorodopa uptake compared with the familial cases ?

Brooks: Normal ^{18}F-dopa uptake is Gaussian in distribution, i.e. 1% of normal subjects will fall outside a 2.5 SD cutoff. We have examined 40 or 50 normal patients. Occasionally one is very aberrant and Calne has reported one such subject who went on to develop PD.

Rajput: In the familial cases that we have studied, movement disorders were similar in about 80% of cases, but the other 20% had a different disorder. For example, I have seen a patient with a 56-year history of non-parkinsonian tremor whose son has PD.

Brooks: There is clearly a relationship between the presence of postural tremor in relatives of PD patients and abnormal fluorodopa uptake and I would not be surprised if your tremor patient had an abnormal scan. However, we have not examined sufficient numbers of tremor cases to be confident about this and we cannot yet say that an elderly person with postural tremor and a familial history of PD will have fluorodopa abnormalities.

Leenders: Was the increased frontal lobe fluorodopa uptake relative or absolute?

Brooks: We re-examined the untransformed images and did a region-of-interest analysis on the cingulate. The uptake was increased by about 30% on both transformed and non-transformed datasets, suggesting that it is an absolute increase.

Leenders: The point here is that although the levels might be more or less normal, they may be significant in terms of functional capacity. A little while ago we compared neuropsychologic function with medial prefrontal lobe uptake, and found that the better the fluorodopa uptake in the medial frontal lobe, the worse was the performance. This is what Robbins found in the monkey. The presence of a neurotransmitter in the frontal lobe may not necessarily be advantageous; it may even be a pathologic phenomenon.

Olanow: In the DATATOP study in which 800 untreated PD patients were followed, postural tremor was initially more common than resting tremor suggesting it may be the earliest change in PD. Hornykiewicz suggests that striatal changes may antedate nigral cell loss. Do you see changes in the striatum prior to the nigra in 3D PET?

Brooks: We do not see changes with ^{18}F-dopa PET in the nigra in the stage I group, only in stage III and IV.

Melamed: Have you looked at PD patients with and without marked postural instability, to determine the whereabouts of lesions associated with falls in PD patients? This phenomenon does not respond to levodopa, and in fact may be aggravated by it.

Brooks: We did not, but we will do so now.

Obeso: Where will you look, because there are so many things which are extradopaminergic?

Brooks: The problem is that dopaminergic changes are bound to correlate anyway with onset of instability simply because all symptoms progress in tandem with loss of nigral cells.

Obeso: Have you looked at activational studies in the patients in the early stages with increased dopamine in the cingulate ?

Brooks: We have looked at early PD patients in stage I and II. In these patients the frontal areas are underactive, so this drive of dopamine is not being translated into preserved prefrontal metabolic function.

Leenders: We are now studying so-called healthy people selected from a group of 8000 who had some sort of tremor but not bad enough for them to consult their doctor, i.e. possibly an extremely mild stage of early PD. We have scanned these people and compared them with matched individuals from the same population, and found that almost all those with slight tremor showed slightly decreased dopaminergic uptake in the striatum. Those with no tremor did not. We have to follow them up, of course, but it is possible that very mild neurological symptoms are strong predictors of the disease.

Rajput: How many of your subjects without tremor had abnormal PET scan ?

Leenders: None.

Rajput: I am surprised, because in the general population between 30% and 50% of patients with PD are not readily diagnosed. You did not detect any preclinical PD patients who were not suspected?

Leenders: The selection criteria were normal individuals with no parkinsonian signs or symptoms, and those who had possible parkinsonian features. Those who had no sign of any symptoms were all normal but those who might have had symptoms had suspicious PET scans.

Calne: This might just be a numbers problem. How many normal subjects were there without any symptoms ?

Leenders: Fifteen, a lot of work.

Calne: Out of 15 patients, you may not have detected preclinical PD patients by chance alone.

CHAPTER FIVE

Dopamine agonists as first line therapy of parkinsonism in MPTP monkeys

PAUL J. BÉDARD[1], MD, PHD, FRCP(C), BALTAZAR
GOMEZ–MANCILLA[1], MD, PHD, PIERRE BLANCHET[1], MD,
PHD, FRÉDÉRIC CALON[2], MSc, RICHARD GRONDIN[1], MSc,
CÉLINE GAGNON[2], PHD, PIERRE FALARDEAU[2], PHD, MARTIN
GOULET[2], MSc, MARC MORISSETTE[2], PHD, CLAUDE
ROUILLARD[1], PHD AND THÉRÈSE DI PAOLO[2], PHD

[1] Centre de Recherche en Neurobiologie, Hôpital de l'Enfant-Jésus,
Québec, [2] Centre de Recherche du Centre Hospitalier de l'Université Laval,
Québec, [1] Department of Pharmacology, Faculty of Medicine and
[2] School of Pharmacy, Laval University, Québec, Canada

ABSTRACT

Although levodopa has proven to be a valuable agent in the treatment of Parkinson's disease, complications such as dyskinesia can arise with prolonged use. The resulting dyskinesia may continue to be experienced by affected patients transferred to the D_2 agonist bromocriptine. Dyskinesias are, however, rarely seen when bromocriptine is used as initial therapy. These observations have led to an hypothesis that dopamine agonists, when administered as initial therapy, have a better therapeutic profile. This better outcome could be due to the selectivity of the agonist for one type of receptor or to the longer duration of action of certain agonists. This hypothesis was tested in MPTP-treated monkeys treated from the beginning with either (1) levodopa, (2) D_1 agonists including SKF38393, SKF82958 or CY208243 or (3) D_2 agonists such as bromocriptine, (+)-PHNO, quinpirole or U91356A. The results indicate that treatment with long-acting D_2 agonists provides an excellent antiparkinsonian response with virtually no dyskinesia. Long-acting D_1 agonists are more likely to induce desensitization and this limits their long-term use.

Levodopa therapy has undoubtedly had a major impact on the treatment of Parkinson's disease (PD). However, a majority of patients, especially younger ones, develop complications in the form of motor fluctuations and dyskinesia.[1-4] In our own clinic, the incidence of dyskinesia is 56%.[5] They rarely occur with the first doses of levodopa but require regular daily exposure to the drug over months or years, suggesting that treatment itself may induce changes in the response pattern to dopamine. A retrospective study[5] suggested that in susceptible individuals, once levodopa is initiated, the appearance of dyskinesia can be expected after an average interval of about three years. Similar findings have been reported by Peppe et al.[6]

One of the most interesting clinical observations is the fact that parkinsonian patients treated from the beginning with only the D_2 agonist bromocriptine seldom develop dyskinesia.[7,8] Interestingly, initiating treatment with a dopamine agonist appears to have the same effect as withholding levodopa in delaying the onset of complications.[9] In most studies, however, the rate of drop-outs in patients treated with bromocriptine alone was high, either due to side effects or to perceived insufficient efficacy. This raises the possibility of a selection bias towards a subgroup of patients with a more favorable response to bromocriptine or less severe disease. On the other hand, in patients having already developed dyskinesia on levodopa, substituting a large dose of bromocriptine will produce similar dyskinesia, suggesting that this abnormal acquired response is transferred to other agents, which by themselves may have a lower dyskinesiogenic potential. The implication of this observation is that to study the dyskinesiogenic potential of a new dopaminergic agent, the drug must be administered to patients or animals (1-methyl 4-phenyl 1,2,3,6 tetrahydropyridine (MPTP)-treated monkeys) which have not been previously exposed to levodopa or other agonists.

The apparently better therapeutic profile of the dopamine D_2 receptor agonist bromocriptine has led to the assumption that the D_2 receptor was associated with the therapeutic response and the D_1 receptor with the unwanted dyskinesia. If so, this principle should generalize to other agents acting on the same receptor families, with all agents acting on the D_2 receptor family having a better therapeutic response, particularly with respect to dyskinesia, and the opposite for the D_1 receptor family.

To test this hypothesis, we studied the effect of daily treatment of large doses of levodopa or various selective agonists of the D_1 or D_2 receptor families in MPTP-treated monkeys.

We used female *Macaca fascicularis*, in which the parkinsonian syndrome was induced by a series of injections of MPTP, 0.3 mg/kg subcutaneously.[10] The animals were then observed for the appearance of a parkinsonian syndrome in the form of akinesia, tremor, rigidity, and aphagia. A significant proportion recovered motorically in the first week after MPTP. They were then reinjected with the same dose of the toxin at weekly intervals until the syndrome was stable for at least a month. This is defined as a score of at least 6 on the disability scale (see below). A clear, observable parkinsonian syndrome requires the loss of 90% or more of the striatal dopamine level.[11-13] The parameters evaluated were locomotion, and a general disability score. During the experimental protocol, the animals were kept in a special observation room located in the animal quarters. They were placed singly in cages equipped with two photocells relayed to a computer which counted the number of interruptions (movements) every 15 minutes and the total for each 24 hour period. The disability score is based entirely on parameters which can be evaluated without manipulating the animals. Eating, climbing, vocalization, social interactions and tremor are scored as present or absent for a maximum disability of 10. A score of at least 6 over at least a month is required for diagnosis of a parkinsonian syndrome. Relief of the syndrome is defined as an improvement of at least three points on the scale. Dyskinesia is assessed as chorea (a random brief movement of a body part), or dystonia (a more sustained contraction of the agonists and antagonists causing torsion movements due to dominance of one group of muscles). These are scored according to our Abnormal Involuntary Movement Scale which scores dyskinesia on a scale of 0 (none) to 3 (severe) in the four limbs, trunk and face. Sequences of each experiment were recorded on video.

At the end of the experiment, the animals were sacrificed by an overdose of pentobarbital and the brains rapidly frozen until assay. In early experiments, the hindbrain was kept in 10% formaldehyde for standard histological staining such as the Nissl or the Kluver-Barrera (Luxol-Fast blue) stains. More recently, we have relied on determinations of dopamine in the striatum by HPLC coupled with electrochemical detection.

In the first series of experiments, levodopa/carbidopa was given orally at 30–50 mg/kg. Several dopamine D_2 agonists were also tested – bromocriptine, 5 mg/kg orally; (+)-PHNO, 6 μg/kg subcutaneously; quinpirole, 0.5 mg/kg subcutaneously. The D_1 agonists SKF38393, (5 mg/kg orally) and CY208243 (0.5 mg/kg subcutaneously) were included. All drugs were administered once daily over at least one month.

In a second series of experiments we compared the effect of chronic administration of one D_2 (U91356A) and one D_1 receptor agonist (SKF82958) administered to different groups of MPTP monkeys either by multiple daily injections (pulsatile mode) or by Alzet minipump (continuous mode). These experiments also included a group treated with levodopa and another treated with the long-acting D_2 agonist cabergoline.

Ligand binding and *in situ* hybridization studies were performed according to published procedures.[13,14] Briefly, the animals were sacrificed three days after the last dose of the dopaminergic agent and the rest of the brain was cut sagitally and one half sectioned with a microtome and prepared for autoradiography.[15] In later studies, frozen sections were exposed to 4% paraformaldehyde for *in situ* hybridization. The other half was sectioned in the coronal plane in front of the optic chiasm and the following structures dissected out: caudate nucleus: anterior, mid-section and posterior; putamen: anterior, middle and posterior; nucleus accumbens; globus pallidus: external and internal; amygdala and frontal cortex. All samples were homogenized and put in the presence of specific radioactive ligands.[11–14,16] The ligands used were: ^{3}H-spiperone (D_2 antagonist site), ^{3}H-NPA (D_2 agonist site), ^{3}H-SCH23390 (D_1 antagonist site), ^{3}H-SKF38393 (D_1 agonist site) and ^{3}H-flunitrazepam (GABA$_A$ site).

Levodopa demonstrated excellent efficacy. Peak-dose dyskinesia developed in all animals within weeks (Table 1).[11,13,17] The dyskinesias were similar to those observed in humans, and were more often choreic than dystonic. There was no clear shortening of the motor response corresponding to 'end-of-dose deterioration' during the treatment period. Once they were apparent, they were seen after each dose even after stopping treatment for periods of up to two months.

Bromocriptine, while also demonstrating excellent antiparkinsonian efficacy at high dose, induced no dyskinesia.[11,14,16] Two other D_2 agonists, however, (+)-PHNO and quinpirole, induced dyskinesias within days to weeks in drug-naïve monkeys. These were indistinguishable from those induced by levodopa in other animals. The D_1 agonist SKF38393 was without effect, even after four weeks. However, the D_1 agonist CY208243 displayed strong antiparkinsonian activity, but soon induced dyskinesia in three out of five animals.

Table 1: Summary of chronic treatment with dopamine agonist monotherapy in drug-naïve MPTP monkeys					
Drug (mg/kg)	**N**	**Receptor family**	**Approximate duration of action (h)**	**Antiparkinsonian efficacy**	**Dyskinesia**
Levodopa/carbidopa or benserazide (30/50)	17	D_1/D_2	3–4	Very good	All
Bromocriptine (5)	18	D_2	8	Very good	No
Cabergoline (0.25)	3	D_2	24–36	Very good (mild tolerance)	Transient (initial) 2/3
U91356A by injection (0.6)	3	D_2	3	Very good	All
U91356A by pump	3	D_2	Continuous	Very good (some tolerance)	Transient (initial) 2/3
(+)-PHNO (6µg)	4	D_2	2–3	Very good	All
Quinpirole (0.9)	4	D_2	2–3	Very good	All
SKF38393 (5)	4	D_1	–	None	None
CY208243 (0.5)	5	D_1	3	Very good	3/5
SKF82958 by injection (1)	3	D_1	1	Very good	2/3
SKF82958 by pump	3	D_1	Continuous	None	None

At this point, it appeared clear that dyskinesia could not be ascribed solely to stimulation of D_1 receptors. On the contrary, in experiments where animals rendered dyskinetic with levodopa were switched to one of several D_2 or D_1 agonists, there was a better ratio of therapeutic effect to dyskinesia with D_1 agonists.[18,19]

Pulsatile versus continuous administration

Another aspect of the pharmacologic profile of the dopamine agonists is their duration of action. In fact, it appeared that the short-acting drugs were likely to induce dyskinesia probably due to their 'pulsatile' action on the receptors, whatever the receptor involved.[20,21] The effect of the mode of administration of the same or different agonists was studied in the monkey model.

A first experiment was performed with ((R)-5-(propylamino)-5,6-dihydro-4H-imidazo[4,5,1-jj]-quinolin-2(1H)-1 hydrochloride, The Upjohn Co., Kalamazoo, USA) that binds at micromolar concentrations to both D_2 (K_i = 1.3nM) and 5-HT_{1A} (K_i = 58nM) receptors, but not to other dopamine, 5-HT, or opiate receptors.[17] The drug was administered over a month, either twice a day in a pulsatile manner or continuously through an osmotic minipump.[17] The total daily doses were calculated to be similar and the serum levels were monitored. Continuous administration of the dopamine agonist led to an initial increase in locomotor activity with transient dyskinesia in one animal. This was promptly followed, within days, by a decreased response which nevertheless remained above control level for the 27-day duration of the study. On the other hand, pulsatile administration (two doses a day) of the same daily dose of the same agent led to behavioral sensitization in terms of locomotion and to the development of dyskinesias which persisted until the end of experiment and even increased over time.

A more recent experiment involved a similar comparison of pulsatile (three injections a day) and continuous administration (by 2ML4 Alzet minipump) of the D_1 full agonist SKF82958 (6-chloro-7,8-dihydroxy-3-allyl-1-phenyl-2,3,4,5-tetrahydro-1H-3-benzazepine hydrobromide). Also included was a group of animals treated every other day with the long-acting D_2 agonist cabergoline as well as a control group of untreated MPTP monkeys. Cabergoline produced a sustained antiparkinsonian effect with transient dyskinesia in two of three animals. There was a 50% decrease in the maximum locomotor response, but thereafter stabilization occurred at this level.[22] This was associated with partial downregulation of D_2 receptors. Pulsatile administration of the D_1 agonist led to dyskinesias which increased with time and were associated with significant shortening of the antiparkinsonian response.[23] Continuous administration of the D_1 agonist SKF82958 led to no visible motor response or dyskinesia despite the presence of significant serum levels of the drug. This suggests rapid and profound tolerance or desensitization.

Both D_1 and D_2 receptors were upregulated by denervation due to MPTP.[11,13,16] Treatment with levodopa reversed this so-called supersensitivity of D_2 receptors while D_1 receptors were not significantly affected. Surprisingly, treatment with the D_1 agonist SKF38393 also reversed the increase in D_2 receptors.[14] Chronic treatment with 5 mg/kg of bromocriptine caused an important downregulation of D_2 receptors and to a lesser extent of D_1 receptors.[14]

Biochemical analysis of the brains of the animals from the experiment comparing treatment with a D_2 agonist administered in the pulsatile *versus* continuous mode indicates that the behavioral sensitization does not correlate with an increase in dopamine receptors. However, the desensitization seen in animals treated with continuous dopaminergic stimulation is associated with downregulation of striatal D_2 receptors and its mRNA message.[14,17] This is in line with previous observations in monkeys[24] and in humans.[25] With the D_1 receptors, there was no clear change in receptor binding with any of the treatments. There was a dramatic decrease in mRNA message after denervation but all treatments partly corrected this trend. Thus, while it is difficult to correlate dyskinesias with changes in dopamine receptors, they could be involved in the process of tolerance or desensitization. On the other hand, in the two groups displaying dyskinesia (levodopa and pulsatile D_2), there was a conspicuous increase in ^{3}H-flunitrazepam binding in the internal division of the globus pallidus which was not seen in the group treated by minipump.[26] In as much as it may reflect supersensitivity of $GABA_A$ receptors in this key station of the basal ganglia, this could explain dyskinesia since either D_1 or D_2 stimulation will eventually result in excessive inhibition by GABA of the internal globus pallidus and lead to dyskinesia.

In the most recent experiment comparing pulsatile *versus* continuous administration of the D_1 agonist SKF82958, Western blotting detected, in the striatum of MPTP-treated control monkeys, an increase of the truncated form of FosB, ΔFosB, which was present after several months of denervation.[27] This band was not present in MPTP animals treated chronically with cabergoline. In MPTP monkeys given three injections a day of the short-acting D_1 agonist SKF82958, there was marked induction in the striatum of ΔFosB. In the minipump group, which did not develop dyskinesia, there was no induction of ΔFosB. There is, therefore, an interesting relationship between the induction of persistent dyskinesia and ΔFosB. Other Fos-related proteins are induced transiently but ΔFosB is induced later and its persistence and presence only in monkeys with dyskinesia suggest a casual link.

DISCUSSION

In MPTP monkeys, dyskinesia can be induced by high doses of levodopa in 100% of animals, provided they are sufficiently denervated (>90%). As previously shown in patients,[7,8] high-dose bromocriptine given *de novo* to well-denervated monkeys, although producing a strong antiparkinsonian effect, is far less likely than levodopa to induce dyskinesia. The contention that the D_2 receptor is responsible for the antiparkinsonian effect while the abnormal movements are mediated by the D_1 receptor is not supported by the fact that three other molecules with reported selectivity for the D_2 receptor – (+)-PHNO, quinpirole, and U91356A in the pulsatile mode – rapidly induced dyskinesia while demonstrating good antiparkinsonian efficacy. The outcome was very different when U91356A was administered in the continuous mode by minipump. Partial tolerance was seen in the form of a decrease in the initial hyperlocomotion. This was also the case with the long-acting D_2 agonist cabergoline. However, the animals retained a strong antiparkinsonian response. The transient dyskinesias observed initially with these agents disappeared after a few days indicating that certain biochemical changes caused by denervation alone are sufficient to allow dyskinesia in the face of a strong dopaminergic stimulation. They also suggest that if this stimulation is more continuous than pulsatile, dyskinesia and the associated biochemical changes can be reversed, while the opposite is true of the pulsatile mode. We therefore conclude that the favorable profile of bromocriptine in terms of dyskinesia is due in large part to its long duration of action.

Of the D_1 agonists tested initially, SKF38393 was without effect even after a month, thus confirming earlier reports,[28–30] while CY208243 induced dyskinesia after a few weeks.[31] Another short-acting full D_1 agonist, SKF82958, also rapidly induced prominent dyskinesia while the same daily dose administered by minipump not only did not induce dyskinesia but was associated with rapid and profound tolerance. In fact, we have shown recently that a long-acting D_1 agonist given to levodopa-primed monkeys induces complete and selective tolerance of the D_1 receptors within a matter of hours.[32] This suggests that the D_1 receptor is more prone to desensitization and that if dopaminergic therapy targeted to both receptor families is considered using a single long-acting molecule acting on both receptors, the D_1 receptor may rapidly desensitize and some of the benefits of the combination would then be lost. This would mean that the D_1 agonist should have an 'intermediate' duration of action to avoid dyskinesia by potent short-acting agents.

Taken together, the results obtained in the MPTP monkey model of parkinsonism indicate that treatment with long-acting dopamine agonists (with sufficiently long half-lives for doses to overlap) of the D_2 receptor family provides an excellent antiparkinsonian response with virtually no dyskinesia. Some partial tolerance is seen but at least, within the limits of the experiments, the antiparkinsonian effect was retained. This is associated with correction of biochemical alterations induced by denervation, notable at the level of striatal D_2 receptors and $GABA_A$ receptors in the internal division of the globus pallidus. D_1 agonists, while demonstrating a better therapeutic index in substitution experiments in levodopa-primed animals, are more likely to induce desensitization, particularly in the case of long-acting agents, and this limits their long-term use. Understanding the mechanism and conditions of this desensitization may allow some type of association of agonists of the D_1 and D_2 receptor families, possibly with different duration of action. These results therefore support and extend the clinical reports of a reduced incidence of dyskinesia associated with dopamine agonists given as first line therapy in PD.

References

1. Barbeau, A. High level levodopa therapy in severely akinetic parkinsonian patients twelve years later. In, Rinne UK, Klinger M, Stamm G, eds, Parkinson's disease: current progress, problems and management. Amsterdam: Elsevier, 1980: 229–239.

2. Nutt JG. Levodopa-induced dyskinesia. Neurol 1990; 40: 340–345.

3. Muenter MD, Tyce GM. Levodopa therapy of Parkinson's disease: plasma levodopa concentration, therapeutic response and side effects. Mayo Clin Proc 1971; 46: 231–239.

4. Mones RJ, Elizan TS, Siegel GJ. Analysis of levodopa-induced dyskinesia in 51 patients with Parkinson's disease. J Neurol Neurosurg Psychiatr 1971; 34: 668.

5. Blanchet PJ, Allard P, Gregoire L, Tardif F, Bédard PJ. Risk factors for peak-dose dyskinesia in 100 levodopa-treated parkinsonian patients. Can J Neurol Sci 1996; 23: 189–193.

6. Peppe A, Dambrosia JM, Chase TN. Risk factors for motor response complications in levodopa-treated parkinsonian patients. In, Narabayashi H, Nagatsu T, Yanagisawa N, Mizuno Y, eds, Advances in Neurology, vol 60: Parkinson's disease: from basic research to treatment. New York: Raven Press, 1993: 698–702.

7. Rascol A, Guiraud B, Montastruc JL, et al. Long-term treatment of Parkinson's disease with bromocriptine. J Neurol Neurosurg Psychiatr 1979; 42: 143.

8. Lees AJ, Stern GM. Sustained bromocriptine therapy in previously untreated patients with Parkinson's disease. J Neurol Neurosurg Psychiatr 1981; 44: 1020–1023.

9. Montastruc JL, Rascol O, Senard J, Rascol A. A randomized controlled study comparing bromocriptine to which levodopa was later added, with levodopa alone in previously untreated patients with Parkinson's disease: a five year follow up. J Neurol Neurosurg Psychiatr 1994; 57: 1034–1038.

10. Burns RS, Chiueh CC, Markey SP, et al. A primate model of parkinsonism: selective destruction of dopaminergic neurons in the pars compacta of the substantia nigra by N-methyl-4-phenyl-1,2,3,6-tetrahydropyridine. Proc Nat Acad Sci USA 1983; 80: 4546–4550.

11. Bédard PJ, Di Paolo T, Falardeau P, Boucher R. Chronic treatment with levodopa, but not bromocriptine, induces dyskinesia in MPTP-parkinsonian monkeys: correlation with ^{3}H-spiperone binding. Brain Res 1986; 379: 294–299.

12. Di Paolo T, Bédard PJ, Daigle M, et al. Long-term effects of MPTP on central and peripheral catecholamine and indoleamine concentrations in monkeys. Brain Res 1986; 379: 286.

13. Falardeau P, Bédard PJ, Di Paolo T. Relation between brain dopamine loss and D_2 dopamine receptor density in MPTP monkeys. Neurosci Lett 1988; 86: 225–229.

14. Falardeau P, Bouchard S, Bédard PJ, et al. Behavioral and biochemical effect of chronic treatment with D_1 and/or D_2 dopamine agonists in MPTP monkeys. Eur J Pharmacol 1988; 150: 59–66.

15. Gagnon C, Bédard PJ, Di Paolo T. Effect of chronic treatment of MPTP monkeys with dopamine D_1 and/or D_2 receptor agonists. Eur J Pharmacol 1990; 178: 115–120.

16. Rouillard C, Bédard PJ, Di Paolo T. Behavioral and biochemical effect of chronic treatment of MPTP-monkeys with bromocriptine alone or in combination with SKF38393. Eur J Pharm 1990; 185: 209–215.

17. Blanchet PJ, Calon F, Martel JC, Bédard PJ, Di Paolo T, Walters RR, Piercey

MF. Continuous administration decreases and pulsatile administration increases behavioral sensitivity to a novel dopamine D_2 agonist (U91356A) in MPTP monkeys. J Pharmacol Exp Ther 1995; 272: 854–859.

18. Gomez-Mancilla B, Bédard PJ. Effects of D_1 and D_2 agonists and antagonists on dyskinesia produced by levodopa in 1-methyl-4-phenyl-1,2,3,6-tetrahydropyridine-treated monkeys. J Pharmacol Exp Ther 1991; 259: 409–413.

19. Blanchet PJ, Bédard PJ, Britton DR, Kebabian JW. Differential effect of selective D_1 and D_2 dopamine receptor agonists on levodopa-induced dyskinesia in MPTP monkeys. J Pharm Exp Ther 1993; 267: 275–279.

20. Engber TM, Susel Z, Juncos J, Chase TN. Continuous and intermittent levodopa differentially affect rotation induced by D_1 and D_2 dopamine agonists. Eur J Pharmacol 1989; 168:291–298.

21. Juncos JL, Engber TM, Raisman R, Chase TN. Continuous and intermittent levodopa differentially affect basal ganglia function. Ann Neurol 1989; 25: 473–478.

22. Grondin R, Goulet M, Di Paolo T, Bédard PJ. Cabergoline, a long-acting D_2 receptor agonist, produces a sustained antiparkinsonian effect with transient dyskinesias. Brain Res 1996; 735: 298–306.

23. Blanchet PJ, Grondin R, Bédard PJ. Dyskinesia and wearing-off following dopamine D_1 agonist treatment in drug-naïve and MPTP-lesioned primates. Mov Disord 1995;11: 91–94.

24. Alexander GM, Brainard DL, Gordon SW, et al. Dopamine receptor changes in untreated and (+)-PHNO-treated MPTP parkinsonian primates. Brain Res 1991; 547: 181–189.

25. Cedarbaum JM, Clark M, Toy LH, et al. Sustained-release (+)-PHNO in the treatment of Parkinson's disease: evidence for tolerance to a selective D_2 receptor agonist administered as a long-acting formulation. Mov Disord 1990; 5: 298–303.

26. Calon F, Goulet M, Blanchet PJ, Martel JC, Piercey MF, Bédard PJ, Di Paolo T. Levodopa or D_2 agonist dyskinesia in MPTP monkeys: correlation with changes in dopamine and $GABA_A$ receptors in the striato-pallidal complex. Brain Res 1995; 680: 43–52.

27. Doucet JP, Nakabeppu Y, Bédard PJ, Hope BT, Nestler EJ, Jasmin B, Iadarola M, St-Jean M, Wigle M, Robertson GS. Chronic alterations in dopaminergic neurotransmission produce a persistent elevation of striatal ΔFosB expression. Eur J Neurosci 1996; 8: 365–381.

28. Close SP, Marriott AS, Pay S. Failure of SKF38393A to relieve parkinsonian symptoms induced by MPTP in the marmoset. Br J Pharmacol 1985; 85: 320–322.

29. Nomoto M, Jenner P, Marsden CD. The dopamine D_2 agonist LY-131865 but not the D_1 agonist SKF38393 reverses parkinsonism induced by 1-methyl-4-phenyl-1,2,3,6-tetrahydropyridine (MPTP) in the common marmoset. Neurosci Lett 1985; 57: 37–41.

30. Bédard PJ, Boucher R. Effect of D_1 stimulation in normal and MPTP monkeys. Neurosci Lett 1989; 104: 223–228.

31. Markstein R, Seilers MP, Vigault JM, et al. Pharmacological properties of CY208243, a novel D_1 agonist. In, Sandler M, Dahlstrom A, Belkmaker, eds, Progress in catecholamine research, part B. New York: Alan R. Liss, 1988.

32. Blanchet PJ, Grondin R, Bédard PJ, Shiozaki K, Britton DR. Dopamine D_1 receptor desensitization profile in MPTP-lesioned primates. Eur J Pharmacol 1996; 309: 13–20.

DISCUSSION

Rascol: In those animals that developed tolerance to the effect of the continuous infusion, did you try adding levodopa and what was the response? I have always been surprised by this waning effect in patients on long-term treatment with dopamine agonists which could be explained by this mechanism and yet when you add levodopa, it works very nicely.

Bédard: The design of this experiment was fixed so that only animals in the levodopa group actually received levodopa. In other experiments, however, once animals are desensitized with a long-acting D_1 agonist, they can still respond to a D_2 agonist and, interestingly, the response was stronger than that seen before desensitization.

Obeso: With the long-acting D_2 agonist, what about tolerance in the motor response ?

Bédard: We have been very impressed by tolerance to long-acting D_1 agonists. The tolerance to D_2 agonists, even long-acting ones, is at most partial. As you saw with cabergoline, there was a partial decrease in hyperlocomotion, but the animals were still very active, maintaining their improvement in score. So there may be partial tolerance but there was a relatively good motor response for the duration of the experiment with receding dyskinesia.

Obeso: I agree there is still a response but most of the work is associated with some tolerance.

Bédard: We may have to consider combination with, for example, a D_1 agonist with a medium duration of activity of about four to five hours. This is not too long to induce desensitization and not too short to induce dyskinesia.

Obeso: In the last couple of years, there has been a lot of emphasis, particularly from the NIH and other groups in the USA, on extra-striatal mediation of dopamine action. Do you have any insight into a possible mechanism ?

Bédard: We know that there are D_1 receptors in the subthalamic nucleus and in the GPi but we have not analyzed the changes which occur there.

Gimenez-Roldan: Occasionally, patients on levodopa therapy have disabling dyskinesias with a very narrow therapeutic window. When they are switched to a pure D_2 agonist such as bromocriptine, the dyskinesias are again reproduced. How do you explain that ?

Bédard: This means that functional changes have been induced by denervation plus chronic treatment with levodopa. When D_2 agonist is started, the patient has dyskinesia, as you saw with cabergoline in animals never treated with levodopa. These changes take time, but my guess would be that if patients were treated with a dopamine agonist without levodopa, some of these changes could be reversed and an improvement seen.

Olanow: Are there any enkephalin inhibitors, as some studies indicate that dyskinesia is associated with overexpression of preproenkephalin?

Bédard: There are blockers but they have not been tested.

Aquilonius: What is really meant by 'continuous' and what extrapolations may be made from animal experiments to man with regard to sleep-waking cycle activity? Is continuous infusion performed in the monkeys during sleep also?

Bédard: We put 2ML4 minipumps under the skin which release the agent continuously day and night, for one month. The monkeys are kept on a light cycle which corresponds to day and night, so they have a sleep cycle which is similar to humans.

Aquilonius: There are some publications which suggest that, in man, round-the-clock infusion differs from daytime infusion.

Stocchi: We have some experience with this issue. If a D_2 agonist is given as a continuous infusion to patients with fluctuations and dyskinesias, the dyskinesias are definitely reduced. We used a 12-hour infusion, leaving the patient free at night. This could prevent tachyphylaxis, for example, and it would be interesting to do this experiment in monkeys. Secondly, we treated a *de novo* patient with ropinirole to determine if dopamine agonists show long-lasting effects similar to levodopa. The effects of ropinirole lasted for up to nine days. I wonder, therefore, about the importance of the dopamine agonist half-life in the *de novo* patient, although it becomes very important later on. The MPTP-treated monkey model does mimic the advanced disease in man, with a very long-lasting effect of levodopa.

Bédard: The same is true for MPTP-treated humans, who develop dyskinesia and fluctuations very rapidly, due to the coupling of a young brain with very severe disease from the onset, which is not necessarily the case in most patients. Regarding the ideal duration, the half-life of the drug is not absolutely important. The general principle is that long-acting agents, with a half-life of six to 12 hours, have advantages over drugs with a shorter duration of action (two to three hours).

Olanow: In an attempt to improve parkinsonism by high frequency stimulation of the subthalamic nucleus (STN), Benabid and Pollock initially induced dyskinesia, but this gradually disappeared with chronic STN stimulation although this is associated with a reduction in levodopa dosage. This is an interesting observation and leads to speculation on whether chronic STN stimulation provides benefits through a mechanism similar to continuous dopaminergic stimulation.

Bédard: The mechanisms can operate at several levels. For instance, there could be a striatal mechanism, a molecular mechanism in the neurons, a peptide mechanism in the external globus pallidus and a GABA mechanism in the internal globus pallidus, all of which may be influenced separately. The STN stimulation may affect the globus pallidus more than other regions.

CHAPTER SIX

The preclinical pharmacology of ropinirole – receptor interactions, antiparkinsonian activity and potential to induce dyskinesia

PETER JENNER[1], PhD, DSc, FRPharmS
AND IAN TULLOCH[2], PhD

[1]Neurodegenerative Diseases Research Centre, King's College London, London and [2]SmithKline Beecham Pharmaceuticals, Harlow, UK

ABSTRACT

Levodopa remains the dominant treatment for Parkinson's disease but new selective dopamine agonist drugs are being introduced for early use in this disorder. Ropinirole is a highly selective dopamine agonist with a unique non-ergoline structure. It interacts selectively with D_2-like receptors in vitro *and in* vivo, *showing a predominance for the D_3 subtype but with little or no interaction with other neurotransmitter receptors. Ropinirole produces alterations in motor behavior indicative of antiparkinsonian activity, including contraversive rotation in 6-hydroxydopamine-lesioned rats and the normalization of motor function and reversal of disability in MPTP-treated primates. Importantly, the administration of ropinirole over a four-week period to drug-naïve MPTP-treated primates induced only mild dyskinesia similar to that produced by bromocriptine but far less than observed with the repeated administration of levodopa. Ropinirole is well-absorbed after oral administration but shows varying degrees of first-pass metabolism in different species. Its plasma protein binding is low and there is extensive phase I and phase II hepatic metabolism. The major pathway in man is the formation of the N-despropyl metabolite which is pharmacologically inactive. In summary, the pharmacologic profile of ropinirole suggests that this compound is an effective antiparkinsonian drug with a low propensity to induce dyskinetic side effects.*

Parkinson's disease (PD) is due primarily to the degeneration of pigmented dopamine-containing cells in the zona compacta of substantia nigra with concomitant appearance of Lewy bodies.[1] The resulting loss of striatal dopamine content is thought to be responsible for the primary features of akinesia, rigidity and tremor. The cause of nigral cell loss remains unknown but may involve excessive formation of reactive oxygen species, oxidative stress and oxidative damage to lipids, protein and DNA.[2] Since the late 1960s, effective therapy for PD has been available in the form of the amino acid precursor of dopamine, namely levodopa. Indeed, levodopa remains the mainstay of treatment of PD, being more effective than any other currently available agent. However, long-term therapy with levodopa leads to a series of treatment complications.[3] The efficacy of the drug declines such that patients experience less benefit from each individual dose of levodopa ('wearing off') and the response may become unpredictable ('on-off' phenomenon). In addition, the use of levodopa may precipitate dose-limiting psychotic episodes, and as many as 70% of PD patients treated with levodopa develop unwanted involuntary movements in the form of chorea and dystonias (dyskinesias). These side effects complicate the use of levodopa such that in the later stages of the illness they preclude adequate treatment for those individuals with the most severe symptomatology. In addition, there has been concern that levodopa may itself exert neurotoxic properties which enhance the rate of progression of PD.[4] *In vitro* studies show that levodopa can exert neurotoxic effects on cell cultures but there is little evidence from *in vivo* investigations in rats or primates to indicate such a toxic action. So far, little support for this concept has come from retrospective studies of the use of levodopa in man. However, the issue of the potential toxicity of levodopa remains key to the development of novel therapeutic strategies for treating PD.

An alternative approach to the treatment of PD has been to use dopamine agonist compounds, such as bromocriptine, pergolide and lisuride. The currently utilized agonist drugs act predominantly through D_2 receptors.[5] Some exert effects on D_1-like receptors; bromocriptine is a D_1 receptor antagonist while pergolide has some D_1 agonist activity. However, the beneficial actions of dopamine agonists in PD have been primarily associated with selective D_2 receptor stimulation. So far, no dopamine agonist drug is as effective as levodopa in the treatment of PD, and dopamine agonists have been used mainly in combination with levodopa as adjunct therapy once treatment complications have begun to occur. Available dopamine agonists (bromocriptine, pergolide and lisuride) are ergoline derivatives and as such exert some activity on other receptor systems such as noradrenaline and 5-HT. This in turn may contribute to the common side effects associated with the use of these compounds in the treatment of PD. Thus, all produce hypotension, somnolence and psychotic episodes. Only bromocriptine and pergolide are in routine use as oral medication for PD, with apomorphine and lisuride being mainly utilized by subcutaneous injection or infusion. Monotherapy with bromocriptine induces a low incidence of dyskinesias compared to levodopa,[6] but few patients can be maintained on monotherapy for more than one or two years. Pergolide has an important role as an adjunct to levodopa treatment.[7] However, there is no information available on the use of pergolide as monotherapy in the treatment of PD or on its propensity to induce dyskinesia.

There is, therefore, a need to develop new dopamine agonists for use in PD which are more effective than those currently available and which produce less severe side effects than occur with levodopa therapy. In addition, there is a need to evaluate dopamine agonists early in the treatment of PD in an effort to avoid or delay the onset of dyskinesias and the putative neurotoxic effect of levodopa. One way is to produce dopamine agonist drugs which are highly selective for dopamine receptors with little or no action on other neurotransmitter receptors in the brain. In addition, the recent description of multiple dopamine receptors in the brain (D_1–D_5) allows for the development of drugs which selectively interact with one or more receptor subtypes.[8] Indeed, D_2-like dopamine receptors can be further divided into D_2, D_3 and D_4 receptors, allowing drug targeting within this receptor family. Several new dopamine agonist compounds have recently been described for use in the treatment of PD, namely ropinirole, pramipexole, talipexole and cabergoline. This chapter concentrates on the pharmacologic actions of one of these compounds, ropinirole, its activity in models of PD and in particular on its ability to initiate dyskinesia in a primate model of PD.

ROPINIROLE

Ropinirole is a potent non-ergoline dopamine agonist that binds specifically to D_2-like receptors with a selectivity similar to that of dopamine. Its structure is distinct from those of other currently available dopamine agonists, most of which are ergoline derivatives (Figure 1). Ropinirole has been shown to exert its agonistic activity at D_2-like receptors located at presynaptic and postsynaptic sites and its pharmacologic profile suggests that it will provide an effective treatment for PD with relatively fewer side effects than are seen with existing dopamine agonists.

PHARMACOLOGIC SPECIFICITY

In radioligand binding studies, ropinirole has a high affinity (pKi 7.54) for dopamine D_2-like receptors and shows negligible affinity for the D_1 subtype. In addition, it has insignificant affinity for a wide range of non-dopaminergic receptors in the brain, including α- and β-adrenoceptors, 5-HT$_1$ and 5-HT$_2$, benzodiazepine and GABA$_A$ receptors.[9] In contrast, ergoline dopamine agonists such as pergolide and bromocriptine, in addition to their interaction with dopamine receptors, have affinity for some of these sites, particularly 5-HT$_1$, 5-HT$_2$ and α-adrenoceptors (Table 1).[10–15] This lack of receptor specificity may contribute to the side effect profile of bromocriptine and pergolide in the clinic.

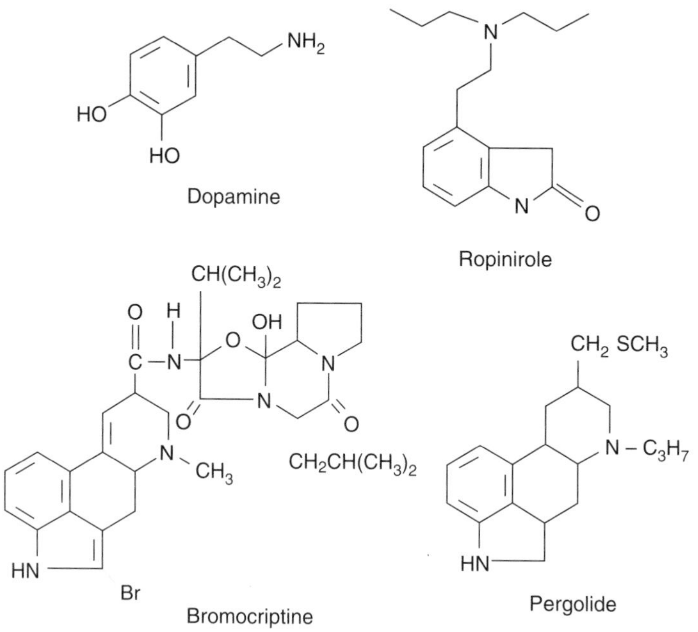

Figure 1: Chemical structures of dopamine, ropinirole and the ergoline dopamine agonists, bromocriptine and pergolide.

Table 1: Dopamine agonist interaction with CNS receptors

Dopamine agonist	Receptor Binding			
	D_2	D_1	$5\text{-}HT_{1/2}$	$\alpha_{1/2}$
Ropinirole	++	0	0	0
Bromocriptine*	++	+	++	++
Pergolide**	+++	+	++	++

*	Bromocriptine is a D_1 antagonist
**	Pergolide is a D_1 agonist
+++	very high
++	high
+	moderate
0	no effect

FUNCTIONAL INTERACTION WITH CLONED HUMAN D_2-LIKE RECEPTORS

Ropinirole interacts with cloned human dopamine receptor subtypes in CHO cell lines transfected with recombinant human D_2, D_3 and D_4 receptors. In binding studies, ropinirole was about 20-fold more selective for

D_3 than D_2 receptors and 50-fold more selective for D_3 than D_4 receptors.[16] The rank order of affinity for ropinirole ($D_3 > D_2 > D_4$) was similar to that of dopamine itself. The functional interaction of ropinirole at cloned human D_2-like receptors can be determined using microphysiometry. This technique detects small changes in the rate of extracellular acidification (reflecting increased cellular metabolism) that occur following activation of cell surface receptors of the D_2 - like family. Ropinirole and dopamine act as full agonists at D_2, D_3 and D_4 receptors as judged by this method (Table 2). Similarly the non-ergoline talipexole produced a maximum response at D_2 and D_3 receptors but a partial agonist effect at D_4 receptors. It is noteworthy that both ropinirole and dopamine showed a higher potency at the D_3 than the D_2 receptor subtype, consistent with the binding data, whereas pergolide showed greater activity at D_2 than D_3 receptors.[17] In this respect, pergolide resembles bromocriptine in showing modest D_2 selectivity in functional assays.[18]

Table 2: Functional potencies of dopamine agonists at cloned human D_2-like receptors in vitro

Dopamine agonist	EC$_{50}$ (nM)			D$_3$/D$_2$ selectivity ratio
	D$_2$	**D$_3$**	**D$_4$**	
Ropinirole	31	3	158	10.3
Dopamine	158	50	100	3.2
Talipexole	12	6	316	2.0
Pergolide	1	6	6	0.16
Bromocriptine*	1.8	12	ND	0.15

Adapted with permission[17]
* Functional mitogenesis assay[18]

EFFECTS MEDIATED BY D_2-LIKE AUTORECEPTORS IN VIVO

Ropinirole also interacts with D_2-like receptors located on presynaptic dopaminergic terminals (autoreceptors). Single doses of ropinirole (0.03–10 mg/kg, p.o.) administered to mice produced dose-dependent reductions in whole brain levels of the dopamine metabolites, homovanillic acid (HVA) and 3,4-dihydroxyphenylacetic acid (DOPAC). Noradrenaline and serotonin turnover were not affected by this treatment.[19] In electrophysiologic studies, ropinirole potently inhibited spontaneously-firing dopaminergic neurons in the substantia nigra pars compacta (ED$_{50}$ = 10–12 μg/kg, i.v.), an effect that was fully blocked by the D_2 receptor antagonist haloperidol (Ashby, personal communication).

The presynaptic effect of D_2 agonists may provide neuroprotection as a result of decreasing dopamine release and a subsequent reduction in the amount of hydrogen peroxide generated through dopamine metabolism.[5] As such, they may have positive effects on disease progression occurring as a result of oxidative stress. Indeed, ropinirole produces a concentration-dependent decrease in hydroxyl radical production in rat striatum evoked by MPP^+-induced dopamine efflux and assessed by *in vivo* microdialysis and salicylate trapping techniques (Jenner, unpublished observations).

ANTIPARKINSONIAN ACTIVITY IN RODENT AND PRIMATE MODELS

Ropinirole produces effects on motor function in normal rodents indicative of pre- and postsynaptic agonist activity. It demonstrated biphasic effects on locomotor activity in both mice and rats.[9] This dose-response profile is consistent with that of a specific, centrally-acting dopamine D_2 receptor agonist. In mice and rats, ropinirole (1–100 mg/kg) caused only mild stereotypic behaviors which were not dose-dependent. In contrast, amphetamine and apomorphine produced marked dose-related stereotypies.[9]

Experimental models of PD in which the nigrostriatal tract is destroyed by either 6-OHDA or MPTP provide evidence that ropinirole is a potent, centrally-acting dopamine agonist with therapeutic potential for the treatment of PD.

6-OHDA-lesioned rodents

In mice and rats lesioned unilaterally with 6-OHDA, postsynaptic dopamine agonists induce circling behavior towards the intact contralateral side. Administration of ropinirole to 6-OHDA-lesioned mice caused contralateral turning across the dose range 0.05–6.4 mg/kg, s.c.[9] Similar results were obtained in 6-OHDA-lesioned rats[20] where ropinirole caused dose-dependent contralateral turning with an ED_{50} of 0.1 mg/kg, s.c.

MPTP-treated common marmosets

1-Methyl-4-phenyl-1,2,3,6-tetrahydropyridine (MPTP) selectively destroys dopamine cell bodies in the zona compacta of the substantia nigra in humans and primates. MPTP treatment produces a marked decrease in locomotor activity, and parkinsonian disability. The MPTP-treated primate is considered the best validated model of PD currently available. Drug action in MPTP-treated primates is consistent with effects observed in man and is highly predictive of antiparkinsonian activity.

In MPTP-treated common marmosets, ropinirole (0.1–1.0 mg/kg, p.o., or 0.05–1.0 mg/kg, s.c.) restored motor function in a dose-related fashion and improved facial expression and movement co-ordination for complex tasks (Figure 2).[9] Onset of activity following ropinirole was within 10–20 minutes of administration and with a duration exceeding two hours. At higher doses, ropinirole induced hyperactivity, emesis and a 'nausea response'. However, lower doses produced some reversal of the motor deficits and no emesis or

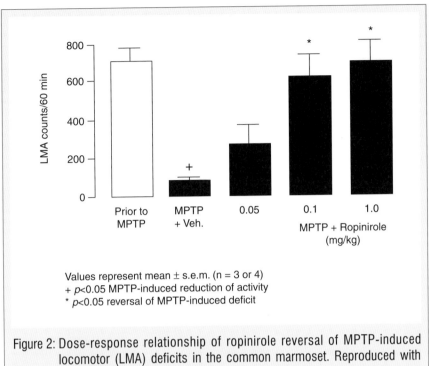

Figure 2: Dose-response relationship of ropinirole reversal of MPTP-induced locomotor (LMA) deficits in the common marmoset. Reproduced with permission.[9]

nausea. Similarly, levodopa plus benserazide also reversed the motor deficits in MPTP-treated marmosets but again, at higher doses, there was emesis and the 'nausea response'.[9]

Chronic administration of ropinirole to MPTP-treated marmosets produced no evidence for the development of tolerance to the antiparkinsonian activity.[9] In contrast, tolerance has been shown to occur to the hypotensive effect of ropinirole in cats and primates.[21] No adverse effects occurred following abrupt cessation of ropinirole after chronic administration (28 days) to cynomolgus monkeys, indicating that the drug has no physical dependence liability (SmithKline Beecham, data on file).

Induction of dyskinesias in MPTP-treated primates

The MPTP-treated primate provides an opportunity not only to determine the antiparkinsonian activity of novel agents but also to assess their ability to induce dyskinesias. The repeated administration of levodopa to MPTP-treated primates rapidly induces dyskinesia since these animals have a severe underlying nigral degeneration.[22] Once dyskinesia is established in response to levodopa treatment, the ability of dopamine agonist drugs to provoke an established dyskinetic response can be ascertained. Previous investigation has shown that all dopamine agonists acting on D_2-like receptors produce an antiparkinsonian response in this model, accompanied by dyskinesia, and that this does not abate on repeated administration.[23,24] This includes bromocriptine which, in clinical use as monotherapy, produces a mild degree of dyskinesia. However, in both the MPTP levodopa-primed primates and in patients with PD previously treated with levodopa, bromocriptine provokes dyskinesia like other dopamine agonist compounds. It is not surprising, therefore, that the acute administration of ropinirole to levodopa-primed MPTP-treated monkeys also initiates dyskinesias as well as producing a significant antiparkinsonian activity (unpublished data).

However, of greater importance is the propensity of dopamine agonist drugs to initiate dyskinesia in otherwise drug-naïve MPTP-treated primates. This has particular relevance to the early use of these compounds in the treatment of PD. Studies with bromocriptine have shown it to induce little or no dyskinesia when administered repeatedly to drug-naïve MPTP-treated primates.[25] This suggests that compounds which have a largely D_2-like receptor action may avoid the onset of dyskinetic phenomena. However, subsequent studies with other D_2-like receptor agonists, namely PHNO and quinpirole, showed the appearance of dyskinesia on repeated administration to MPTP-treated primates.[26] However, bromocriptine has a much longer duration of effect than PHNO or quinpirole. This is important since drugs which have a short pulsatile effect on dopamine receptors are more likely to induce dyskinesias than compounds which produce prolonged or continuous receptor stimulation.[27] This is of particular relevance to alterations in striatal output pathways, particularly the indirect D_2-mediated striatopal-lidal–GABA/enkephalin-containing pathway which is thought to be involved in the initiation of dyskinetic responses.[28] Since ropinirole has a long duration of effect in reversing parkinsonian deficits in MPTP-treated primates, it might be expected to show a low propensity to induce dyskinesia compared to levodopa. Indeed, in a recent investigation of the comparative ability of levodopa, bromocriptine and ropinirole to produce antiparkinsonian activity and to initiate dyskinesia in MPTP-treated primates, this has proved to be correct.[29]

In groups of MPTP-treated drug-naïve common marmosets, levodopa, bromocriptine and ropinirole were administered in doses which produced similar degrees of reversal of motor disability and which, over the 30-day period of administration, produced equivalent alterations in locomotor activity.[29] The repeated administration of levodopa rapidly produced dyskinesias within the first few days of treatment which then intensified in severity over the course of the study. Administration of bromocriptine, as previously reported, produced a much lower intensity of dyskinetic response. Ropinirole produced an even lower incidence of dyskinesia than was observed with bromocriptine and on some days no dyskinesia was apparent. Both bromocriptine and ropinirole produced a significantly lower dyskinetic score than levodopa during the 30-day study but the difference between bromocriptine and ropinirole was not significant although ropinirole had a lower overall score (Figure 3). This study confirms that some D_2 agonist

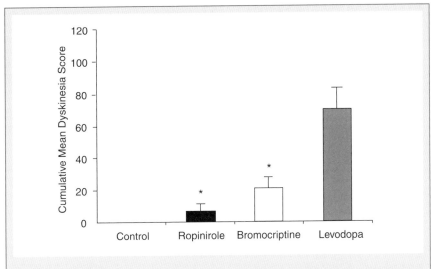

Figure 3: Cumulative mean daily dyskinesia scores in MPTP-treated common marmosets over 30 days receiving levodopa (12.5 mg/kg daily plus carbidopa 12.5 mg/kg p.o.), ropinirole (0.3 mg/kg for seven days then 0.5 mg/kg p.o. daily) or bromocriptine (1.0 mg/kg for seven days then 0.5 mg/kg s.c. daily) against controls (n=4 in each group). *$p<0.01$ vs levodopa. Reproduced with permission.[29]

drugs produce a lower incidence of dyskinesia compared to levodopa and that this may be related to the pharmacokinetic and pharmacodynamic properties of these compounds.

Alterations in striatopallidal activity in this study were assessed by measuring the mRNA for enkephalin (preproenkephalin). The administration of MPTP to common marmosets produces an elevation of preproenkephalin mRNA in the striatum as a result of the removal of the normal inhibitory dopaminergic tone. Following chronic treatment of MPTP-treated primates for 30 days with levodopa, the elevation in preproenkephalin mRNA was unchanged. Similarly, there was little or no change in striatal preproenkephalin mRNA following repeated administration of bromocriptine. However, treatment with ropinirole produced a marked decrease in preproenkephalin mRNA such that levels returned almost to those seen in normal animals. This suggests that ropinirole is able to reverse a key biochemical abnormality which is normally associated with the onset of dyskinetic phenomena (unpublished data).

PHARMACOKINETIC PROFILE OF ROPINIROLE

Extensive studies on the pharmacokinetic profile of ropinirole have been undertaken in a range of species, including man (Table 3). Ropinirole is rapidly and almost completely absorbed in the mouse, rat, monkey and man.

Table 3: Pharmacokinetic profile of ropinirole in rat, monkey and man

Parameter	Rat	Monkey	Man
Time to peak plasma concentration (hours)	1.5–4	1–1.6	1.1–1.4
Plasma protein binding (%)	30	~25	39
Elimination half-life (hours)	~0.5	1.3	5–7**
		11*	

* A second elimination phase was observed in 3 out of 4 animals with a mean half-life of 11 hours
** After oral administration of ropinirole to patients with PD
SmithKline Beecham, unpublished data.

Peak plasma concentrations after oral administration were generally seen within two hours in all species. Blood clearance was high in the rat and monkey, indicating that ropinirole undergoes extensive first-pass metabolism in these species. Because of this metabolism, bioavailability is lower in the rat and monkey. In man, the mean absolute bioavailability of ropinirole (46%) was greater than in the monkey and rat.

Plasma protein binding was low (10–40%) and independent of concentration. Therefore, ropinirole would not be expected to produce drug interactions by displacement of plasma protein-bound drugs, and alterations of its pharmacokinetics as a result of changes in plasma protein levels are unlikely.

Ropinirole is extensively metabolized by conventional phase I and phase II pathways in the liver (Figure 4). In the rat, the major metabolic pathway was via hydroxylation at position 7 to form SK&F89124. In the mouse, non-human primates and man, the major pathway was via N-depropylation to form SK&F104557, which was further metabolized to the inactive metabolites, SK&F97930 and SK&F96990. Metabolites formed by either pathway were then generally metabolized further in phase II by glucuronidation. Studies in human liver microsomes have shown that cytochrome $P_{450}1A2$ (CYP1A2) is the enzyme mainly responsible for metabolism of ropinirole.[30]

Pharmacologic activity of ropinirole metabolites

The major metabolite in mouse, monkey and man, SK&F104557, had a lower affinity than ropinirole for dopamine D_2 and D_3 receptors. Its *in vivo* activity in rats was at least 100-fold lower than that of ropinirole. Neither of the two metabolites of SK&F104557, SK&F97930 and SK&F96990, showed activity at central dopamine D_2 receptors *in vivo*.[20] Thus, it is unlikely that any of these metabolites contribute to the central dopamine D_2 agonist activity of ropinirole in man.

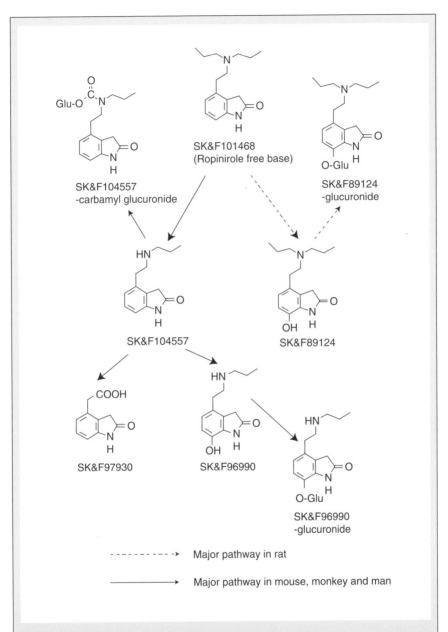

Figure 4: Proposed biotransformation of ropinirole in mouse, rat, cynomolgus monkey and man. SmithKline Beecham, unpublished data.

Conclusion

Dopamine agonist drugs have a significant place in the treatment of PD as adjunct therapy to levodopa in the latter stages of the illness when treatment complications arise. However, they can also provide significant symptomatic benefit in the early stages of the illness by avoiding the early use of levodopa and the onset of treatment complications, in particular dyskinesias. Ropinirole is a highly selective dopamine agonist with little effect on other types of neurotransmitter receptors. Its specific effects on the D_2-like family of receptors confers a selectivity to the compound, not present in those dopamine agonists currently utilized in the treatment of PD. From the pharmacologic profile of ropinirole it is clear that the compound exerts a selective and functional effect on the D_3 receptor, although also having actions on the D_2-like family of receptors in general. The role of the D_3 receptor in the treatment of PD remains unknown but the effects of ropinirole at this site may have relevance to the atypical antidepressant activity shown by the compound in the Porsolt rat swimming test (unpublished data). The ability of ropinirole to produce rotation in 6-hydroxydopamine-lesioned rats and a reversal of motor deficits in MPTP-treated primates is an expected response for an effective dopamine D_2-agonist drug and is predictive of antiparkinsonian activity. The good oral bioavailability of ropinirole, coupled with its low degree of plasma protein binding and lack of active metabolites, suggest that it will be without significant pharmacokinetic or drug interaction problems in clinical use. Of particular interest is the low intrinsic activity of ropinirole in producing dyskinesia in otherwise drug-naïve MPTP-treated primates. This suggests that the use of the compound as monotherapy in the early stages of PD is unlikely to induce significant dyskinetic effects, so avoiding one of the major side effects which occurs as a result of early use of levodopa in this patient population. Indeed, the use of ropinirole alone, as primary therapy followed by the introduction of levodopa when necessary, may limit the onset of dyskinesias for a significant period of time so allowing more effective treatment of PD patients.

ACKNOWLEDGMENTS

This study was supported by the National Parkinson's Disease Foundation, Miami, USA, the Parkinson's Disease Society and the Medical Research Council, UK, and the Medical Research Council, Canada.

REFERENCES

1. Forno LS. Pathology of Parkinson's disease. In, Marsden CD, Fahn S, eds, Neurology 2, Movement Disorders. London: Butterworths Scientific, 1982: 25–40.

2. Jenner P, Olanow CW. Oxidative stress and the pathogenesis of Parkinson's disease. Neurol 1996; 47 (Suppl 3): S161–S170.

3. Marsden CD, Parkes JD, Quinn N. Fluctuations of disability in Parkinson's disease – clinical aspects. In, Marsden CD, Fahn S, eds, Neurology 2, Movement Disorders. London: Butterworths Scientific, 1982: 96–122.

4. Olanow CW. A rationale for the use of dopamine agonists as primary therapy: Parkinson's disease. Can J Neurol Sci 1992;19: 108–112.

5. Jenner P. The rationale for the use of dopamine agonists in Parkinson's disease. Neurol 1995; 45 (Suppl 3): S6–S12.

6. Lees AJ, Stern GM. Sustained bromocriptine therapy in previously untreated patients with Parkinson's disease. J Neurol Neurosurg Psychiatr 1981; 44:1020–1023.

7. Langtry HD, Clissold SO. Pergolide – a review of its pharmacological properties and therapeutic potential in Parkinson's disease. Drugs 1990; 39: 491–506.

8. Schwartz J-C, Giros B, Martres M-P, Sokoloff P. The dopamine receptor family: molecular biology and pharmacology. Semin Neurosci 1992; 4: 99–108.

9. Eden RJ, Costall B, Domeney AM, Gerrard PA, Harvey CA, Kelly ME, Naylor RJ, Owen DAA, Wright A. Preclinical pharmacology of ropinirole (SK&F101468-A), a novel dopamine D_2 agonist. Pharmacol Biochem Behav 1991; 38: 147–154.

10. Silberberg EK, Hrushka RE. Effects of ergot drugs on serotonergic function: behavior and neurochemistry. Eur J Pharmacol 1979; 58: 1–10.

11. Hagan JD, Pierce PA, Peroutka SJ. Differential binding of ergot compounds to human versus rat 5-HT_2 cortical receptors. Biol Sign 1994; 3: 223–229.

12. Beart PM, McDonald D, Cincotta M, De Vries DJ, Gundlach AL. Selectivity of some ergot derivatives for 5-HT_1 and 5-HT_2 receptors of rat cerebral cortex. Gen Pharmacol 1986; 17: 57–62.

13. Ruffolo RR, Cohen ML, Messick K, Horng JS. Alpha-2-adrenoceptor mediated effects of pergolide. Pharmacol 1987; 35: 148–154.

14. Pahwa R, Koller WC. Dopamine agonists in the treatment of Parkinson's disease. Cleveland Clin J Med 1995; 62: 212–217.

15. Jackson DM, Mohell N, Georgiev J, Bengtsson A, Larsson L-G, Magnusson O, Ross SB. Time course of bromocriptine-induced excitation in the rat: behavioral and biochemical studies. Naunyn-Schmiedeberg's Arch Pharmacol 1995; 351: 146–155.

16. Bowen WP, Coldwell MC, Hicks FR, Riley GJ, Fears R. Ropinirole, a novel dopaminergic agent for the treatment of Parkinson's disease, with selectivity for cloned D_3 receptors. Br J Pharmacol 1993; 110 (Suppl): 93P.

17. Coldwell MC, Hagan J, Middlemiss D, Tulloch I, Boyfield I. Ropinirole is a D_3 selective agonist at cloned human D_{2long}, D_3 and $D_{4.4}$ receptors in functional studies using microphysiometry. Br J Pharmacol, in press.

18. Sautel F, Griffon N, Levesque D, Pilon C, Schwartz J-C, Sokoloff P. A functional test identifies dopamine agonists selective for D_3 versus D_2 receptors. Neuroreport 1995; 6: 329–332.

19. Fears R, Bowen WP, Eden RJ, Kay S. Neurochemical selectivity and D_3 affinity of the novel dopaminergic agonist ropinirole. New Trends Clin Neuropharmacol 1994; 8: 298.

20. Reavill C, Esmail A, Williamson IJ, Nelson P. The effect of ropinirole (SK&F101468) and its metabolites SK&F89124, SK&F104557, SK&F97930 and SK&F96990 in the *in vivo* circling rat model of Parkinson's disease. Neuropharmacol, submitted.

21. Parker SG, Raval P, Yeulet S, Eden RJ. Tolerance to peripheral, but not central effects of ropinirole, a selective dopamine D_2-like receptor agonist. Eur J Pharmacol 1994; 265: 17–26.

22. Bédard PJ, Di Paolo T, Falardeau P, Boucher R. Chronic treatment with levodopa, but not bromocriptine, induces dyskinesia in MPTP-parkinsonian monkeys. Correlation with ^{3}H-spiperone binding. Brain Res 1986; 379: 294–299.

23. Gomez-Mancilla B, Bédard PJ. Effect of D_1 and D_2 agonists and antagonists on dyskinesia produced by levodopa in 1-methyl-4-phenyl-1,2,3,6-tetrahydropyridine-treated monkeys. J Pharmacol Exp Ther 1991; 259: 409–413.

24. Pearce RKB, Jackson M, Smith L, Jenner P, Marsden CD. Chronic levodopa administration induces dyskinesias in the 1-methyl-4-phenyl-1,2,3,6-tetrahydropyridine-treated common marmoset (*Callithrix jacchus*). Mov Disord 1995; 10: 731–740.

25. Falardeau P, Bouchard S, Bédard PJ, Boucher R, Di Paolo T. Behavioral and biochemical effect of chronic treatment with D_1 and/or D_2 dopamine agonists in MPTP monkeys. Eur J Pharmacol 1988; 150: 59–66.

26. Bédard PJ, Gomez-Mancilla, Blanchette P, Gagnon C, Falardeau P, Di Paolo T. Role of selective D_1 and D_2 agonists in inducing dyskinesia in drug–naïve MPTP monkeys. In, Narabayshi H, Nagatsu T, Yanagisawa N, Mizuno Y, eds, Advances in Neurology, Vol 60. New York: Raven Press, 1993: 113–118.

27. Blanchette P, Bédard PJ, Matsumura M, Richard H, Filion M. Pathophysiology of levodopa-induced dyskinesia: changing concepts. In, Percheron G, *et al.*, eds, The Basal Ganglia. New York: Plenum Press, 1994: 539–548.

28. Crossman AR. A hypothesis on the pathophysiological mechanisms that underlie levodopa- or dopamine agonist-induced dyskinesia in Parkinson's disease: implications for future strategies in treatment. Mov Disord 1990; 5: 100–108.

29. Pearce RKB, Banerji T, Jenner P, Marsden CD. Effects of repeated treatment with levodopa, bromocriptine and ropinirole in drug-naïve MPTP-treated common marmosets. Br J Pharmacol 1996; 118 (Suppl): 37P.

30. Bloomer JC, Clarke SE, Chenery RJ. *In vitro* identification of the P450 enzymes responsible for the metabolism of ropinirole. Drug Metab Disposit, submitted.

DISCUSSION

Bédard: Do you think that any of the behavioral effects you describe in your animals are due to stimulation of D_3 receptors, since in rodents D_3 agonism decreases locomotor activity?

Jenner: The function of D_3 receptors is not known. It has been suggested that blockade of D_3 receptors may have antipsychotic effects, but this has not as yet been proven. It should also be considered that D_3 agonism may modulate D_1 and D_2 activity, as seen in mice.

Melamed: The highest concentration of D_3 receptors is seen in the islands of Calleja. Do you know the significance of this region?

Jenner: You are correct, but unfortunately no-one knows what these cells do. They are diffusely distributed throughout the ventral striatum and are therefore difficult to study.

Ogawa: Do you see any evidence of neuroprotection with ropinirole and do you think this might account for the reduced incidence of dyskinesia seen in ropinirole-treated parkinsonian monkeys?

Jenner: Stimulation of D_2 autoreceptors on presynaptic dopaminergic neurons may reduce dopamine turnover and decrease oxidative stress. In human patients, it is possible that a drug which prevents degeneration of dopamine terminals could permit a more normal or physiologic regulation of dopamine uptake, storage and release in the striatum and in this way protect against the development of dyskinesia. This is an important area to investigate but our studies were confined to simply testing the antiparkinsonian effects and propensity for dyskinesia associated with administration of ropinirole.

Leenders: Is it possible that the difference in dyskinesia between bromocriptine- and ropinirole-treated monkeys was due to the administration of relatively lower doses of ropinirole in the early stages of the study?

Jenner: We increased the dose of ropinirole after one week in order to induce comparable motor responses in our animals. We do not claim that ropinirole induces less dyskinesia than bromocriptine. While there was less dyskinesia in ropinirole-treated monkeys, differences between the ropinirole and bromocriptine groups were not statistically significant.

Sanchez-Ramos: Were the animals 'rewarded' by ropinirole, as they are with levodopa?

Tulloch: We have no evidence that ropinirole causes self-administration and there was no physical dependency.

Rascol: What is the half-life of ropinirole? I have seen wearing-off of its clinical effects within hours in parkinsonian patients.

Tulloch: Ropinirole has a half-life of six to seven hours in man, and one hour in rodents. The ergot dopamine agonists have metabolites with activities at different receptor types. This is not the case for ropinirole. As you know, however, pharmacokinetic and pharmacodynamic half-lives may differ. Both pergolide and bromocriptine also have shorter periods of benefit than would be predicted by the pharmacokinetic half-life.

Calne: Does ropinirole penetrate biological membranes, and is there any first-pass metabolism?

Tulloch: Ropinirole does penetrate biological membranes, and can penetrate the skin. It is metabolized in the liver by P_{450} and there is 30–40% first pass metabolism.

Olanow: Would you comment on the evidence that levodopa can induce dyskinesia in normal monkeys?

Jenner: Yes. We have recently shown that a high daily dose (80 mg/kg) of levodopa can induce dyskinesia in normal monkeys. Previous studies which did not show this effect used lower doses of levodopa and indeed we did not see dyskinesia in monkeys receiving 20–40 mg/kg of levodopa per day. Interestingly, expression of preproenkephalin was increased in those animals showing dyskinesia but not in those who did not develop this complication.

CHAPTER SEVEN

Mechanisms of motor complications in Parkinson's disease – a discussion

Olanow: We will now discuss the mechanisms that may be responsible for the motor complications seen with drug treatments in PD. So with that in mind, we will address the issue of what factors are responsible for the motor complications that plague patients and physicians. As a starting point, see Figures 3a–c in Chapter 1.

Obeso: I would like to begin by trying to address the concern about how pallidotomy might improve both parkinsonism and dyskinesia. The current model of the organization of the basal ganglia predicts that increased basal ganglia output is associated with parkinsonism and reduced output from the basal ganglia is associated with dyskinesia. This concept comes from the work of many investigators, particularly Alan Crossman and Mahlon DeLong. In summary, it has been shown that GPi neuronal and metabolic activity is increased in parkinsonism. It is thought that in parkinsonism, dopamine depletion induces disinhibition of the STN which excessively stimulates or drives the GPi. We have been very happy with that idea because it is very simple. Now comes the paradox of pallidotomy which improves parkinsonism but also improves dyskinesia. According to the model, a lesion in the GPi in a normal animal or person should reduce basal ganglia output and produce dyskinesia. This is consistent with the development of hemichorea or ballism after lesions in the STN which cause a reduction in the excitatory innervation of the GPi. This paradox may be explained by a recent paper from Filion and colleagues in *Neuroscience* which showed variable firing patterns in GPi neurons of normal monkeys rendered dyskinetic by bicuculline infusion into the GPe. In a previous paper they reported that in parkinsonian monkeys apomorphine induced a variable pattern of neuronal firing in the GPi. Indeed, single cell recordings indicate that neighboring neurons may show patterns of increased or decreased firing. This is a crucial observation in my view. Thus, overall firing frequencies may be misleading as activity can be reduced while firing in individual neurons is increased. So if an aberrant signal is emanating from the GPi, this could lead to dyskinesia despite the fact that this abnormality is not reflected in the increased overall firing rate and metabolic activity of the GPi. Vitek *et al.* have shown that in a patient with hemiballism, the abnormal firing pattern in a single neuron correlated precisely with dyskinetic movements. Pallidotomy relieved the movement disorder in this patient. Thus, one could envision how pallidotomy might improve parkinsonian features by reducing the excessive pallidal inhibitory output while at the same time eliminating the aberrant firing pattern in individual pallidal neurons that are associated with dyskinesia. So I think that the problems we have with the model may be because we have tried to oversimplify.

Brücke: The problem remains that if the thalamus is lesioned, akinesia does not occur.

Obeso: Marsden and I have considered this issue in our publication in *Brain*, 1994. The thalamocortical projection is thought to be underactive in PD and this is supported by the metabolic studies in PD patients and MPTP-treated monkeys. Thus, it is unlikely that a thalamic lesion will worsen parkinsonism as the pathway is already underactive. It is different in the normal state. Dick Passingham produced large bilateral thalamic lesions in normal monkeys and initially saw profound akinesia. The monkeys gradually recovered and were not akinetic but had residual motor learning problems.

Olanow: I think you see that clinically with bilateral thalamic hemorrhages or infarcts. These patients can be profoundly akinetic. This syndrome is somewhat uncommon, and it may be that bilateral thalamic lesions are required. I have been struck by the observation that unilateral stimulation of the STN induces bilateral benefits. Thus, dysfunction may not be associated with a unilateral thalamic lesion thereby accounting for the relative rarity of this syndrome.

Obeso: Yes, that is part of the problem. One should also consider that akinesia is a complex phenomenon and there may be multiple pathways that must be affected prior to its development.

Calne: I agree entirely with your thesis that one is dealing with a complex situation. That is the basis of my criticism of the model that has been discussed at such great length. It is obviously an over-simplification. What I want to emphasize is that we need to make models that fit the facts, and not force the facts to fit the models. I think we have to modify the model as the information becomes available and we may have to modify this model a lot further because I suspect that even the example you gave is a great over-simplification and there will be other things that have to be built into it.

Olanow: To illustrate this further, our group including Dr. Calne, recently described a profound increase in 'on' time with a reduction in dyskinesia following fetal nigral transplantation despite the fact that there was no alteration in the dose of levodopa. That patient had virtual elimination of 'off' time and the dyskinesia went away. So, in keeping with your idea that we really need to make a model that fits the facts, we need to have a model that explains these findings.

Jenner: Three points I would like to raise. Firstly, as one who has chased output pathways around the rat basal ganglia, I can assure you that it is very difficult to come to the conclusion that there is one single output pathway responsible for any of these phenomena. We could induce transient changes in motor behavior by lesioning any one of a number of nuclei and in most cases, within a few days or a few weeks, the animal has compensated and exhibits normal motor function. Secondly, I would like to return to the question of over-simplification and I do think the model is an over-simplification. We have put blinkers on. We have heard about the cholinergic input today. Where are these featured in our model? We have heard about the topographical glutamatergic input from the cortex. Where does this come into play? We talk about D_1 and D_2 receptors as though they are only in the striatum. They are not; they are in the globus pallidus and the subthalamic nucleus; there is a major population of D_1 receptors and output neurons in the substantia nigra reticularis. Not a word about those because it is too complicated. Third is the crucial question of why dyskinesias, once they develop, are permanent. Once you have them, certainly in animals, the pattern of behavior is laid down and every time you probe the animal with a dopamine agonist or with levodopa you get the same abnormal patterns of behavior. What makes them permanent? That is not in the wiring diagrams either.

Aquilonius: I think that presynaptic mechanisms have been underestimated in regard to their possible relationship to motor fluctuations. It has been shown that after intravenous infusion of levodopa into advanced parkinsonian patients, there is an instant displacement of raclopride binding in the striatum which is not seen in early parkinsonian patients. In my view this proves that in the advanced parkinsonian patient, exogenous levodopa is rapidly decarboxylated and synaptically available almost instantly after administration.

Obeso: I think the major criticism of the model is that it appears to be static when obviously it is not. But I do not think one should get too pessimistic. The model has played a fundamental role in some therapeutic advances such as predicting that lesions in the STN will improve parkinsonism.

Gerfen: In the wiring diagrams that we use in our working models, we do in fact include the cholinergic interneurons and the GABAergic interneurons. We feel these play a role in how information is processed within the striatum. The reason I don't include them in my diagrams is that the work is incomplete. Physiologists correctly give us a hard time with our diagrams. Michel Filion showed in the late 1970s and early 1980s that the pattern of activity in globus pallidus neurons is altered dramatically after dopamine lesions. More recently, he has noted that the patterns of activity differ from one neuron to the other in the GPi. So those of us utilizing this model show simple diagrams and yet we know the real data have a rich complexity. I make the case for a simple model because we try to isolate specific components within these circuits. The point I would make is that we know there are two populations of neurons with different connections. Neurons that provide direct projections are different in their connections from those that provide indirect projections and so we can say that there are direct and indirect pathways. Whether they are solely responsible for akinesias and dyskinesias remains to be established and is probably an over-simplification. Nonetheless, it is important to ask the question of how these different neuronal populations are regulated in their activity. We use the dopamine-depleted model because the groups act in a homogenous, almost stereotypic, way. When you give a D_1 agonist to dopamine-depleted animals, the entire population of D_1 neurons behaves in a homogeneous way. However, in the normal striatum there are subtypes of D_1 neuron and if you look at the distribution of responses in a normal animal to a D_1 agonist, some neurons show huge increases, while most do not show any increase at all. Another aspect of the firing of these spiny projection neurons comes from the work of Charlie Wilson who showed that they flip back and forth between two different states: a 'down' state and an 'up' state. This is an important aspect of the function of spiny neurons. So the point I would make is that the models are overly simplistic but they have some utility, particularly if you are aware of the underlying complexity.

Olanow: I think you have to consider that these models have allowed us to generate putative therapies that can be tested in animal models and eventually human patients. For example, based on the current model, it might be beneficial to electrically stimulate the GPe. Such an approach would be expected to induce inhibition of the subthalamic nucleus and the GPi through direct GABAergic axons. This might be preferable to stimulating the STN where it is not yet clear whether benefits are due to inhibition of STN output or excitation of STN neurons with stimulation of the GPe through backfiring and indirect inhibition of the GPi. The advantages of these kinds of models are that they allow us to come up with hypotheses which are testable and potentially can generate new therapies for our patients, even though refinements still need to be made to the model.

Calne: No, I cannot entirely agree that the models provide utility. They provide utility in generating hypotheses, getting grants, and in getting papers published but one should not be seduced by thinking that the models provide the truth.

Bédard: I would like to add another perspective to the discussion about models. In my view, the occurrence in the same patients of dyskinesia and fluctuations may be seen as two separate mechanisms. First of all, one could consider the response to dopaminergic agents. What we are seeing is the shortening of the motor response because the action starts later and ends sooner. This could be explained by certain dopamine receptors becoming subsensitive. On the other hand, dyskinesia, in my mind, seems more like a defect of collateral inhibition. When we perform a movement, it is likely that there is a preceding signal surrounded by an area of inhibition so that the message is clear. The fact that a lesion of the internal pallidum is capable of alleviating dyskinesias suggests that there may be a defect in collateral inhibition at a higher level. For example, a defect in the striatum, the STN, or the GPe could lead to an abnormal firing pattern that can be suppressed by a lesion in the GPi. This hypothesis would predict that if you can restore the sensitivity of dopamine receptors or normalize the threshold, you could restore neurochemical activity.

Sanchez-Ramos: This is reminiscent of the era in the 1950s when opiate dependence and withdrawal were treated with surgical procedures. But the chemists never gave up hope and they ended up synthesizing a series of mixed agonists–antagonists such as nalorphine and naloxone, and surgery is now rarely performed. I would like to suggest that probably there will be some mixed agonist or partial agonist–antagonist dopaminergic drugs such as 3PPP, that will tend to downregulate overactive dopamine receptors of one type and upregulate others.

Obeso: I would like to ask what would be the mechanism whereby a dopaminergic drug could avoid priming for dyskinesia?

Bédard: Unfortunately, the mechanism responsible for priming is not known. Our work suggests that dyskinesias are associated with pulsatile stimulation of the dopamine receptors and that continuous dopaminergic stimulation may be protective.

Jenner: My personal view is that the pharmacokinetics of the drug are one important component and based on Dr. Bédard's work, longer-acting drugs are less likely to prime than shorter-acting drugs. This is a very simplistic view, but what Dr. Bédard said about the priming phenomenon is the key to it all. We do not understand what the priming phenomenon is, nor do we understand what biochemical changes take place in the neuron. It is very difficult to avoid a phenomenon if you do not know the cause of that phenomenon.

Calne: I would like to suggest an experiment based on the transplant patient that you mentioned. I would like to reinforce the observation in the transplant patient with Cheung Lee's findings in rodents that transplanted tissue protects them from stereotypy induced by dopaminergic agents. It would be interesting to do a transplant procedure in an animal with mild parkinsonism to see if the graft would protect against the induction of dyskinesia by levodopa. The obvious clinical application of that would be to transplant an early patient to see if that would protect from dyskinesia.

Olanow: It is reasonable to consider that the experiment would be successful and that transplant might protect against development of dyskinesia. This could be a reflection of the observation that the two factors which promote the development of dyskinesia are disease severity and pulsatile administration of a dopaminergic drug. Transplant may effectively diminish the degree of disease severity.

Tolosa: I would agree that priming for dyskinesia occurs in parkinsonian patients. Cotzias noted that when he stopped levodopa for a month, patients would re-develop dyskinesias after the first two doses. One question I would like to ask is whether denervation of the striatum is necessary for priming? We know it is quite important for inducing dyskinesias. If so, do different degrees of lesions in the striatum induce different degrees of priming?

Jenner: I think one of the answers is that dyskinesia can be induced in normal monkeys but very high doses of levodopa must be administered.

Tolosa: But once you induce them, do you get priming?

Jenner: Yes, once they are induced they are primed and every dose of levodopa subsequently produces the same pattern of behavioral response, even in the normal monkey.

Obeso: Would you say that the opposite is true: that the more severe the denervation, the lower the threshold?

Jenner: Certainly the more severe the lesion, the shorter the time to the onset of dyskinesia.

Garcia de Yebenes: I would like to make a comment regarding Dr. Jenner's statement about the necessity for higher doses of dopamine agonists in normal animals. I believe that we should differentiate between the different types of dyskinesias. In normal animals, if you increase the dose of levodopa you can induce increased activity or hyperactivity. You can also get stereotypic behavior and dyskinesias of chorea type but in normal monkeys you do not get dystonia.

Melamed: I would like to redraw the attention of this audience to another fascinating phenomenon which may also involve priming. That is the initial response to levodopa. When we give levodopa to patients, we do not get an immediate response. It takes days and sometimes even weeks before we get a response and this is usually long before they develop dyskinesia. I am talking about levodopa-induced benefit. How does the parkinsonian patient get a response to levodopa? Priming in the induction of a response to levodopa may differ from the priming associated with dyskinesias.

Olanow: Dr Melamed, when you say that we do not get an effect in the first days, are you talking about patients with early, mild disease?

Melamed: Patients with more severe disease who are initiated on levodopa may have a good response with the first dose.

Calne: I agree with the observation that you make, but I think the explanation is simple. We generally start patients on a low dose and gradually increase the dose in order to reduce the incidence of side effects. Certainly in the old days, when you started levodopa in severe patients, the results were spectacular.

Obeso: Has anyone here seen dyskinesias in PD or in a monkey with MPTP PD induced with the first exposure?

All: General agreement – yes.

Obeso: I have also seen it so we agree that it occurs, but it is rare.

Olanow: The rapid onset of dyskinesia in these animals may relate to their degree of denervation and may not be directly comparable to what is seen in PD patients. Most patients with PD do not have the degree of nigral damage that is present in the MPTP monkey and do not receive the same dose of levodopa that is administered to the monkey. So it may not be a parallel comparison.

Bédard: I think that priming, as we understand it, relates to induction of transcription factors which in turn leads to changes in peptides. It is probably no accident that many of our patients, when the effect of their levodopa dose is over, not only have motor deterioration but a crash with pain, and a syndrome similar to that observed in people who have been addicted to cocaine or other opiates. I believe that these manifestations are due to induced chemicals in the striatum or elsewhere.

Rajput: With respect to the normal substantia nigra and dyskinesias, I have never seen one. I have several patients now whom I have followed for erroneous diagnoses that received high doses of levodopa. One of them has just come to autopsy after 27 years of treatment. He never had dyskinesias.

Olanow: This is only one case and the dose of levodopa employed may have been substantially less than that employed in the normal monkeys who developed dyskinesia following extremely high doses of levodopa (80 mg/kg).

Jenner: Can I come back to that? The dose is very important, in my view, in terms of dyskinesias and normal basal ganglia because at 40 mg/kg, which is 2.8 g of levodopa a day in human terms, plus a decarboxylase inhibitor, we saw no dyskinesia. When the dose is doubled to the equivalent of 5.6 g of levodopa a day plus a decarboxylase inhibitor, we started to see dyskinesia. So this response, at least in normal monkeys, is dose-dependent.

Obeso: Dr. Jenner, why did you give such a high dose of levodopa to a monkey?

Jenner: There were 48 Macaque monkeys in this study and it was a regulatory toxicology study. We were not involved in the design of the protocol.

Tolosa: We have been discussing the mechanism responsible for dyskinesias and the significance of priming. I have been impressed in my Parkinson's clinic by a problem that is even more important than dyskinesia – the mental side effects induced by levodopa and dopamine agonists. I would like to suggest that there is a certain priming effect here as well and once patients begin to have hallucinations or confusion, it quickly becomes an unmanageable problem. In a few weeks or months, many patients can hardly tolerate levodopa or dopamine agonists.

Olanow: I do not know if there is any evidence of priming for mental side effects. I think a lot of patients with PD develop dementia with psychosis and at post-mortem have Alzheimer's pathology or cortical Lewy bodies. It is likely that the neuropsychiatric adverse effects of levodopa that you are seeing are due to the background of dementia rather than a priming effect.

Tolosa: I would agree with you. It is difficult to use the term 'priming' for this problem. But the problem is that you give levodopa, induce confusion, and trigger it very quickly in subsequent weeks once it has developed. It is hard to think that this is from a concomitant Alzheimer's disease or other problem, but I agree with you, perhaps we should not be using this term.

Gershanik: In the matter of side effects with dopamine agonists, you have to remember that the main localization of D_4 receptors is gating the output of GABA neurons in the cortex, so probably the effect of dopaminergic agents mediating psychiatric side effects has nothing to do with the antiparkinsonian effect of dopaminergic agonists but is acting through a cortical mechanism.

Stocchi: I would like to comment on the issue of how long it takes for levodopa to become effective. We did a single-blind study in which we gave a fixed dose of 400 mg to a group of 10 *de novo* PD patients until they reached maximum effect. The patients took between three and 12 days to reach the maximum benefit, despite a constant dosage. Interestingly, the patient who took the least time was the most affected one. We also did a single-tablet levodopa dosing test at the beginning and end of the study. At the beginning of the study we could not detect any significant improvement. When we redid the experiment after they reached the maximum benefit, once again the single tablet did not induce any benefit because the patient had not deteriorated from his previous dosage. It took approximately 15 days for patients to return to their previous motor state. So there is a sort of relationship between the time to reach the maximum effect and the time to lose the effect which is the long-lasting effect of levodopa.

Calne: If you take into account the fact that the half-life in brain tissue must be much longer than in blood, then I think three days would be just what you would expect, from the principles of basic pharmacology, to build up a sufficient level in the brain to induce a pharmacodynamic effect.

Melamed: We have looked at the effect of the first-ever dose of levodopa by quantitative analysis of motor function. We also looked at the pharmacokinetics of the first-ever dose of levodopa. The results are fascinating. It takes time for levodopa to become effective. The priming, if we can use that term, could be at many levels. There could be priming of the absorption of the next dose of levodopa; maybe the absorption improves. Priming could be due to changes in dopa decarboxylase activity. And, of course, there could be priming of presynaptic or postsynaptic mechanisms.

Aquilonius: I think it is very important to have objective measurement of movement analysis because this is more sensitive than clinical examination and conventional scoring systems. With tests for posture, locomotion and manual function, you can observe the effect of levodopa after the first dose in any early parkinsonian patient.

Olanow: I think that if you are going to talk about priming you have to eliminate the pharmacokinetic contribution. We could design a study where you give a patient a dose of levodopa once every 14 days or an interval that far exceeds its elimination half-life. It would then be interesting to see if the same dose behaved differently when administered after the person had already been exposed to the initial dose. At present it is not possible to say that the delay in reaching maximal benefit is due to priming.

Calne: Dr. Obeso, you should be able to throw light on this, with apomorphine. You must have given apomorphine to *de novo* patients and I would have thought you get an immediate response, but tell me if I am wrong.

Obeso: Yes, that is correct. *De novo* patients respond to apomorphine. One has to focus on a patient with disease severity sufficient to be able to detect a benefit. The more advanced the patient, the more striking is the benefit.

Bonuccelli: We did this kind of trial in our *de novo* patients. We gave them 50 µg/kg of apomorphine at 8, 24, 48 and 72 hours, just to see if we could detect this kind of priming. We did not see anything at all, and there was no potentiation. I did not publish these studies because it was a negative study.

Rascol: I have a practical comment. Most of the clinical studies with dopamine agonists assess long-term motor side effects. The inclusion criteria allow patients to have received levodopa for a few weeks. I think this is wrong because we do not really know how long it takes for priming to occur. Thus, if you see dyskinesia or motor fluctuations in the agonist group, you cannot be sure if they are related to the agonist or to a pre-existing priming effect secondary to previous levodopa exposure.

Olanow: I think this is a very important point. In other words, a patient who starts on an agonist, having taken levodopa, may not be the same as a patient who starts on an agonist having never taken levodopa. I believe it is very important to design a clinical trial measuring efficacy and motor complications in untreated PD patients who are randomized to receive levodopa, a dopamine agonist having never seen levodopa, and a dopamine agonist having been previously exposed to levodopa.

SECTION III

Clinical Issues

CHAPTER EIGHT

Dopamine agonists in Parkinson's disease: a clinical review

EDUARDO TOLOSA AND CONCEPCIÓ MARIN

Department of Neurology, University of Barcelona,
Barcelona, Spain

ABSTRACT

Dopamine agonists have been used for the treatment of Parkinson's disease since 1974. Experience gained over this period has shown that the main benefits from the use of dopamine agonists are a reduction in levodopa dose, reduced dyskinesia and improved early morning dystonia. The major drawbacks of current dopamine agonist use are an increased incidence of hallucinations and delusions. Both advantages and disadvantages are dose-dependent and reversible and, in newly-diagnosed patients, dopamine agonists may be used in lower doses than those required to treat those with advanced disease. Any nausea resulting from dopamine agonist use may be reduced by the administration of domperidone, while apomorphine may be employed to rescue patients from 'off' periods, despite oral dopamine agonist use.

The first to use a dopamine agonist in the clinical management of Parkinson's disease (PD) was Schwab[1] who gave the emetic drug apomorphine to PD patients and showed improvement. At that time, he was unaware of the dopaminergic properties of apomorphine shown later.[2] Dopamine agonists were introduced as a practical tool in the management of PD in the 1970s in an attempt to overcome the problems encountered with long-term levodopa treatment. In 1974, the ergot derivative bromocriptine was shown to significantly alleviate parkinsonian disability.[3] Numerous studies have since confirmed the antiparkinsonian effect of bromocriptine and assessed its usefulness in PD patients both as monotherapy and when given in conjunction with levodopa. More recently, other dopamine agonists have been shown to be at least equally effective in PD. These agonists include the ergot derivatives pergolide and lisuride which have been approved for the treatment of PD in many countries. Several other promising agonists are still under investigation, such as ropinirole, pramipexole and cabergoline, but are likely to be available soon for use in the clinic.

The main pharmacologic characteristics of the dopamine agonists are summarized in Tables 1 and 2. Dopamine agonists offer several theoretical advantages over levodopa for the treatment of PD. For example, several of them have longer half-lives than levodopa and a high degree of receptor specificity, suggesting that a more prolonged and selective motor effect with less side effects can be obtained. To date, five different dopamine receptors, D_1 to D_5, have been identified.[4] Improvement in motor function is generally attributed to stimulation of D_1 and D_2 receptors.[5]

Table 1: Pharmacologic aspects of dopamine agonists

- Directly stimulate dopamine receptors bypassing degenerating nigrostriatal neurons
- Longer striatal half-life than levodopa
- Selective receptor activation
- Do not require enzymatic conversion to active agent
- Do not compete for transport in the gut or at the blood-brain barrier
- Alternate routes of administration may be possible
- Possible protective effects
- May decrease dopamine turnover
- Delay the appearance of levodopa side effects

Table 2: Activity of dopamine agonists on dopamine receptors D_1–D_5

Agonist	D_1	D_2	D_3	D_4	D_5
Bromocriptine	−	++	++	+	+
Lisuride	+	++	?	?	?
Pergolide	+	++	++++	?	+
Cabergoline	−	+++	?	?	?
Ropinirole	−	++	++++	+	−
Pramipexole	−	++	++++	++	?

+	minimal agonist effect
++++	maximal agonist effect
−	no activity, partial activity or antagonist

This paper reviews clinically relevant information on the use of the dopamine agonists in the management of PD. Emphasis will be given to those dopamine agonists currently available and in widespread use in most countries, e.g. bromocriptine and pergolide. Apomorphine, a non-ergot agonist that can be effective when administered by non-oral routes, will also be discussed.

DOPAMINE AGONISTS AS MONOTHERAPY

Dopamine agonists can be given as monotherapy, under two circumstances. They can be used, on the one hand, at the onset of therapy. This strategy permits delaying the introduction of levodopa, a drug that with the passage of time induces incapacitating dyskinesias and motor fluctuations in most patients and on theoretical grounds could accelerate PD by increasing neuronal degeneration. Dopamine agonists can also be used as a substitute for levodopa in patients with advanced PD and severe motor fluctuations and dyskinesias. Such an approach would seem reasonable, since from laboratory studies with dopamine agonists given as monotherapy, we know that these drugs induce much less motoric complications than levodopa.

Several clinical studies have shown that dopamine agonists are useful when given as monotherapy in *de novo* patients, with some reports suggesting that they can be as potent as levodopa.[6–8] Bromocriptine has been by far the most extensively studied, and the information available suggests that the various ergot derivatives do not differ dramatically in their clinical effects when given in equipotent doses.[9]

Virtually all studies demonstrate a markedly reduced incidence of motor complications in PD patients treated with bromocriptine monotherapy *versus* levodopa. Monotherapy with bromocriptine also improves the cardinal symptoms of PD and prolonged treatment results in strikingly less dyskinesias and motor fluctuations than levodopa.[10–12] The dosages needed for an effective symptomatic effect vary among patients, but with mild disability even small doses can be useful. Some studies have reported efficacy of bromocriptine similar to that of levodopa in the first few months but generally the antiparkinsonian effects are less than those obtained with levodopa therapy.[11,13,14]

Unfortunately, bromocriptine tends to lose efficacy with the passage of time. In the series of Lees and Stern,[10] only 28 of 50 patients were still improved by more than 25% after one year of treatment with bromocriptine alone (mean dose 70 mg/day). After a mean bromocriptine treatment duration of 2.6 years, only 17 patients (34%) were still taking bromocriptine with benefit. For these reasons, eventually levodopa needs to be added to the agonist.[15,16] Another disadvantage for some patients with the use of bromocriptine in early treatment is the time to achieve optimal benefit which is longer than that needed when using levodopa. While these observations would argue against the early use of a dopamine agonist as monotherapy, early introduction of an agonist is favored in the case of a young PD patient (e.g. less than 55 years old). Younger patients are more prone to early development of dyskinesias and motor fluctuations and will also have to be medically managed for a longer period of time. Also, younger patients are less likely to develop major side effects from dopamine agonists.[17]

Since a possible neuroprotective effect has been postulated for dopamine agonists, a large clinical trial evaluated one year of bromocriptine *versus* levodopa therapy on clinical disease progression. Both drugs were withdrawn before final clinical scoring in order to compare the unmedicated state after one year of medication with that of baseline. In this study the progression of the disease was the same in the two groups.

Lisuride is an ergoline that stimulates D_2 dopamine receptors, but it also acts on the D_1 and the 5-HT$_1$ serotonergic receptors.[18] Its potency has been estimated to be 13–15 times that of bromocriptine.[19,20] Experience with lisuride in previously untreated patients is limited.[21-23] These patients have usually obtained a mild to moderate improvement which has persisted in a small number for more than two years. All features of parkinsonism have improved although some investigators have found that tremor responds best[22] while others report that tremor is minimally affected.[23] Giovannini et al.[24] have reported the results of four years of monotherapy with lisuride. Initially it proved effective in 15 untreated patients, but after some time seven patients required additional levodopa and three others dropped out for other reasons.

Pergolide is another dopamine receptor agonist used in PD treatment. This ergot derivative stimulates both D_1 and D_2 dopamine receptors and has a much longer half-life than lisuride or bromocriptine. Information on the use of pergolide as monotherapy in the early stages of PD is very limited but suggests that, like other agonists, it has important antiparkinsonian properties although to a lesser degree than levodopa.[25] The use of pergolide as monotherapy has also been evaluated in occasional patients with relatively advanced PD and in whom effectiveness from levodopa has waned.[26] While effective in this setting in alleviating the main signs of parkinsonism, only very rarely can pergolide or any of the other orally-administered agonists substitute for levodopa for significant periods of time in patients with severe dyskinesias and motor fluctuations. Such attempts are invariably met with rapid re-emergence of disabling parkinsonism. Structural and functional abnormalities in the brains of patients with advanced disease probably limit the efficacy of the agonists. Furthermore, large doses of the agonists are frequently needed in these patients which may result in mental aberrations or other unwanted side effects. Only in the young patient with moderate disease who cannot tolerate levodopa can total substitution of levodopa by pergolide or another agonist be contemplated based on existing knowledge.

DOPAMINE AGONISTS AS ADJUNCTS TO LEVODOPA

Numerous studies have shown that dopamine agonists are useful as adjuncts to levodopa in the management of advanced PD patients suffering from levodopa-induced motor fluctuations and dyskinesias.[27] In patients with wearing-off or 'on-off' oscillations, the addition of bromocriptine reduces the number, intensity and duration of the 'off' periods. Moreover, it permits a reduction in levodopa dosage by one quarter to one half, according to some studies. This reduction in levodopa dose results in less dyskinesias or dystonia when present.[10,28]

In many of these studies,[29-32] gains in control of parkinsonism generally followed the build-up of bromocriptine dosage to 30 mg/day or more. While some reports have claimed no additional benefits or even declining effects from further advance of bromocriptine dosage,[33–35] most investigations report a correlation between dose and the degree of improvement derived from the drug.[30,36] Higher doses of bromocriptine are needed to improve 'on-off' oscillations than the less disabling end-of-dose deterioration.

Bromocriptine has been reported to be useful in alleviating a number of specific problems that can occur in parkinsonian patients on long-term levodopa treatment. It can provide relief for nocturnal akinesia and early morning dystonia[37,38] and also ameliorate daytime end-of-dose dystonic reactions.[39]

A slow-release form of bromocriptine was examined in a multicenter double-blind comparison with traditional bromocriptine. The slow-release form was associated with fewer side effects, but the effects on individual parkinsonian features were comparable.[40] However, other studies on this formulation of bromocriptine are not available.

Lisuride causes an improvement in parkinsonian symptoms similar to that of bromocriptine when added to levodopa.[19,41–43] In the study conducted by Caraceni et al.[42] lisuride induced a significant improvement in akinesia, rigidity and tremor. It allows for a reduction of the levodopa dosage, reduces frequency and intensity of peak-dose dyskinesias, and prolongs daily 'on' time.[42,44–46] The effect of lisuride on levodopa-induced motor fluctuations has been investigated in patients in advanced stages of the disease. Several studies have been carried out with lisuride in aqueous solution, delivered either intravenously or subcutaneously with the goal of achieving continuous dopaminergic stimulation.[47–50] The results of these investigations have shown that in the majority of patients, parenteral delivery of lisuride dramatically smoothed out severe levodopa-associated fluctuations. Lightweight pumps were devised for portable use with abdominal subcutaneous infusion.[48] Psychiatric side effects associated with sustained lisuride administration have been the reason for the need to discontinue this treatment modality.[51,52]

Several recent studies have found that pergolide, when added to a levodopa regimen, also improves disability associated with motor fluctuations. In every study, pergolide reduced motor fluctuations by decreasing 'off' time and/or increasing 'on' time by 50% or more,[53–55] with fluctuations even disappearing in some patients. Gait and bradykinetic symptoms have been shown to improve during both 'on' and 'off' phases[53–55] or not to be modified.[26] Tremor is, for the most part, unaffected by pergolide treatment. A number of studies[56–58] have found clinical benefit at doses ranging from 0.1 to 7.2 mg/day and have concluded that three dose/day regimens are adequate for most patients. Pergolide is 10 times more potent on a milligram per milligram basis than bromocriptine and is up to four times longer-acting. Although no difference in efficacy between pergolide and bromocriptine could be demonstrated in a short-term study,[56] patients who no longer benefit from bromocriptine may improve when pergolide is substituted.[59]

There is some controversy as to the long-term efficacy of the dopamine agonists when combined with levodopa. When bromocriptine is begun in low doses and built up slowly, peak efficacy occurs within the first six months of treatment and then may decline. Decreased efficacy is more pronounced in patients with advanced disease treated with high doses than in patients with mild to moderate disease treated with low doses.[41] Long-term effects of pergolide were assessed in 66 patients treated for 16 months with a mean daily dose of 2.6 mg. All 66 patients improved initially, but eventually 23 patients (35%) deteriorated. The decrease in efficacy after chronic treatment with pergolide is similar to that after chronic treatment with other dopamine agonists. When the natural progression of PD is taken into account, however, pergolide or bromocriptine, if given in combination with levodopa, appear to retain significant therapeutic value for at least two to three years. Proper studies to evaluate the long-term efficacy of the various dopamine agonists are needed.

EARLY COMBINATION OF DOPAMINE AGONISTS WITH LEVODOPA – A STRATEGY TO DELAY MOTOR FLUCTUATIONS

Although some patients obtain substantial benefit from dopamine agonists when given as monotherapy in the early stages of the disease,[6,11,60] it is generally acknowledged that these drugs are less efficacious than levodopa. Several investigators have reported that the early treatment of PD patients with a combination of a dopamine agonist and levodopa is well-tolerated and results in fewer motor complications such as dyskinesias and fluctuations than does treatment with levodopa alone. A combination of bromocriptine from the start with a standard levodopa regimen gave comparable antiparkinsonian efficacy to that of levodopa alone,[11,61] plus the added benefit of a much lower incidence of dyskinesia and fluctuations after several years.[11] This therapeutic strategy of combining a dopamine agonist with levodopa in the early stages of PD could result in fewer motor complications by modifying the development of tolerance and dopamine receptor desensitization.[62] Combined therapy could also decrease the production of free radicals generated by the oxidative metabolism of dopamine.[63]

Factor and Weiner and their colleagues[64,65] have recently criticized the routine early use of dopamine agonists. They pointed out major flaws in the existing literature which purport to show a lower incidence of motor complications with early dopamine agonist therapy. In addition, they have reported a double-blind study evaluating outcomes from early combination of bromocriptine with levodopa and have concluded that this strategy may not be effective.[65] Nevertheless, the number of patients included in their study (seven) was too small for confidence about the reliability and statistical significance of their conclusions.

A recent European study, the PRADO study,[66] comparing levodopa/benserazide monotherapy with bromocriptine plus levodopa/benserazide as the initial treatment of PD, had to be terminated prematurely because of a significantly greater cardiac mortality in the levodopa monotherapy group. The significance of these results, unexpected and contrary to all past experience with the drug, is unclear.

Combination of levodopa with lisuride in early disease has also been suggested to prevent or postpone the development of the motor fluctuations that occur after high dosage levodopa therapy,[23,24] but these studies are also subject to the same methodological flaws as those using bromocriptine under the same treatment paradigm. Further work aimed at demonstrating the hypothetical preventive effect of dopamine agonists on levodopa-induced motor fluctuations is necessary.

SIDE EFFECTS OF ORALLY – ADMINISTERED DOPAMINE AGONISTS

The most frequent adverse side effects of the ergot derivative dopamine agonists are listed in Table 3. The most important ones, nausea and vomiting, postural hypotension and psychiatric aberrations are qualitatively similar to those seen with levodopa. With the use of domperidone, nausea and vomiting can be averted.[38] Psychiatric side effects have been the most common reason for the need to discontinue lisuride or other dopaminergic ergots.[51] Hallucinations and similar psychotic phenomena are experienced by up to one-quarter of patients treated with dopaminergic ergots.[67] Clozapine, an atypical antipsychotic which has little tendency to cause extrapyramidal side effects,[68] has proven useful in treating dopamine agonist-induced psychosis.[69] Clozapine's side effects include sedation, sialorrhea and postural hypotension and severe agranulocytopenia in occasional patients. Olanzapine, another atypical neuroleptic with a similar pharmacologic profile to clozapine, does not induce bone marrow suppression and has been recently shown to be effective in treating levodopa-induced psychosis[70] and

Table 3: Side effects of dopamine agonists	
Frequency	**Side effect**
Common	Nausea, vomiting
	Psychiatric reactions
	Postural hypotension
	Fatigue
	Sedation
	Constipation
	Chest pain
	Subcutaneous nodules (subcutaneous lisuride or apomorphine)
	Nasal vestibulitis (intranasal apomorphine)
Less common	Erythromelalgia-like reactions
	Worsening of dyskinesias
Rare	Pleural thickening

can also be expected to alleviate similar problems induced by dopamine agonists. Occurrence of dose-related or idiosyncratic side effects often influences the ability to use dopaminergic drugs. Gradual increase of the dopamine agonist and taking the drug after a meal slows absorption and may lessen potential side effects.

A number of less common effects can result from these drugs. Erythromelalgia-like reactions have been reported with ergot derivatives.[55] Rarely, pleural thickening, pulmonary infiltrates and retroperitoneal fibrosis have developed in patients maintained on chronic, high-dose bromocriptine regimens.[56,71–73]

When added to levodopa, a dopamine agonist can trigger first-time abnormal involuntary movements,[74] or more commonly exacerbate existing levodopa-induced dyskinesias.[75] Both peak dose and diphasic dyskinesias can be aggravated by orally administered agonists.[42,74] This effect frequently requires reduction of levodopa dose for optimal control of the patient's symptoms. The enhancement of levodopa-induced dyskinesias is not inevitable and in some patients peak-dose involuntary movements have been observed to improve with addition of an agonist.[42,76,77] The effect of an agonist on levodopa-induced dyskinesias might be related to the doses of the agonist used. Bromocriptine, for example, at doses of 20 mg/day which produced antiparkinsonian effects, failed to enhance levodopa-induced dyskinesias in a large group of patients.[39] In general, worsening of dyskinesias is not a serious consequence of the addition of dopaminergic antiparkinsonian therapy, as long as levodopa dosages are reduced appropriately.[53]

Oral administration of a dopamine agonist does not induce 'off'-period dystonia in patients on levodopa and several authors have found that such agents can actually improve this levodopa-related side effect.[39] This antidystonic effect may be attributed to the prolonged half-life of some of the agonists which results in a more constant stimulation of dopamine receptors despite fluctuating plasma levels of levodopa.

APOMORPHINE

Apomorphine is a non-selective dopamine agonist acting at both the D_1 and D_2 subfamilies of dopamine receptors. Decades ago, it was used for the treatment of parkinsonian symptoms,[1] but abandoned due to its side effects and short duration of action. Recently, apomorphine has been administered by intramuscular or subcutaneous injection as a rapidly-acting remedy for refractory 'off' periods,[78–80] and by subcutaneous infusion using portable pumps to achieve a more continuous effect[78,81] in patients with levodopa-related disabling motor fluctuations. Following subcutaneous injection, its antiparkinsonian effects occur within 5–15 minutes and last for 40–90 minutes.[78] Subcutaneous administration by continuous waking-day infusion, or by repeated intermittent injection, can be well-tolerated during chronic use and can greatly improve 'on' time in patients with marked motor fluctuations.[82–84] Tolerance to the beneficial effects of apomorphine does not seem to be a clinically significant problem, even after five years of therapy with continuous infusion.[80]

Apomorphine is readily absorbed through both the sublingual[83,85–87] and intranasal mucosa routes.[83,84,88,89] Sublingual administration can be as effective as parenteral routes in alleviating 'off' periods and associated dystonia,[82,86,87] although aphthous ulceration of the oral mucosa may result. Apomorphine can also be administered via the intranasal route using a metered-dose nebulizer.[83,88–90] This mode of administration provides a duration and magnitude of motor response comparable to subcutaneous injection, but the dose needed to reverse the 'off' period is doubled, on average. The presence of crusting of nasal mucous membranes is a limiting side effect for long-term use.[84] Some patients alternate the subcutaneous and intranasal routes of application depending on the side effects encountered. Even though the use of subcutaneous or intranasal apomorphine offers an effective treatment strategy in patients with motor fluctuations, patients must be selected carefully for this treatment.[90] The best candidates are younger patients with predictable 'off' periods, good quality 'on' periods, a definite pattern of dyskinesias, and no neuropsychiatric manifestations.

Side effects produced by apomorphine can include allergic reactions, nausea and vomiting, postural hypotension, sedation, confusional states and dyskinesias.[91] Concomitant use of domperidone abolishes nausea and vomiting in most instances.[38,92] Domperidone is usually started before administration of the agonist but can usually be discontinued after several weeks as tolerance to the peripheral side effects of apomorphine develops. Unlike lisuride, hallucinations are generally not a problem with apomorphine, but subcutaneous nodules are frequently encountered at the infusion site.[78,93] More recently, there has been increasing interest in the use of subcutaneous injections of apomorphine for aiding the diagnosis of PD, and differentiating it from the Parkinson-plus syndromes that do not show an appreciable response to apomorphine.[94,95]

OTHER DOPAMINE AGONISTS IN THE TREATMENT OF PD

Following the successes of bromocriptine, there have been continuing efforts to improve the effectiveness of dopaminergic therapy. These attempts have resulted in the development and clinical testing of more than a dozen dopaminergic compounds. Experience with the first of these, lergotrile,[33] provided evidence that alternative dopaminergic compounds might offer some advantages over bromocriptine. This notion was supported by the results of studies conducted with the 8-alpha-ergoline **mesulergine** (CU32-085), a compound with agonism at both the D_1 and D_2 receptors.[96] Mesulergine is unique in that a demethylation metabolite rather than the parent drug is responsible for its antiparkinsonian action.[97] Its clinical usefulness against parkinsonism was comparable to that of bromocriptine,[98] and it exerted additional desirable properties, including an antidepressant action and effectiveness against postural instability for some patients. Mesulergine also tended to produce less orthostatic blood pressure drop than did other dopaminergic drugs.[99] Although promising, this drug was discontinued from further clinical trials because of animal toxicology results. Another ergoline compound **CQA206-291**, also required conversion to produce a metabolite with potent D_1 and D_2 agonism.[100] CQA206-291 proved to be as effective as other dopaminergic agonists in both *de novo* and adjunctive therapy study paradigms.[101–103]

Among other developments in dopaminergic ergot derivatives have been analogs with modifications to the tetracyclic structure of lisuride, thereby altering its therapeutic profile. For instance, the addition of a 6-N-propyl adduct made for more sustained properties than those of the parent compound.[47] Clinical trials with trans-9,10-dihydrolisuride, **terguride**, showed that this compound produced fewer side effects compared with lisuride.[104,105] Terguride differs from lisuride in possessing mixed agonist-antagonist properties. Studies using small doses of terguride, either alone or in combination with levodopa, have reported net agonistic effects, improving parkinsonism and increasing dyskinesias.[104] However, clinical trials of the drug using higher doses and as an adjunct to levodopa demonstrated a mild antagonistic effect reducing the severity of dyskinesias.[50,106]

Several other compounds with potent D_2 dopamine receptor agonist properties have been investigated for their antiparkinsonian potential. These include **CQP210-403**[107] and **CV205-502**.[108] Although each compound was effective against parkinsonism, further development of these compounds has not continued. Like other compounds which have increased potency at supersensitive postsynaptic D_2 receptors, (-)**3-PPP**[109] and **B-HT 920**,[110] **ciladopa** was tested in parkinsonian patients. Some pilot studies with ciladopa were encouraging,[111] but others found little effect.[112] The drug had to be withdrawn because of carcinogenicity in experimental animals.

(+) 4-propyl-9-hydroxynaphthoxazine (**PHNO**) is the most potent D_2 dopaminergic compound known. PHNO showed promising antiparkinsonian efficacy in patients when given orally, intravenously or transdermally.[113–115] This drug was studied as a monotherapy and as an adjunctive therapy to levodopa, using a controlled-release oral preparation,[116] and it induced the same types of adverse effects as other dopaminergic agonists. In comparison to pergolide, however, PHNO appeared to be less effective.[117] PHNO was canceled from further development because of animal toxicity.

Although D_2 stimulation has been the primary focus of agonist research, D_1 agonists are also under investigation, especially for their putative role in controlling dyskinesias. Furthermore, some activation of D_1 systems seems necessary to enable the effect of D_2 agonists to occur.[118] Clinical trials with a partial D_1 agonist, the benzazepine **SKF38393**, were initiated based on the results of trials in MPTP-parkinsonian monkeys.[119] However, this compound conferred little benefit either by itself or in combination with bromocriptine.[120,121] Trials with **CY208-243**, a dopaminergic compound with a selective D_1 receptor agonism,[122] revealed considerable effectiveness in two double-blind, placebo-controlled trials.[123,124] By itself, the drug exerted antiparkinsonian effects, mostly against tremor.[124] Drug toxicity halted its clinical development.

Several other dopamine agonists are currently being tested in clinical trials. Among the most promising agents are cabergoline and the non-ergoline agents ropinirole and pramipexole. Cabergoline has a longer duration of action than other dopaminergic drugs previously tested.[125,126] It has been used as monotherapy for parkinsonism and as an adjunct to levodopa in patients for improving motor fluctuations and dyskinesias.[127–129] In early studies it significantly reduced the duration and severity of 'off' periods, and periods of total immobility were abolished in more than 85% of patients.[130] As monotherapy or as adjunctive treatment, ropinirole is effective at improving parkinsonism.[126,131] In open-label evaluations, patients could lower levodopa doses without loss of function when ropinirole was added.[132] This is discussed in more detail in the next chapter.

Pramipexole is a new direct-acting full dopamine agonist which binds to the D_3 dopamine receptor with a seven-fold greater affinity than the D_2 and D_4 receptors.[133] Preliminary clinical trials with pramipexole have revealed significant efficacy in reducing the severity of parkinsonian symptoms in patients who were not receiving levodopa, as well as in advanced parkinsonian patients with motor fluctuations and/or drug-resistant rest tremor.[134]

CONCLUSION

Dopamine agonists have been in use for the treatment of PD since 1974 when it was demonstrated that the addition of bromocriptine to the regime of parkinsonian patients already receiving optimal conventional therapy, including levodopa, led to improvement in clinical benefits. Bromocriptine and two other ergot derivatives with dopaminergic properties, pergolide and lisuride, have since been extensively studied in PD, and it is generally agreed that all three are similarly efficacious drugs in the early stages as well as in the advanced stages of the disease. From review of the available literature on the clinical use of dopamine agonists, as well from personal experience (ET) in treating patients with dopamine agonists for almost two decades, we can conclude the following:

- addition of a dopamine agonist frequently requires decreasing the intake of levodopa in patients with fluctuations and dyskinesias;
- the main benefit from adding a dopamine agonist and reducing levodopa are decreased wearing-off, reduced dyskinesias and improvement in early morning dystonia;
- the major drawbacks of dopamine agonists are the increased incidence of hallucinations and delusions and, rarely, postural hypotension and erythromelalgia;
- the advantages and disadvantages of dopamine agonists are dose-dependent and reversible;

- domperidone frequently reduces nausea and vomiting that can occur with initiation of dopamine agonist treatment by blocking dopamine receptors at the brainstem level but outside the blood–brain barrier;
- in general, when used in newly-diagnosed patients, the dopamine agonists are helpful at lower doses than those required to treat advanced disease and their use as monotherapy is associated with a very low incidence of dyskinesias. Their therapeutic index is still lower than that of levodopa and most patients need addition of the drug in relatively short periods of time;
- apomorphine, when given subcutaneously or intranasally, reproduces transiently the effects of levodopa and can consistently and rapidly rescue patients from their 'off' periods. It is therefore of great value in some patients disabled by this phenomenon, despite treatment with oral dopamine agonists.

There are numerous unanswered questions about the dopamine agonists. Does the clinical efficacy of the various ergot agonists differ? How do the ergot agonists compare to the newer agents currently being tested in patients? Which agent should we use first? Do the dopamine agonists have some 'neuroprotective' effect when given to patients? Are the non-ergot agonists better tolerated than the ergot-derived dopamine agonists? Only properly designed and executed studies, some of which are already under way, will eventually answer these, as well as other questions that are so important in order to properly treat PD patients.

References

1. Schwab RS, Amador LV, Lettvin LY. Apomorphine in Parkinson's disease. Trans Am Neurol Assoc 1951; 76: 251–253.

2. Cotzias GC, Papavasiliou PS, Tolosa ES, et al. Treatment of parkinsonism with apomorphine: possible role of growth hormones. N Engl J Med 1976; 294: 567–572.

3. Calne DB, Teychenne PF, Claveria LE, Eastman R, Greenacre JK, Petrie A. Bromocriptine in parkinsonism. Brit Med J 1974; 4: 442–444.

4. Sibley DR, Monsma FJ. Molecular biology of dopamine receptors. Trends Pharmacol Sci 1991; 13: 61–69.

5. Robertson HA. Dopamine receptor interactions: some implications for the treatment of Parkinson's disease. Trends Neurosci 1992; 15: 201–205.

6. Tolosa E, Blesa R, Bayes A, Forcadell F. Low-dose bromocriptine in early phases of Parkinson's disease. Clin Neuropharmacol 1987; 10: 169–174.

7. Montastruc JL, Rascol O, Rascol A. A randomized controlled study of bromocriptine versus levodopa in previously untreated parkinsonian patients: a three-year follow-up. J Neurol Neurosurg Psychiatr 1989; 52: 773–775.

8. Nakanishi T, Mizuno Y, Goto I, et al. A nationwide collaborative study on the long-term effects of bromocriptine in patients with Parkinson's disease. Eur Neurol 1991; 31: 3–16.

9. Gawell MJ, King DB, Libman I, McLean DR, Paulseth R, Raphy B, Riopelle RJ, Bouchard S. Bromocriptine in de novo Parkinson's disease patients. Arch Neurol 1988; 45: 204–208.

10. Lees AJ, Stern GM. Sustained bromocriptine therapy in previously untreated patients with Parkinson's disease. J Neurol Neurosurg Psychiatr 1981; 44: 1020–1023.

11. Rinne UK. Early combination of bromocriptine and levodopa in the treatment of Parkinson's disease: a 5-year follow-up. Neurol 1987; 37: 826–828.

12. Riopelle RJ. Bromocriptine and the clinical spectrum of Parkinson's disease. Can J Neurol Sci 1987; 14: 455–459.

13. Rascol A, Montastruc JL, Guirard-Chaumeil B, Clanet M. Bromocriptine as first treatment of Parkinson's disease. Long-term results. Rev Neurol 1982; 138: 402–408.

14. Rinne UK. Combined bromocriptine–levodopa therapy early in Parkinson's disease. Neurol 1985; 35: 1196–1198.

15. Staal-Schrenemachers AL, Wesselring H, Kamphuis DJ, Burg WRD, Lake JPWF. Low dose bromocriptine therapy in Parkinson's disease: double-blind, placebo-controlled study. Neurol 1986; 36: 291–293.

16. Stern GM, Lees AJ. Long-term effects of bromocriptine given to de novo patients with idiopathic Parkinson's disease. Adv Neurol 1986; 45: 525–527.

17. Olanow CW, Hauser RA, Gauger L, et al. The effect of deprenyl and levodopa on the progression of Parkinson's disease. Ann Neurol 1995; 38: 771–777.

18. Kehr W. Effect of lisuride and other ergot derivations on monoaminergic mechanisms in rat brain. Eur J Pharmacol 1976; 41: 261–273.

19. LeWitt PA, Gopinathan G, Ward CD, et al. Lisuride versus bromocriptine treatment in Parkinson's disease. Neurol 1982; 32: 69–72.

20. Schachter M, Sheehy MP, Parkes JD, Marsden CD. Lisuride in the treatment of parkinsonism. Acta Neurol Scand 1980; 62: 382–385.

21. Agnoli A, Suggieri S, Baldasarre M, *et al*. Dopaminergic ergots in parkinsonism. In, Calne DB, Horowski R, McDonald RJ, Wuttke W, eds, Lisuride and other dopamine agonists. New York: Raven Press, 1983: 407–418.

22. Rinne UK. New ergot derivatives in the treatment of Parkinson's disease. In, Calne DB, Horowski R, McDonald RJ, Wuttke W, eds, Lisuride and other dopamine agonists. New York: Raven Press, 1983: 431–442.

23. Martignioni E, Suchy I, Pacchetti C, *et al*. Lisuride in Parkinson's disease: naïve and long-term treatment. Curr Ther Res 1986; 39: 696–708.

24. Giovannini P, Scigliano G, Piccolo I, Soliveri O, Suchy I, Caraceni T. Lisuride in *de novo* parkinsonian patients: a four-year follow-up. Acta Neurol Scand 1988; 77: 322–327.

25. Rinne UK. Dopamine agonists as primary treatment in Parkinson's disease. Adv Neurol 1986; 45: 519–523.

26. Lieberman AN, Goldstein M, Gopinathan G, Leibowitz M, Neophytides A, Walker R, Heisinger E, Nelson J. Further studies with pergolide in Parkinson's disease. Neurol 1982; 32: 1175–1179.

27. Lieberman AN, Gopinathan G, Neophytides A, Nelson J, Goldstein M. Dopamine agonists in Parkinson's disease. In, Stern GM, ed, Parkinson's disease. Baltimore: Johns Hopkins Univ Press, 1990: 509.

28. Teychenne PF, Bergsrud D, Elton RL, Racy A. Bromocriptine: long-term low dose therapy in Parkinson's disease. Clin Neuropharmacol 1986; 9: 138–145.

29. Kartzinel R, Teychenne P, Gillespie MM, Perlow M, Gielen AC, Sadowsky DA, Calne DB. Bromocriptine and levodopa (with or without carbidopa) in parkinsonism. Lancet 1976; ii: 272–275.

30. Lieberman AN, Kupersmith M, Estey E, Goldstein M. Treatment of Parkinson's disease with bromocriptine. N Engl J Med 1976; 295: 1400–1403.

31. Lees AJ, Haddad S, Shaw KM. Bromocriptine in parkinsonism: a long-term study. Arch Neurol 1978; 35: 503–505.

32. Jansen NH. Bromocriptine in levodopa response-losing parkinsonism: a double-blind study. Eur Neurol 1978; 17: 92–99.

33. Teychenne PF, Pfeiffer R, Bern SM, McIntruff D, Calne DB. Comparison between lergotrile and bromocriptine in parkinsonism. Ann Neurol 1978; 3: 319–324.

34. Koller WC, Weiner WJ, Nausieda PA, Klawans HL. Bromocriptine: decreased clinical effects at higher doses. Neurol 1979; 29 (Suppl 1): 1439.

35. Grimes JD. Bromocriptine in Parkinson's disease: results obtained with high and low dose therapy. Can J Neurol Sci 1984: 11: 225–228.

36. Larsen TA, Newman RP, LeWitt PA, Calne DB. Severity of Parkinson's disease and the dosage of bromocriptine. Neurol 1984; 34: 795–797.

37. Lander CM, Lees AJ, Stern GM. Oscillations in performance in levodopa-treated parkinsonians: treatment with bromocriptine and L-deprenyl. Clin Exp Neurol 1979; 16: 197–203.

38. Quinn N, Illas A, L'Hermitte F, Agid Y. Bromocriptine and domperidone in the treatment of Parkinson's disease. Neurol 1981; 31: 662–667.

39. Hoehn MM, Elton RL. Low dosages of bromocriptine added to levodopa in Parkinson's disease. Neurol 1985; 35: 199-206.

40. Mannen T, Mizuno Y, Iwata M, *et al*. A multicenter double-blind study on slow release bromocriptine in Parkinson's disease. Neurol 1991; 41: 1598–1602.

41. Lieberman AN, Gopinathan G, Neophytides A. Bromocriptine and

lisuride in Parkinson's disease. Ann Neurol 1983; 13: 44–47.

42. Caraceni T, Giovannini P, Parati E, *et al.* Bromocriptine and lisuride in Parkinson's disease. Adv Neurol 1984; 40: 531–536.

43. Laitinen A, Rinne UK, Suchy I. Comparison of lisuride and bromocriptine in the treatment of advanced Parkinson's disease. Acta Neurol Scand 1992; 86: 593–595.

44. Lees AJ, Stern GM. Pergolide and lisuride for levodopa-induced oscillations. Lancet 1981; ii: 577.

45. Lieberman AN, Leibowitz M, Gopinathan G, Walker R, Hiesiger E, Nelson J, Goldstein M. Review: The use of pergolide and lisuride, two experimental dopamine agonists in patients with advanced Parkinson's disease. Am J Med Sci 1985; 290: 102–106.

46. Rinne UK. Early dopamine agonist therapy in Parkinson's disease. Mov Disord 1989; 4 (Suppl 1): 86–94.

47. LeWitt PA. Clinical and pharmacological aspects of the antiparkinsonian ergoline lisuride. In, Fahn S, Marsden CD, Jenner P, Teychenne P, eds, Recent developments in Parkinson's disease. New York: Raven Press, 1986: 347–354.

48. Obeso JA, Luquin MR, Martinez-Lage JM. Lisuride infusion pump: a device for the treatment of motor fluctuations in Parkinson's disease. Lancet 1986; i: 467–470.

49. Horowski R, Obeso JA. Lisuride, a direct dopamine agonist in the treatment of Parkinson's disease. In, Koller WC, Paulson G, eds, Therapeutics in Parkinson's disease. New York: Marcel Dekker, 1990: 269–309.

50. Baronti F, Mouradian MM, Conant KE, *et al.* Partial dopamine agonist therapy of levodopa-induced dyskinesias. Neurol 1992; 42: 1241–1243.

51. Obeso JA, Luquin MR, Vaamonde J, Martinez-Lage JM. Subcutaneous administration of lisuride in the treatment of complex motor fluctuations in Parkinson's disease. J Neurol Transm 1988; 27 (Suppl): 17–25.

52. Critchley P, Parkes D. Transdihydrolisuride in parkinsonism. Clin Neuropharmacol 1987; 10: 57–64.

53. Sage JL, Duvoisin RC. Pergolide therapy in Parkinson's disease. A double-blind, placebo-controlled study. Clin Neuropharmacol 1985: 8: 260 2–2665.

54. Jankovic J, Orman J. Parallel double-blind study of pergolide in Parkinson's disease. Adv Neurol 1986; 45: 551–554.

55. Olanow CW, Alberts MJ. Double-blind controlled study of pergolide mesylate as an adjunct to Sinemet® in the treatment of Parkinson's disease. Neurol 1986; 36: 555–560.

56. LeWitt PA, Ward CD, Larsen TA, *et al.* Comparison of pergolide and bromocriptine therapy in parkinsonism. Neurol 1983; 33: 1009–1014.

57. Lieberman AN, Goldstein M, Leibowitz M, Gopinathan G, Neophytides A, Hiesiger E, Nelson J, Walker R. Long-term treatment with pergolide: decreased efficacy with time. Neurol 1984; 34: 223–226.

58. Lieberman AN, Neophytides A, Leibowitz M, Gopinathan G, Pact V, Walker R, Goodgold A, Goldstein M. Comparative efficacy of pergolide and bromocriptine in patients with advanced Parkinson's disease. Neurol 1983; 33: 95–108.

59. Goetz GC, Tanner CM, Glantz R, Klawans HL. Chronic agonist therapy for Parkinson's disease: a five-year study of bromocriptine and pergolide. Neurol 1985; 35: 749–751.

60. Calne DB, Rinne UK. Controversies in the management of Parkinson's disease. Mov Disord 1986; 1: 159–162.

61. Gimenez-Roldan S, Tolosa E, Burguera JA, Chacón-Liano H, Forcadell F. Early combination of bromocriptine and

levodopa in Parkinson's disease. A prospective randomized study of two parallel groups over a total follow-up period of 44 months including an initial eight month double-blind stage. Clin Neuropharmacol, in press.

62. Murata M, Kanazawa I. Repeated levodopa administration reduces the ability of dopamine storage and abolishes the supersensitivity of dopamine receptors in the striatum of intact rats. Neurosci Res 1993; 16: 15–23.

63. Olanow CW. A rationale for dopamine agonists as primary therapy for Parkinson's disease. Can J Neurol Sci 1992; 19: 108–112.

64. Factor SA, Weiner WJ. Early combination therapy with bromocriptine and levodopa in Parkinson's disease. Mov Disord 1993; 8: 267–272.

65. Weiner WJ, Factor SA, Sanchez-Ramos JR, Singer C, Sheldon C, Cornelius L, Ingenito A. Early combination therapy (bromocriptine and levodopa) does not prevent motor fluctuations in Parkinson's disease. Neurol 1993; 43: 21–27.

66. Przuntek H, Weizel D, Blumner E, et al. Bromocriptine lessens the incidence of mortality in L-dopa-treated parkinsonian patients: PRADO study discontinued. Eur J Clin Pharmacol 1992; 43: 357–363.

67. Serby M, Angrist B, Lieberman A. Mental disturbances during bromocriptine and lergotrile treatment of Parkinson's disease. Am J Psychiatr 1978; 135: 1227–1229.

68. Baldessarini RJ, Frankenburg FR. Clozapine: a novel antipsychotic agent. N Engl J Med 1991; 324: 746–754.

69. Kahn N, Freeman A, Juncos JL, Manning D, Watts RL. Clozapine is beneficial for psychosis in Parkinson's disease. Neurol 1991; 41: 1699–1700.

70. Wolters EC, Jansen ENH, Tuynman-Qua HG, Bergmans PLM. Olanzapine in the treatment of dopaminomimetic psychosis in patients with Parkinson's disease. Neurol 1996; 47: 1085–1087.

71. Melamed S, Braunstein GD. Bromocriptine and pleuropulmonary disease. Arch Int Med 1989; 149: 258–259.

72. Demonet JF, Rostin M, Dueymes M, Ioualalen A, Montastruc JL, Rascol A. Retroperitoneal fibrosis and treatment of Parkinson's disease with high doses of bromocriptine. Clin Neuropharmacol 1986; 9: 200–201.

73. LeWitt PA, Calne DB. Recent advances in the treatment of Parkinson's disease: the role of bromocriptine. J Neural Transm 1981; 51: 175–184.

74. Quinn NP. Antiparkinsonian drugs today. Drugs 1984; 28: 236–262.

75. Quinn NP, Lang AE, Thompson C, et al. Pergolide in the treatment of Parkinson's disease. Adv Neurol 1984; 40: 509–514.

76. Teychenne PF, Bergstud D, Racy A, Elton RL, Vern B. Bromocriptine: low dose therapy in Parkinson's disease. Neurol 1982; 32: 577–583.

77. Ilson J, Fahn S, Mayem R, et al. Pergolide treatment in parkinsonism. In, Calne DB, Horowski R, McDonald RJ, Wuttke W, eds, Lisuride and other dopamine agonists. New York: Raven Press, 1983: 443–451.

78. Stibe CMH, Lees AJ, Kempster PA, Stern GM. Subcutaneous apomorphine in parkinsonian 'on-off' oscillations. Lancet 1988; i: 403–406.

79. Lees AJ. Dopamine agonists in Parkinson's disease: a look at apomorphine. Fund Clin Pharmacol 1993; 7: 121–128.

80. Lees AJ. Dopamine agonists – a look at apomorphine. In, Agid Y, ed, Current trends in the treatment of Parkinson's disease. John Libbey and Company Ltd, 1992: 69–76.

81. Obeso JA, Grandas F, Vaamonde J, Luquin MR, Martinez-Lage JM. Apomorphine infusion for motor fluctuations in Parkinson's disease. Lancet 1987; i: 1376–1377.

82. Hughes AJ, Bishop S, Kleedorfer B, Turjanski N, Fernandez W, Lees AJ, Stern GM. Subcutaneous apomorphine

in Parkinson's disease: response to chronic administration for up to five years. Mov Disord 1993; 8: 165–170.

83. Kapoor R, Turjanski N, Frankel J, Kleedorfer B, Lees A, Stern G. Intranasal apomorphine; a new treatment in Parkinson's disease. J Neurol Neurosurg Psychiatr 1990; 53: 1015.

84. Munoz E, Marti MJ, Marin C, Tolosa E. Long-term treatment with intermittent intranasal or subcutaneous apomorphine in patients with levodopa-related motor fluctuations. Clin Neuropharmacol, in press.

85. Lees AJ, Montastruc JL. Turjanski N, Rascol O, Kleedorfer B, Peyro Saint-Paul H, et al. Sublingual apomorphine and Parkinson's disease: J Neurol Neurosurg Psychiatr 1989; 52: 1140.

86. Deffond D, Durif F, Tournilhac M. Apomorphine in treatment of Parkinson's disease: comparison between subcutaneous and sublingual routes. J Neurol Neurosurg Psychiatr 1993; 56: 101–103.

87. Durif F, Paire M, Deffond D, Eschalier A, Dordain G, Tournilhac M, Lavarenne J. Relation between clinical efficacy and pharmacokinetic parameters after sublingual apomorphine in Parkinson's disease. Clin Neuropharmacol 1993; 16: 157–166.

88. Kleedorfer B, Turjanski N, Ryan R, et al. Intranasal apomorphine in Parkinson's disease. Neurol 1991; 41: 761–762.

89. Van Laar T, Jansen ENH, Essink AWG, et al. Intranasal apomorphine in parkinsonian 'on-off' fluctuations. World Med Rev Parkinson's Dis 1992; 1: 14–15.

90. Tolosa ES, Valldeoriola Marti MJ. New and emerging strategies for improving levodopa treatment. Neurol 1994; 44 (Suppl): S35–S44.

91. Ruggieri S, Stocchi F, Carta A, Agnoli A. Side effects of subcutaneous apomorphine in Parkinson's disease. Lancet 1989; i: 556.

92. Corsini GU, Del Zompo M, Gessa GL, Mangoni A. Therapeutic efficacy of apomorphine combined with an extracerebral inhibitor of dopamine receptors in Parkinson's disease. Lancet 1979; i: 954–956.

93. Poewe W, Kleedorfer B, Wagner M, Benke T, Gasser T, Oertel W. Side effects of subcutaneous apomorphine in Parkinson's disease. Lancet 1989; i: 1084–1085.

94. Barker R, Duncan J, Lees A. Subcutaneous apomorphine as a diagnostic test for dopaminergic responsiveness in parkinsonian syndromes. Lancet 1989; 1: 675.

95. Oertel WH, Gasser T, Ippisch R, Trenkwalder C, Poewe W. Apomorphine test for dopaminergic responsiveness. Lancet 1989; i: 1262–1263.

96. Jellinger K. Adjuvant treatment of Parkinson's disease with dopamine agonists: open trial with bromocriptine and CU32-085. J Neurol 1982; 227: 75–88.

97. Markstein R. Mesulergine and its 1,20-N-N-bimethylated metabolite interact with D_1 and D_2 receptors. Eur J Pharmacol 1983; 95: 101–107.

98. Burton K, Larson TA, Robinson RG, et al. Parkinson's disease: a comparison of mesulergine and bromocriptine. Neurol 1985; 35: 1205–1208.

99. Pfeiffer R. The pharmacology of mesulergine. Clin Neuropharmacol 1985; 8: 64–72.

100. Jaton A, Enz A, Vigouret J, Pfaffle P, Markstein R. CQA206-291, an ergot derivative with biphasic dopaminergic action. Experientia 1987; 43: 705.

101. Lang AE, Riley D, Vachon L, Lataste X. CQA296-291 in Parkinson's disease: an acute single escalating dosage study. Can J Neurol Sci 1990; 17: 416–419.

102. Rascol O, Fabre N, Teravainen H, Poewe W, Lucking C, Rinne U, Dupont E, Hirt D, Hoyer M, Lataste X. CQA206-291: a novel dopamine

agonist in the treatment of Parkinson's disease. Clin Neuropharmacol 1990; 13: 303–311.

103. Pfeiffer RF, Hofman R. CQA206-291 in Parkinson's disease. Clin Neuropharmacol 1991; 14: 170–178.

104. Brücke T, Danielezyk W, Simany M, Sofic E, Reiderer P. Terguride: partial dopamine agonist in the treatment of Parkinson's disease. Adv Neurol 1986; 45: 573–576.

105. Suchy I, Rinne UK, Wachtel H. Evaluation of terguride in patients with Parkinson's disease. Adv Neurol 1986; 45: 577–581.

106. Ruggieri S, Stocchi F, Baronti F, Viselli F, Horowski R, Lucarelli C, Agnoli A. Antagonist effect of terguride in Parkinson's disease. Clin Neuropharmacol 1991; 14: 450–456.

107. Pfeiffer R, Herrera JH, Glaeske CS, Hofman RE. CQP201-403 in Parkinson's disease: an open-label study. Mov Disord 1989; 4: 278–281.

108. Olanow CW, Werner EG, Gauger LL. CV205-502: safety, tolerance and efficacy of increasing doses in patients with Parkinson's disease on a double-blind, placebo crossover study. Clin Neuropharmacol 1989; 12: 490–497.

109. Nomoto M, Jenner P, Marsden CD. Alterations in motor behavior produced by isomers of 3-PPP in the MPTP-treated marmoset. Eur J Pharmacol 1986; 121: 123–128.

110. Hinzen D, Hornykiewiez O, Kobinger W, et al. The dopamine autoreceptor agonist B-HT 920 stimulates denervated postsynaptic dopamine receptors in rodent and primate models of Parkinson's disease: a novel approach to treatment. Eur J Pharmacol 1986; 131: 75–86.

111. Lieberman AN, Gopinathan G, Neophytides A, Pasternack P, Goldstein M. Advanced Parkinson's disease: use of partial dopamine agonist, ciladopa. Neurol 1987; 37: 863–865.

112. Aminoff MJ, Goodin DS, Habermann-Little B, et al. Treatment of Parkinson's disease with ciladopa. Ann Neurol 1987; 21: 311.

113. Stoessl AJ, Mak E, Calne DB. (+)-4-propyl-9-hydroxynaphthoxazine (PHNO), a new dopaminomimetic, in treatment of parkinsonism. Lancet 1985; ii: 1330–1331.

114. Grandas FJ, Jenner PG, Nomoto M, Stahl S, Quinn NP, Parkes JD, et al. (+)-4-propyl-9-hydroxynaphthoxazine in Parkinson's disease. Lancet 1986; i: 906.

115. Lieberman AN, Chin L, Baumann G. MK-458, a selective and potent D_2 receptor agonist in advanced Parkinson's disease. Clin Neuropharmacol 1988; 11: 191–200.

116. Ahlskog JE, Muenter MD, Bailey PA, Miller PM. Parkinson's disease monotherapy with controlled-release MK-458 (PHNO): double-blind study and comparison to carbidopa/levodopa. Clin Neuropharmacol 1991; 14: 214–227.

117. Ahlskog JE, Muenter MD, Bailey PA, Stevens PM. Dopamine agonist treatment of fluctuating parkinsonism: D_2 (controlled-release MK-458) vs. combined D_1 and D_2 (pergolide). Arch Neurol 1992; 49: 560–568.

118. Stoof JC, Kebabian JW. Opposing roles for D_1 and D_2 dopamine receptors in efflux of cAMP from rat neostriatum. Nature 1981; 294: 366–368.

119. Nomoto M, Jenner P, Marsden CD. The dopamine D_2 agonist LY141865, but not the D_1 agonist SKF38393, reverses parkinsonism induced by 1-methyl, 4-phenyl-1,2,3,6-tetrahydropyridine (MPTP) in the common marmoset. Neurosci Lett 1985; 57: 37–41.

120. Braun AR, Fabbrini G, Mouradian MM, Barone P, Chase TN. Selective D_1 dopamine receptor agonist treatment of Parkinson's disease. J Neurol Transm 1987; 68: 41–50.

121. LeWitt PA, Schlick P, Hussain M, et al. Selective D_1 agonist SKF38393 in parkinsonism. Neurology 1988; 38 (Suppl 1): 258.

122. Karobath M. The pharmacology of CY208-243, a CNS active dopamine$_1$ receptor agonist. In, Calne DB, Fahn S, Marsden CD, Goldstein M, eds, Recent developments in Parkinson's disease. New Jersey: MacMillan, 1987: 241–248.

123. Tsui JKC, Wolters EC, Peppard RF, Calne DB. A double-blind placebo controlled dose-ranging study to investigate the safety and efficacy of CY208-243 in patients with Parkinson's disease. Neurol 1989; 39: 856–888.

124. Emre M, Rinne UK, Rascol A, Lees A, Agid Y, Lataste X. Effects of a selective partial D$_1$ agonist, CY208-243, in *de novo* patients with Parkinson's disease. Mov Disord 1992; 7: 239–243.

125. Rabey JM, Nissipeanu P, Inzelberg R, *et al.* Beneficial effect of cabergoline in the treatment of Parkinson's disease. Adv Neurol 1990; 53: 451–455.

126. Burn DJ, Anderson T, Bottomley J, Haran S, Brooks DJ. Treatment of Parkinson's disease with a selective D$_2$ agonist, ropinirole, as adjunct therapy. Neurol 1991; 41 (Suppl 1): 399.

127. Jori MC, Franceschi M, Giusti MC, Canal N, Piolti RR, Frattola L, Bassi S, Calloni E, Mamoli A, Camelingo M. Clinical experiences with cabergoline, a new ergoline derivative in the treatment of Parkinson's disease. Adv Neurol 1990; 53: 539–543.

128. Obeso JA, Lera G, Vaamonde J, Martinez-Lage JM. Cabergoline for the treatment of motor complications in Parkinson's disease. Neurol 1991; 41 (Suppl): 172.

129. Hutton JT, Morris JL, Brewer MA. Controlled study of the antiparkinsonian activity and tolerability of cabergoline. Neurol 1993; 43: 613–616.

130. Poewe W, Luef G, Kleedorfer B, *et al.* Antiparkinsonian activity of a non-ergot dopamine agonist, CV205-502, in patients with fluctuating Parkinson's disease. Mov Disord 1990; 5: 257–259.

131. Eden RJ, Costall B, Domeney AM, Gerrard PA, Harvey CA, Naylor RJ, Owen DAA, Wright A. Preclinical pharmacology of ropinirole (SKF101-468-A), a novel dopamine D$_2$ agonist. Pharmacol Biochem Behav 1991; 38: 147–154.

132. Kapoor R, Pirtosek D, Frankel J, *et al.* Treatment of Parkinson's disease with novel dopamine D$_2$ agonist SKF1-01468. Lancet 1989; i: 1445–1446.

133. Sautel F, Griffon N, Levesque D, Pilon C, Schwartz JC, Sokoloff P. A functional test identifies dopamine agonists selective for D$_3$ versus D$_2$ receptors. Neuro Report 1995; 6: 329–332.

134. Albani C, Popescu R, Lacher R, *et al.* Single dose response to pramipexole in patients with Parkinson's disease. Mov Disord 1992; 7 (Suppl 1): 98.

CHAPTER NINE

Ropinirole: clinical profile

OLIVIER RASCOL, MD, PHD

Department of Clinical Pharmacology, Clinical Investigation Center
and INSERM U455, CHU Toulouse, France.

ABSTRACT

Ropinirole is a new, structurally unique, selective D_2 agonist, active in a dose-dependent manner both peripherally and centrally in the treatment of Parkinson's disease (PD). After oral administration, the drug is rapidly absorbed (median T_{max} 1.4 hours), with a bioavailability of 46% and mean apparent elimination half-life of 6 hours, predominantly via the hepatic route. Three doses per day are recommended. Plasma protein binding is low (10–39%) and concentration-independent and the drug is oxidatively metabolized mainly via CYP 1A2. Potential hypotensive and gastrointestinal effects are more likely at higher doses (>0.8 mg) and may be prevented by the use of domperidone. The results of initial studies suggest that, in the treatment of early PD (Hoehn & Yahr stages I and II), ropinirole has efficacy similar to that of levodopa. As an adjunct to levodopa, ropinirole allows at least a 20% reduction of levodopa dose, while reducing the 'off' time experienced by patients.

Ropinirole is a new, potent, orally active D_2 dopamine agonist which is active peripherally in the treatment of Parkinson's disease (PD).[1] It has recently received marketing approval for this indication in the UK, France and other Western countries.

Ropinirole has several theoretically interesting properties compared to the other marketed dopamine agonists. Its structure is uniquely different from other currently available dopamine agonists, most of which are ergoline derivatives, and this difference may result in fewer side effects. It is a selective drug for the D_2 family of dopamine receptors, with little affinity or no affinity for binding at D_1, α_2 and β adrenoceptors, 5-HT$_1$, 5-HT$_2$, benzodiazepine and GABA receptors.[1] This may contribute to reduced side effects. Ropinirole has a dose-dependent antiparkinsonian activity that has been claimed to be comparable to that of levodopa in PD patients deprived of their usual antiparkinsonian treatment and receiving acute oral single dose challenges of the compound.[2] It induces less dyskinesia than levodopa in the MPTP model of parkinsonism in the monkey.[3]

Clinical Pharmacodynamics in Healthy Volunteers

Clinical pharmacology studies have shown ropinirole to lower serum prolactin levels, an expected effect of a D_2 dopamine agonist. This effect is seen at a single oral dose of 0.08–2.5 mg.[4] Single low doses of ropinirole (0.08 mg) in healthy volunteers do not induce significant changes in supine resting heart rate or blood pressure. Similarly, the drug has no effect at this dosage on supine or plasma catecholamine concentrations. At higher doses (over 0.25 mg) symptomatic postural hypotension with a blunting of the increase in noradrenaline, which normally occurs upon standing, is frequently observed.[5,6] It is likely that tolerance to the hypotensive effects of the compound develops in humans as has been observed in the rat and the monkey.[7] Moreover, it has been shown in healthy volunteers that domperidone can reduce such hypotensive effects.[8]

As expected with a dopamine agonist, gastrointestinal effects, particularly nausea, are seen at doses greater than 1 mg.[4] Digestive dopaminergic symptoms are also likely to be prevented by the peripheral dopamine antagonist domperidone, and to be subject to tolerance with chronic treatment. A progressive up-titration is thus recommended when initiating treatment with ropinirole, as is the case for any other effective dopaminergic drug, in order to reduce these potential side effects.

Pharmacokinetics

Because of frequent nausea and postural effects above 0.8 mg, the pharmacokinetics of ropinirole have been evaluated over a limited single oral dose range in healthy volunteers. Pre-treatment with domperidone 20 mg, one hour before administration of ropinirole, does not alter the pharmacokinetics of ropinirole.[8] Consequently, the oral pharmacokinetics above 1 mg have been characterized under domperidone cover. Pharmacokinetics after single oral administration of ropinirole in parkinsonian patients are within the range of values reported in healthy individuals.

After oral administration, ropinirole is rapidly absorbed, with median T_{max} observed at about 1.4 hours after dosing. Bioavailability of ropinirole from the tablet formulation is approximately 46%. Both C_{max} and $AUC_{(0-t)}$ increase with a corresponding dose increase over the evaluable range of single doses. The overall mean apparent elimination half-life is calculated to be 3.5 hours.[9] The average terminal phase elimination half-life of ropinirole in parkinsonian patients is six hours. This is longer than that of levodopa, but shorter than that of other dopamine agonists such as bromocriptine or pergolide. It is recommended that ropinirole be administered three times daily. As expected for a drug being administered approximately every half-life, there is on average a two-fold higher steady-state plasma concentration of ropinirole after repeat oral dosing. As the dose is individually titrated for each patient, this does not affect the use of the drug in the clinic.

Co-administration of food does not markedly affect the bioavailability of steady-state ropinirole. C_{max} was decreased by 25% on average and T_{max} was delayed by 2.6 hours in 12 PD patients treated with 6 mg of ropinirole per day.[10] The reduction in C_{max} with food may perhaps help to reduce the severity of peripheral dopamine side effects such as nausea. The reduction of C_{max} and the delay in T_{max} may delay or reduce the 'on' periods in some patients with motor fluctuations. On the other hand, because of the reduction in C_{max} in the fed condition, dyskinetic patients may theoretically have less abnormal movement when ropinirole is given after food. However, no clinical data support these theoretical predictions at present.

Plasma protein binding of ropinirole is low (10–39%) and is independent of concentration over the therapeutic range. Drug interactions, related to plasma protein binding, are thus unlikely. The metabolism of ropinirole is extensive and does not appear to be dependent on the route of administration. Based on *in vitro* enzymology data, the cytochrome P_{450} 1A2 (CYP 1A2) enzyme is mainly responsible for the oxidative metabolism of ropinirole. None of the known metabolites are expected to be pharmacologically active over the proposed dose range. Elimination of ropinirole is believed to be mostly due to hepatic rather than to renal clearance mechanisms. In the absence of specific data, ropinirole should not be used in subjects with severe renal or hepatic impairment.

The potential exists for drug interactions when ropinirole is co-administered with either a substrate or inhibitor of the CYP 1A2 enzyme. Ropinirole has little potential to inhibit cytochrome P_{450} at therapeutic doses but it is possible that co-substrates (e.g. theophylline) or inhibitors (e.g. ciprofloxacin) of CYP 1A2 may influence the steady-state oral clearance of ropinirole. However, co-administration of oral theophylline at therapeutic doses under steady-state conditions in 12 parkinsonian patients did not induce significant changes in the rate or extent of availability of ropinirole (manuscript in preparation).

Ropinirole has no significant effect on the steady-state pharmacokinetics of the combination of levodopa 100 mg/carbidopa 10 mg twice daily and *vice versa*.[11]

EFFICACY

Since 1967, the mainstay of treatment for PD has been replacement therapy for dopamine deficiency with levodopa.[12] After a few years, however, patients develop a range of disabling dyskinesias and motor fluctuations.[13–15] The limitations of levodopa therapy have led to the introduction of other therapeutic strategies, such as the use of dopamine agonists.

Originally introduced as adjunct therapy to levodopa in patients with a fluctuating or deteriorating response to levodopa, dopamine agonists are now increasingly proposed as initial treatment. This strategy is supported by the rarity of motor fluctuations and dyskinesias observed as long as levodopa-naïve patients can be managed with a dopamine agonist as monotherapy.[16–18] The reason why such motor complications are less frequent with dopamine agonists compared with levodopa is poorly understood, but may be related to pharmacokinetic (longer half-life) or pharmacodynamic (receptor subtype selectivity) differences.

The antiparkinsonian effects of dopamine agonists, however, are often perceived to be less than those of levodopa and, after a few years of treatment, levodopa is generally introduced for most patients. This observation led to a strategy whereby levodopa and a dopamine agonist are administered together for the first months of treatment – this is known as the 'early combination' strategy.[19] Another option is to treat the patients with an agonist as monotherapy for as long as possible, adjuncting levodopa only when and if the efficacy of the agonist wanes; this generally occurs after two to four years.[20] Both strategies are claimed to be as effective as levodopa monotherapy but with significantly fewer motor fluctuations and dyskinesias. This assumption is based upon a small number of pilot studies, all of which suffer from methodological shortcomings.[21] Consequently, the early use of dopamine agonists and the possible advantages of delayed treatment with levodopa are still open to question[22–25] and well-designed trials are necessary to confirm or refute the results of these pilot studies. The development of a new compound such as ropinirole provides a unique opportunity to conduct such needed long-term prospective, double-blind, randomized, controlled studies.

Efficacy of ropinirole in patients with early PD

One of the major interests in developing ropinirole was to set up and conduct prospective controlled studies evaluating the activity of a dopamine agonist as an initial treatment in PD, rather than as a late adjunct therapy to levodopa, once long-term motor problems have already occurred. Two main questions must be addressed – (1) is ropinirole monotherapy potent enough to improve the symptoms in order to replace or significantly delay the need for levodopa, and for how long, and (2) does this strategy actually delay the incidence or reduce the severity of dyskinesias and/or motor fluctuations on long-term follow-up? A pilot phase II study, conducted in 63 patients with early PD, showed that ropinirole, at up to 5 mg b.i.d., was superior to placebo in controlling the symptoms.[26]

Subsequently, three large controlled studies have been conducted in patients with early PD. These were double-blind, prospective, multicenter, randomized trials. Patients were included if they suffered from PD, had not been treated previously with levodopa (or for no more than six weeks) and required a symptomatic dopaminergic treatment. Ropinirole and the comparator were titrated as monotherapy through 13 levels (ropinirole: up to 24 mg/day, levodopa: up to 1200 mg/day, bromocriptine: up to 40 mg/day, or placebo) according to the patients' clinical response. If the maximal dose (dose 13) was reached, or if dose-limiting side effects occurred, and further symptomatic improvement was needed, the maximal or highest tolerated dose was maintained and levodopa was then added in an open way, as a 'rescue' treatment. The UPDRS motor score (part III) was chosen as the principal measure of efficacy.[27] Three other criteria were also analyzed: the percentage of 'responders', defined as those patients who achieved at least a 30% improvement on their UPDRS motor score, the percentage of patients 'improved' according to a seven-point clinician's global evaluation scale (CGI) (patients 'improved' or 'very much improved' being defined as 'improved') and the percentage of patients requiring levodopa rescue during the study. To date, only the six-month data are available. Consequently, most of the answers to the initial questions concerning long-term efficacy and adverse events are not yet available.

Study 054: This is a six-month placebo-controlled study conducted in 241 PD patients. After six months, patients treated with ropinirole (n=116, mean dose=16 mg/day) showed a significantly greater improvement in motor function (−24% in UPDRS motor score) than the placebo-treated group (n=125, +3% in UPDRS motor score) ($p<0.001$). There was also a significantly larger percentage of 'responders' in the ropinirole group (47%) than in the placebo group (20%) (odds ratio 4.45, 95% CI 2.26, 8.78). Similarly, more patients were 'improved' on the CGI in the ropinirole group (33%) than in the placebo group (12%) (odds ratio 4.06, 95% CI 2.00, 8.22). Finally, levodopa rescue was significantly less frequent in the ropinirole group (11%) than in the placebo group (29%) (odds ratio 0.30, 95% CI 0.14, 0.61).

Study 056: This is an ongoing five-year levodopa-controlled study performed on 268 PD patients (ropinirole, n=179; levodopa, n=89). The main objective of this study is to compare the incidence of late motor complications (motor fluctuations or dyskinesias) between the two groups after five years. A six-month interim analysis showed that the percentage improvement in the UPDRS motor score was 44% in the levodopa group (464 mg/day) and 32% in the ropinirole group (10 mg/day).[28] This −12% difference in favor of levodopa is significant (95% CI −20%, −5%). The proportion of 'responders' did not, however, differ significantly between groups (levodopa 58%, ropinirole 48%) (odds ratio 0.64, 95% CI 0.37, 1.09). The 'improver' analysis on the CGI revealed that disease severity had a significant effect on the efficacy of treatments. There was no difference between the two treatments in patients with Hoehn & Yahr stages I and II but patients with stages II.5 and III had a greater probability of being an 'improver' on levodopa (odds ratio 0.11, 95% CI 0.04, 0.35). Few patients received rescue therapy with levodopa (4% for ropinirole, 1% for levodopa), a difference that was not statistically significant.

Study 053: This is a three-year bromocriptine-controlled study conducted in 335 PD patients (ropinirole, n=168; bromocriptine, n=167). It was prospectively stratified for concurrent selegiline use. At six months there was a marked treatment by selegiline interaction and the results from each stratum were therefore considered separately. After six months, the mean dose of ropinirole was 8 mg/day while that of bromocriptine was 17 mg/day.[29] Without selegiline, ropinirole was significantly superior to bromocriptine in terms of UPDRS improvement (35% *vs.* 20%) (difference=15%, 95% CI 6%, 21%), 'responder' analysis (55% *vs.* 33%) (odds ratio 2.81, 95% CI 1.53, 5.14) and 'improver' analysis (46% *vs.* 30%) (odds ratio 2.26, 95% CI 1.24, 4.13). In patients receiving selegiline, however, there was no longer any significant difference in UPDRS improvement (34% *vs.* 37%), 'responder' analysis (63% *vs.* 63%) and 'improver' analysis (50% *vs.* 58%). If the results are analyzed in the population as a whole, outcome variables overall are still significantly in favor of ropinirole for UPDRS improvement (35% *vs.* 27%) (difference=8%, 95% CI 1.5%, 13.8%) and 'responder' analysis (58% *vs.* 43%) (odds ratio 1.93, 95% CI 1.29, 2.89). 'Improver' analysis demonstrates a similar but non-significant tendency (48% *vs.* 40%). Although the three-year results are not yet available, it is interesting to note that, after 2.5 years of follow-up, nearly 60% of the patients are still receiving a dopamine agonist blindly (ropinirole or bromocriptine) as monotherapy. This information suggests that, in spite of what is generally claimed in open studies,[19,30,31] a majority of patients with early PD can be correctly managed over more than two years with a dopamine agonist alone, without requiring levodopa rescue and without side effects preventing continuation of treatment.

In summary, studying the efficacy of ropinirole as monotherapy during the first six months of treatment of early PD demonstrates that the compound is significantly superior to placebo. Overall, levodopa was more effective than ropinirole, although they had a similar efficacy in the less severely affected patients. Ropinirole was superior to bromocriptine, particularly in patients not receiving selegiline.

The mean dose of bromocriptine at six months is comparable with the mean doses of 18 mg and 16.4 mg used by other investigators[23,32] after one year. The mean dose of levodopa was similar to or higher than the mean doses reported in other early therapy studies – Libman *et al.* reported a dose of 252 mg at five months,[34] Montastruc *et al.* reported a dose of 393 mg at six months,[20] and the Parkinson's Disease Research Group in the UK reported a dose of 420 mg in the absence of selegiline after 12 months.[31] It is interesting to note, however, that for all treatment groups in the ropinirole studies, the mean doses reached by endpoint were considerably less than the maximum permitted by the protocol. The small number of patients who withdrew early before complete titration contribute to this finding, but for patients who did not reach six months, one could conclude that (a) these patients had satisfactorily responded on this dose, or (b) the investigator had reached a 'psychologic limit', or (c) a fear of treatment-related side effects led to an acceptance of suboptimal response and an unwillingness to increase the dose. In a further analysis, however, no difference was found between the group of patients treated with at least 12 mg ropinirole or 20 mg bromocriptine, and patients treated with less than these doses in terms of the proportion of patients classed as 'responders'.

Despite the promising low rate of rescue with levodopa in all active treatment groups, the main goal is to compare the long-term benefit/risk ratio of ropinirole versus bromocriptine and levodopa, but as the studies are ongoing, conclusions cannot be drawn before their completion.

Efficacy of ropinirole as an adjunct treatment to levodopa

This indication corresponds to the most 'classical' use of dopamine agonists in PD. In several countries, dopamine agonists are often only approved for this indication. According to this strategy, the dopamine agonist is introduced to minimize levodopa motor fluctuations, once they have occurred.

Several open pilot studies have suggested that ropinirole is useful in treating PD patients who are already on levodopa.[34,35] Four controlled clinical studies have been performed, three of which are placebo-controlled (030, 034 and 044) and one is bromocriptine-controlled (043). Patients included in these studies had received levodopa for a mean duration of five to eight years and were considered as not optimally controlled. Levodopa doses had been stably maintained before entering into the study and no other dopamine agonist was co-administered.

Study 030: This is a three-month placebo-controlled randomized (1:1) study conducted in 46 patients. All patients were experiencing mild to moderate 'on-off' fluctuations. The mean duration of 'off' periods was four hours per day. Efficacy was assessed by using diary cards as the primary evaluation criterion. Levodopa doses were kept constant. Ropinirole administered twice daily (mean dose 7 mg/day) was associated with a marked reduction in the proportion of awake time spent 'off' (–50%) which was significantly larger than the placebo effect (–20%) ($p<0.01$).[36]

Study 034: This study included 68 patients randomized 2:1 to ropinirole or placebo. All patients had motor fluctuations. Ropinirole was used at a mean daily dose of 7 mg. Efficacy was sought primarily in terms of reduction in total daily dose with concomitant improvement or maintenance of clinical symptoms on a CGI. There was no significant change in the proportion of awake time spent 'off' in either group. Similarly, the mean percentage reduction in levodopa daily dose was not significantly reduced (–22%) compared to placebo (–18%). The patients may have been 'over-treated' with levodopa before entering into the study, which might explain why it was possible to reduce the daily dose of levodopa by nearly 20% without deterioration in clinical symptoms in the placebo group.

Study 044: This is a six-month study including 149 PD patients not optimally controlled by levodopa and randomized 2:1 to ropinirole or placebo. Levodopa doses were flexible and could be decreased during the study. The main assessment criterion was the percentage of 'responders', defined as patients who achieved at the same time a reduction of at least 20% in the amount of 'off' time and a reduction of at least 20% in daily levodopa dose. This is a rather complex and difficult end-point, combining two theoretically contradictory objectives. The mean daily dose of ropinirole was 16 mg/day after six months of treatment, a dose larger than that used in other studies. After six months of therapy, there were significantly more 'responders', as defined previously, in the ropinirole group (28%) than in the placebo group (11%) (odds ratio 4.41, 95% CI 1.53, 12.7).

Study 043: This is a six-month study comparing ropinirole and bromocriptine in 555 patients not optimally controlled on levodopa. Randomization was 2:1. The design of the study allowed enrolment of a large variety of patients, including those not optimally controlled on levodopa, with or without motor fluctuations, and those who were satisfactorily controlled on levodopa but wished to reduce its daily dose by means of a dopamine agonist, as well as those already treated with another oral dopamine agonist and who accepted the switch to ropinirole. The primary outcome variable of this study was safety; efficacy was a secondary goal. Therefore, the heterogeneity of the inclusion criteria dictated a large variety of judgment criteria: reduction in levodopa daily dose, reduction in time spent 'off' (there were no diary cards but the proportion of awake time spent 'off' was determined by questioning the patients) and improvement in the UPDRS score. Consequently, the efficacy results of this study are unclear and there is no convincing evidence of superiority of either agonist.[37]

To summarize, studying ropinirole as an adjunct to levodopa in patients with advanced PD and motor fluctuations shows that the drug reduces the awake time spent 'off' by an average of two to three hours when levodopa is not reduced.[35] The addition of ropinirole to levodopa allows an average reduction in daily levodopa dose of 20%, once a therapeutic dose of the agonist has been reached. Even when the two above criteria are combined, ropinirole is still superior to placebo in generating significant improvement in patients with motor fluctuations. The results comparing ropinirole to bromocriptine as adjunct treatment are unclear.

CLINICAL SAFETY

A total of 1423 PD patients and 110 healthy volunteers have been exposed to ropinirole during its clinical development program. In the majority of these patients, exposure exceeded six months. Over 600 patients were exposed for at least one year and several patients have now been followed for up to five years. Table 1 gives the main emergent adverse events reported in the early therapy studies with an incidence equal or superior to 10% in any treatment group. Table 2 gives the list of adverse events leading to drop-outs in the same population. Many more patients were exposed to ropinirole than to the comparators, which is important to consider when comparing the safety variables.

Most of the reported adverse events are in the range of what is currently expected with a dopamine agonist. Nausea was the most common adverse event for ropinirole and levodopa and less with bromocriptine. Nausea generally occurs early, when treatment is started, and tolerance develops with time. In the early therapy studies, severity was mainly reported as 'mild' to 'moderate'. Nausea was generally well-tolerated and importantly caused few drop-outs. Domperidone, where available, may reduce this side effect. In the adjunct therapy studies, nausea occurred at a much lower rate, which is not

Table 1: Emergent adverse events in the early therapy studies (incidence ≥10% any treatment group)

	Ropinirole n=732		Placebo n=181		Levodopa n=94		Bromocriptine n=167	
	n	%	n	%	n	%	n	%
Patients with adverse events	630	86	170	94	88	94	151	90
Anxiety	46	6.3	20	11	6	6.4	14	8.4
Arthralgia	53	7.2	22	12.2	8	8.5	12	7.2
Constipation	56	7.7	23	12.7	10	10.6	18	10.8
Dizziness	175	23.9	49	27.1	20	21.3	25	21.0
Dyskinesia*	18	2.5	11	6.1	16	17.0	3	1.8
Headache	84	11.5	31	17.1	15	16.0	25	15.0
Infection (viral)	59	8.1	6	3.3	10	10.6	22	13.2
Injury	50	6.8	13	7.2	12	12.8	15	9.0
Insomnia	117	16.0	30	16.6	16	17.0	18	10.8
Nausea	324	44.3	47	26.0	43	45.7	42	25.1
Pain	52	7.1	7	3.9	12	12.8	15	9.0
Parkinsonism aggravated	51	7.0	10	5.5	10	10.6	19	11.4
Somnolence	183	25.0	28	15.5	17	18.1	13	7.8
Vomiting	85	11.6	15	8.3	10	10.6	12	7.2

* includes patients after levodopa was added to treatment.

Table 2: Adverse events leading to drop-out (early therapy studies)

	Ropinirole n=515 %	Placebo n=147 %	Levodopa n=89 %	Bromocriptine n=167 %
Nausea	4.1	1.4	3.4	2.4
Vomiting	1.7	0.7	2.2	1.8
Hallucination	1.7	0	1.1	2.4
Dizziness	1.4	1.4	1.1	0
Parkinsonism aggravated	1.4	0.7	0	0.6
Hypertension	0.6	1.4	0	0.6
Syncope	0.6	0	1.1	0
Dyskinesia	0.6	0	1.1	0
Headache	0.6	2.0	0	0.6
Anxiety	0.6	0.7	1.1	0

surprising since these patients had the opportunity of developing tolerance to this adverse event because of previous exposure to levodopa and other dopaminergic agents.

Orthostatic hypotension was frequently seen in healthy volunteers. Dizziness, postural hypotension and syncope were also observed in a number of PD patients. These adverse events were seen in the ropinirole group as well as in the active comparator groups. The clinical significance in PD patients is however less clear, because such symptoms were also frequently reported in patients on placebo.

Somnolence was observed in a proportion of patients. This is an interesting finding for a D_2 agonist, since the central dopaminergic systems are not known to be involved in sleep mechanisms. However, it should be remembered that sedation is a prominent effect of a mixed D_1/D_2 agonist such as apomorphine. Somnolence may be troublesome in some patients, especially during the day, but it may also be a beneficial effect in the large number of patients complaining of insomnia during the night.

There was a low incidence of psychiatric episodes in the early therapy studies but this is not surprising after only six months of follow-up in *de novo* patients. There was no clear difference between confusion and hallucinations compared to levodopa or bromocriptine, although the selective D_2 profile of ropinirole may be expected to result in a lower incidence of psychiatric adverse events. Longer follow-up and post-marketing surveillance may show some differences in the future.

Dyskinesias were observed in a small proportion of patients treated with ropinirole and the comparators, as well as those on placebo, in the early therapy studies. As expected, the percentage was higher in the levodopa group. Prospective long-term follow-up results will provide more interesting information when studies 056 and 053 are complete. However, after only six months of treatment with placebo and each of the dopamine agonists, the percentage of patients suffering from dyskinesia is not nil, even though these drugs alone are not supposed to provoke dyskinesia. There are several explanations for this observation. Several patients received levodopa as a rescue treatment within the first six months of treatment, so it is likely that levodopa induced the dyskinesia in most of the cases. In some other cases, levodopa had been previously prescribed prior to entry into the studies, because the inclusion criteria allowed a history of levodopa therapy of less than six weeks' duration. This may have been enough to 'prime' the patients to the pro-dyskinetic effect of the drug, which may account for the subsequent use of dopamine agonists also inducing dyskinesia. This was observed when both dopamine agonists, ropinirole as well as bromocriptine, were used in the late adjunct therapy studies in levodopa-treated patients, dyskinesia being a frequent adverse event reported in the ropinirole and bromocriptine treatment groups.

In conclusion, ropinirole is a new non-ergoline selective D_2 dopamine agonist. It has antiparkinsonian effects as monotherapy in the early stages of the disease and as adjunct therapy to levodopa in more advanced patients. 'Peripheral' dopaminergic adverse events (nausea, orthostatic hypotension) are in the range of what is expected with a dopamine agonist. As an early treatment, ropinirole can delay the need for levodopa. Whether this is significant in terms of the incidence of long-term motor side effects such as dyskinesia or motor fluctuations remains to be demonstrated. The final results of the ongoing three- and five-year prospective comparative studies with bromocriptine and levodopa will help to answer this question. Until now, only the symptomatic antiparkinsonian effects of ropinirole have been analyzed. There is a growing interest in the potential neuroprotective properties of different dopamine agonists. This hypothesis is now being tested in PD patients treated with ropinirole using ^{18}F-dopa as a marker of striatal dopamine nerve terminals (D. Brooks, personal communication).

REFERENCES

1. Eden RJ, Costall B, Domeney AM, Genard PA, Harvey CA, Kelly ME, Naylor RJ, Owen DAA, Wright A. Preclinical pharmacology of ropinirole (SKF101468-A) a novel dopamine D_2 agonist. Pharmacol Biochem Behav 1991; 38: 147–154.

2. Vidailhet MJ, Bonnet AM, Belal S, Dubois B, Marle C, Agid Y. Ropinirole without levodopa in Parkinson's disease. Lancet 1990; 336: 316–317.

3. Jenner P, Tulloch I, this volume

4. Acton G, Broom C. A dose rising study of the safety and effects on serum prolactin of SKF101468, a novel dopamine D_2 receptor agonist. Br J Clin Pharmacol 1989; 28: 435–441.

5. Acton G, Broom C, Howland K, Manchee K. Effects of the dopaminergic D_2 receptor agonist ropinirole on posturally-induced changes in plasma catecholamines and hemodynamics. Br J Clin Pharmacol 1990; 29: 619.

6. de Mey C, Enterling D, Meineke I, et al. Effects of the novel D_2 dopaminergic agonist ropinirole on supine resting and stimulated circulatory and neuroendocrine variables in healthy volunteers. Arzneim-Forsch/Drug Res 1990; 40: 7–13.

7. Parker SG, Raval P, Yeulet, Eden RJ. Tolerance to peripheral, but not central, effects of ropinirole, a selective dopamine D_2-like receptor agonist. Eur J Pharmacol 1994; 265: 17–26.

8. de Mey C, Enterling D, Meineke I, Yeulet S. Interactions between domperidone and ropinirole, a novel dopamine D_2 receptor agonist. Br J Clin Pharmacol 1991; 32: 483–488.

9. Boothman BR, Spokes EG. Pharmacokinetic data for ropinirole. Lancet 1990; 336: 814.

10. Thalamas C, Rayet S, Brefel C, Eagle S, Lopez-Gil A, Fitzpatrick K, Beerahee A, Montastruc JL, Rascol O. Effect of food on the pharmacokinetics of ropinirole in patients with Parkinson's disease. Mov Disord 1996; 11 (Suppl 1): 138.

11. Taylor AC, Beerahee A, Cyronak M, et al. Lack of a pharmacokinetic interaction between ropinirole and levodopa in parkinsonian patients [abstract]. Pharmacother 1996; 16: 512–513.

12. Cotzias GC, Van Woert MH, Schiffer LM. Aromatic amino acids and modification of parkinsonism. N Engl J Med 1967; 276: 374–379.

13. Marsden CD, Parkes JD. 'On-off' effects in patients with Parkinson's disease on chronic levodopa therapy. Lancet 1976; i: 292–296.

14. Hardie RJ, Lees AJ, Stern GM. 'On-off' fluctuations in Parkinson's disease: a clinical and neuropharmacological study. Brain 1984; 107: 487–506.

15. Nutt JG. Levodopa-induced dyskinesia: review, observations, and speculations. Neurol 1990; 40: 340–345.

16. Rascol A, Guiraud B, Montastruc JL, David J, Clanet M. Long-term treatment of Parkinson's disease with bromocriptine. J Neurol Neurosurg Psychiatr 1979; 42: 143–150.

17. Lees AJ, Stern GM. Sustained bromocriptine therapy in previously untreated patients with Parkinson's disease. J Neurol Neurosurg Psychiatr 1981; 44: 1021–1023.

18. Montastruc JL, Rascol O, Rascol A. A randomized controlled study of bromocriptine versus levodopa in previously untreated parkinsonian patients: a 3-year follow-up. J Neurol Neurosurg Psychiatr 1989; 52: 773–775.

19. Rinne UK. Brief communications: early combination of bromocriptine and levodopa in the treatment of Parkinson's disease: a 5 year follow-up. Neurol 1987; 37: 826–828.

20. Montastruc JL, Rascol O, Senard JM, Rascol A. A randomized controlled study comparing bromocriptine to which levodopa was later added, with levodopa alone in previously untreated patients with Parkinson's disease: a five-year follow up. J Neurol Neurosurg Psychiatr 1994; 57: 1034–1038.

21. Factor SA, Weiner WJ. Viewpoint: early combination therapy with bromocriptine and levodopa in Parkinson's disease. Mov Disord 1993; 8: 257–262.

22. Rascol A, Montastruc JL, Rascol O. Should dopamine agonists be given early or late in the treatment of Parkinson's disease? Can J Neurol Sci 1984; 11: 229–232.

23. Fahn S, Bressman SB. Should levodopa therapy of parkinsonism be started early or late? Evidence against early treatment. Can J Neurol Sci 1984; 11: 200–206.

24. Hachinski V. Timing of levodopa therapy. Arch Neurol 1986; 43: 407.

25. Melamed E. Initiation of levodopa therapy in parkinsonian patients should be delayed until the advanced stages of the disease. Arch Neurol 1986; 43: 402–405.

26. Brooks DJ, Turjanski N, Burn DJ. Ropinirole in the symptomatic treatment of Parkinson's disease. J Neurol Transm 1995; 455: 231–238.

27. Fahn S, Elton R and Unified Parkinson's Disease Rating Scale Development Committee. Unified Parkinson's Disease Rating Scale. In: Fahn S, Marsden CD, Calne D, eds. Recent developments in Parkinson's disease, vol 2. New York: Raven Press, 1987: 153–163.

28. Rascol O, Brooks DJ, Brunt ER, Korczyn AD, Poewe WH, Stocchi F on the behalf of the 056 study group. Ropinirole in the treatment of early Parkinson's disease: a 6-month interim report of a 5-year levodopa-controlled study. Mov Disord, submitted.

29. Korczyn AD, Brooks DJ, Brunt ER, Poewe WH, Rascol O, Stocchi F. Ropinirole versus bromocriptine in the treatment of early Parkinson's disease: a 6-month interim report of a 3-year study. Mov Disord submitted.

30. Lieberman A. Dopamine agonists used as monotherapy in de novo PD patients: comparisons with selegiline. Neurol 1992; 42 (Suppl): 37–40.

31. Parkinson's Disease Research Group in the United Kingdom. Comparison of the therapeutic effects of levodopa, levodopa and selegiline and bromocriptine in patients with early, mild Parkinson's disease: three-year interim report. Br Med J 1993; 307: 469–472.

32. Hoehn MM, Elton RL. Low dosages of bromocriptine added to levodopa in Parkinson's disease. Neurol 1985; 35: 199–206.

33. Libman I, Gawel MJ, Riopelle RJ, Bouchard S. A comparison of bromo-criptine (Parlodel®) and levodopa-carbidopa (Sinemet®) for treatment of de novo Parkinson's disease patients. Can J Neurol Sci 1987; 14: 576–580.

34. Kapoor R, Pirtosek Z, Frankel JP, Stern GM, Lees AJ, Bottomley JM, Sree Haran N. Treatment of Parkinson's disease with novel dopamine D_2 agonist SKF101468. Lancet 1989; i: 1445–1446.

35. Kleedorfer B, Stern GM, Lees AJ, Bottomley JM, Sree Haran N. Ropinirole (SKF101468) in the treatment of Parkinson's disease. J Neurol Neurosurg Psychiatr 1991; 54:10.

36. Rascol O, Lees AJ, Senard JM, et al. Ropinirole in the treatment of levodopa-induced motor fluctuations in patients with Parkinson's disease. Clin Neuropharmacol 1996; 19: 234–245.

37. Ropinirole 043 study group. A double-blind comparative study of ropinirole vs. bromocriptine in the treatment of parkinsonian patients not optimally controlled on levodopa. Mov Disord 1996; 11 (Suppl 1): 188.

CHAPTER TEN

The need to delay the use of levodopa in patients with Parkinson's disease

ELDAD MELAMED, MD, RUTH DJALDETTI, MD,
DANIEL OFFEN, MD, AND ILAN ZIV, MD

Department of Neurology, Rabin Medical Center,
the Felsenstein Research Center, Beilinson Campus, Petah Tiqva,
and the Sackler School of Medicine,
Tel Aviv University, Tel Aviv, Israel

ABSTRACT

Long-term administration of levodopa has both beneficial and detrimental consequences in Parkinson's disease (PD) patients. The drug reduces the severity of parkinsonian signs and symptoms and may improve patient survival. However, the initial beneficial effects may not be maintained, many patients developing a variety of adverse reactions two to five years after the initiation of therapy. These include motor oscillations which, in the advanced stages of the illness after prolonged levodopa use, may become intolerable. Damage to the surviving nigral dopaminergic neurons may also occur, thereby accelerating disease progression. It is likely that the emergence of response fluctuations after chronic use of levodopa is related to the use of the drug, in addition to disease progression per se. In view of this likely association, it would appear prudent to withhold levodopa from patients with only mild, early PD, delaying its use until the condition becomes more advanced. Other drugs, such as dopamine agonists, should be used in this interim period.

Several decades after its revolutionary introduction, levodopa continues to be the most powerful and widely-used drug in the treatment of Parkinson's disease (PD). Its unrivaled therapeutic success depends on a unique and fortunate combination of several features related to both the disease and the drug. Unlike dopamine, the missing neurotransmitter, orally-administered levodopa can cross the blood–brain barrier from the systemic circulation into the basal ganglia. This entry is highly facilitated by the combined use of peripheral dopa decarboxylase inhibitors. Despite the massive degeneration of nigrostriatal dopaminergic nerve terminals that normally contain most of the striatal dopa decarboxylase, enzyme activity remains in the caudate and putamen in extradopaminergic compartments which is sufficient to convert exogenous levodopa to dopamine. Unlike tyrosine hydroxylase, dopa decarboxylase is not a rate-limiting enzyme in the biosynthesis of catecholamines. It has a low affinity for its substrate and converts available levodopa to dopamine in an unlimited manner. Finally, postsynaptic dopaminergic receptors located on target neurons for the nigrostriatal nerve endings are not lost in the parkinsonian caudate and putamen nuclei. They are even hypersensitive and thus are able to respond to the dopamine molecules formed from exogenous levodopa.

Consequences of Chronic Levodopa Therapy in Patients with PD

Long-term administration of levodopa has a profound and complex impact on many aspects of PD. It carries both good and potentially harmful consequences. The interactions of levodopa with the illness can be concentrated in four major domains.

Effect on morbidity. There is no doubt that levodopa has a marked beneficial effect on parkinsonian signs and symptoms. It improves bradykinesia, rigidity, tremor, and postural stability. Thus, it highly ameliorates function and quality of life of afflicted patients.

Possible effect on mortality. Levodopa therapy may increase life span and improve survival of patients with PD.[1,2]

Possible effect on the development of dyskinesias and response fluctuations. Unfortunately, the initial smooth and stable beneficial effect of levodopa may not be maintained. After a problem-free period lasting two to five years on average (the so-called 'levodopa honeymoon'), many patients develop a variety of disabling adverse reactions including dyskinesias and response fluctuations.[3,4] The latter may be complex and include predictable and random motor oscillations such as the 'wearing-off' phenomenon – shortening of duration of benefit induced by individual doses of levodopa; 'delayed on' – prolongation of duration of latency from ingestion of an oral dose of levodopa to turning on;[5] 'no-on' – complete failure of an oral dose of levodopa to induce a beneficial effect;[6] 'on-off' phenomenon – sudden, random, unpredictable and transitory 'shut down' of a successful effect of an individual dose of levodopa. In the advanced stage of the illness and after prolonged treatment with levodopa, these adverse phenomena may become predominant and intolerable. Daily function of the patients is then dominated by swings between more functional 'on' hours when mobility is possible but intermingled with various disabling dyskinesias, and 'off' periods manifested by severe slowness and rigidity. The duration of satisfactory 'on' periods greatly declines and the patients are severely incapacitated with an extremely poor quality of life.

Possible effect on the natural history of the illness. Finally, since levodopa can produce toxic metabolic agents and, in particular, free radical species, there

[178]

has been a persistent concern that long-term administration may damage the surviving nigral dopaminergic neurons.[7] Thus, it may accelerate rates of nigral degeneration and disease progression.

The question of whether chronic levodopa therapy causes the emergence of dyskinesias and motor response fluctuations and hastens the loss of remaining dopaminergic neurons in the nigra and the deterioration of illness is not only of academic interest, but is extremely important for many practical reasons. If levodopa does indeed have a causative role in the development of motor complications and a harmful effect on the natural history of the disease, it would provide a strong argument against the early introduction of levodopa therapy. Rather, it would support a cautious approach with a delay in the initiation of this treatment modality until the more advanced stages of the disease.[8]

Are Response Fluctuations Caused by Mechanisms Related to the Disease or to Long-Term Treatment with Levodopa?

The causes of the loss of the initial smooth and stable effect of levodopa, the switch to beneficial responses induced by single doses of the drug on a 'one-to-one' basis, and the emergence of the more complex response fluctuations (the 'wearing off', 'on-off', 'delayed-on' and 'no-on' phenomena) are still unclear. Most likely these cannot all be explained on the basis of one single mechanism but are, in all probability, the result of a combination of several causative factors which involve central and/or peripheral mechanisms that are associated with the basic illness or with the levodopa treatment itself.

It is generally accepted that the beneficial effects of exogenous levodopa in PD are due to its conversion to functional, receptor-accessible dopamine molecules in the basal ganglia and to the restoration of the diminished nigrostriatal dopaminergic neurotransmission. It can therefore be assumed that the response fluctuations are due to failure in delivery of dopamine formed from exogenous levodopa to, and activation of, target striatal dopaminergic receptors. Therefore, a central hypothesis suggests that the loss of levodopa efficacy is predominantly due to disease progression with increasing disappearance of surviving dopaminergic nerve terminals, leading to a decreasing capacity to form and store dopamine derived from exogenous levodopa in the striatum.[9] Under normal circumstances, most of the dopa decarboxylase in the striatum is contained within dopaminergic nerve endings. Also, most of the dopamine formed from endogenous tyrosine and levodopa is stored in vesicles within dopamine neurons for release into the synapse when the neuron fires. In the early stages of PD, it is possible that there are still sufficient numbers of surviving dopaminergic terminals so that decarboxylation of exogenous levodopa can still occur predominantly within this compartment, and that most of the formed dopamine can be stored in vesicles for a slow and protracted physiologic release. As long as these circumstances prevail, there will be a smooth and stable response to levodopa. Later, when the disease has progressed and the continued loss of dopaminergic terminals has reached a critical point, most of the decarboxylation of exogenous levodopa is shifted to the dopa decarboxylase present in 'extra-dopaminergic' sites (e.g. serotoninergic and non-aminergic neurons, and glia).[10] Because most of the vesicular apparatus is lost, the formed dopamine is not stored but immediately leaks out and is spilled into the synapse. Consequently, the success and duration of benefit induced by each individual levodopa dose now depends on the ability of this dose to be absorbed, reach the striatum, be decarboxylated and form dopamine, and for these dopamine molecules to reach and activate responding receptors. Such a theory would rule out any role for treatment with levodopa itself (unless, of course, levodopa accelerates the loss of the terminals – see below). In this case, response fluctuations would be linked only to the duration and severity of the illness and not to the duration of levodopa therapy, and complications would invariably emerge independently of when treatment was initiated. If indeed this is the only operative mechanism, there would be no point in delaying levodopa administration and preventing patients from enjoying its benefits early in the course of their illness. It is beyond the scope of this discussion to review the pros and cons of this theory.

By contrast, many investigators believe that levodopa treatment itself and the duration of treatment is far more important in causing response fluctuations than the progression of disease. The following mechanisms have been implicated. (1) Prolonged levodopa administration may affect its own utilization in the striatum. Several studies in experimental animals (with intact nigrostriatal projections) have demonstrated that repeated levodopa administration can result in a decreased striatal accumulation of dopamine from exogenous levodopa, perhaps because of interference with dopa decarboxylase activity.[11-14] The enzyme itself may be suppressed or there may be depletion of co-factors.[15] Such a mechanism could contribute to the 'wearing off' phenomenon. (2) Prolonged 'bombardment' with levodopa and the formed dopamine can cause changes in postsynaptic dopaminergic receptors.[14,16,17] It may cause sensitization of one subclass of receptors (e.g. D_2) and downregulation of another (e.g. D_1).[18,19] (3) Chronic treatment with levodopa may give rise to excess activation of dormant metabolic pathways with increased formation of aberrant metabolites within the striatum. Most of these by-products would be inert but some could act as false inhibitory agents, block dopaminergic receptors and interfere with the action of the dopamine formed from exogenous levodopa at these receptor sites.[20,21] This could participate in the cause of the 'wearing off' phenomenon but could also be instrumental in the abrupt and random premature and transitory termination of a successful dose effect as occurs in the 'on-off' phenomenon.

Although central pharmacodynamic mechanisms are probably extremely important, the role of peripheral pharmacokinetic factors is very significant. Certain subtypes of motor fluctuations, particularly the 'delayed-on' and 'no-on' phenomena, are linked to faulty absorption of orally-administered levodopa.[22,23] The latter may be associated with poor solubility of levodopa, competition with neutral amino acids formed from protein and peptide breakdown and with 3-0-methyldopa formed by the COMT metabolism of levodopa, and intraluminal pH changes. However, recent evidence points to decreased gastric motility and emptying as a major obstacle for the absorption of oral levodopa.[24] When the stomach does not contract, a poorly-soluble dose of ingested levodopa may stagnate for a long time before it is transferred to the duodenum (where absorption is rather immediate) causing the 'delayed-on' phenomenon. Certain doses (particularly those taken in the afternoon) may not leave the stomach at all by the time of the next dose intake, leading to a total dose failure, the so-called 'no-on' phenomenon. As with central mechanisms, delayed gastric emptying may be caused by factors related to the disease and/or to treatment with levodopa. It is now well-established that Auerbach's and Meissner's cholinergic plexuses in the stomach wall become involved in the pathologic process of PD and progressively degenerate. Indeed, Lewy bodies have been identified within gastric cholinergic neurons.[25] Loss of these neurons could be responsible, at least in part, for the gastric atony in parkinsonians. However, dopaminergic receptors are also present within the stomach walls.[26,27] Although their physiologic role is not yet known, they may participate in the control and regulation of gastric motility. It is, therefore, not impossible that their chronic bombardment by oral levodopa may play a role in the development of delayed gastric emptying and some of the response fluctuations.[28]

Does Long-Term Treatment with Levodopa Damage Nigrostriatal Neurons and Accelerate Progression of PD?

Levodopa is a powerful toxin. Its enzymatic or auto-oxidation can produce various harmful free radical species including superoxide, hydrogen peroxide, semiquinones and quinones.[29] Levodopa is extremely lethal to neuronal and non-neuronal cells *in vitro*.[30,31] It can cause cell membrane lipid peroxidation and death by necrosis. We have recently shown that exposure of various cell cultures (e.g. chick sympathetic neurons and PC 12 cells) to levodopa killed the cells by apoptosis (programmed cell death).[32] Dopamine has the same toxic effect *in vitro*.[33] In the parkinsonian striatum, at least part of the exogenous levodopa is taken up and decarboxylated to dopamine by the surviving nigrostriatal dopaminergic nerve terminals.[10] Theoretically, its oxidation or the oxidation of the formed dopamine could produce massive amounts of toxic free radicals that overload and exceed the neutralizing capacity of the natural intracellular scavenging protective mechanisms. Part of the administered levodopa may be metabolized to dopamine and oxidized in other striatal compartments such as glial cells and the formed oxidants could reach the dopaminergic neurons by diffusion. These toxic products could kill the cells by necrosis or apoptosis by damaging the membrane, the mitochondria and particularly the nuclear DNA. Thus, it is hypothetically possible and has been a constant worry, that prolonged levodopa could accelerate nigrostriatal degeneration, alter the predetermined natural course of the illness and hasten its progression.[7] However, while levodopa is toxic in the cell culture situation, it is still not completely settled whether it is harmful *in vivo*. When large oral doses of levodopa were administered to normal mice for 18 months, no damage to the integrity of nigrostriatal neurons was observed.[34] Long-term systemic administration of levodopa failed to induce any destruction of dopaminergic neurons, even if these neurons were rendered more vulnerable to the possible toxic effects by combined administration of MPTP, haloperidol or central blockade of superoxide dismutase.[35] Similar negative findings were reported by other investigators.[36] However, a few studies show dopaminergic neuronal damage by systemic administration of levodopa. Long-term levodopa enhanced the damage in rat ventral tegmental (A10) dopaminergic neurons following exposure to 6-hydroxydopamine.[37,38] Repeated systemic levodopa injections in rats were toxic to, and damaged, fetal dopaminergic neurons that had been grafted into the striatum.[39] By contrast, repeated administration of levodopa to pregnant mice did not destroy dopaminergic neurons in the fetus or interfere with their postnatal development.[40] Likewise, the very few available clinical studies in humans suggest that the nigra is not damaged by chronic administration of levodopa. For instance, a non-parkinsonian patient treated with high-dose levodopa for several years showed no evidence of nigral damage.[41] Likewise, an autopsy investigation in a parkinsonian patient who had a fetal nigral transplantation showed that large numbers of grafted dopaminergic cells survived and formed dense axonal outgrowths despite continued post-operative treatment with levodopa.[42] Although most of the available *in vivo* studies are reassuring, we still cannot completely rule out the possibility that chronic levodopa treatment adversely affects dopaminergic neurons in PD because of the unknown cause of the illness and the potential for dopaminergic neurons to be specifically vulnerable to this drug.

SOME CONCLUDING ARGUMENTS IN FAVOR OF DELAYING INITIATION OF LEVODOPA THERAPY IN EARLY STAGES OF PD

There is no doubt that levodopa is the most effective drug for the treatment of most of the motor signs and symptoms of PD. This feature would make levodopa the best therapeutic strategy at any stage, early or late, of the disease. Secondly, levodopa may improve survival and increase the life span of afflicted patients. This feature would make a particularly strong case for an early start of levodopa treatment. However, recent studies now question whether the early use of levodopa indeed delays death in parkinsonians, particularly in the early stages of the disease.[43] It is most likely that improved mortality seen in the older levodopa studies is related to benefits conferred to patients with advanced stages of the illness where it may prevent life-threatening complications associated with immobility such as pneumonia, pulmonary embolism, and pressure sores. Thirdly, it is likely that the emergence of response fluctuations after chronic administration of levodopa is related to treatment with levodopa itself as well as disease progression. It is becoming increasingly clear that the early use of levodopa has a deleterious and irreversible priming effect for the later generation of dyskinesias.[44] In addition, concerns still linger regarding the possibility that chronic levodopa can damage surviving nigrostriatal neurons and accelerate disease deterioration. Eventually, as the illness advances, all patients will sooner or later require levodopa. However, in view of the above considerations, it seems wise and prudent to withhold levodopa in patients with mild, early PD and delay its initiation for the more advanced stages when functional and social disability justifies this approach.[8,45] Other drugs such as dopamine agonists, which provide symptomatic benefit and have a reduced potential for inducing motor complications and oxidative stress, should be used in this interim period. It would naturally be ideal if a dopamine agonist or other agent could be developed that was as effective as levodopa, capable of preventing the later development of dyskinesias and response fluctuations, and neuroprotective.

ACKNOWLEDGMENT
Supported, in part, by the National Parkinson's Disease Foundation, Miami, Florida, USA.

REFERENCES

1. Yahr MD. Evaluation of long-term therapy in Parkinson's disease: mortality and therapeutic efficacy. In, Birkmayer W, Hornykiewicz O, eds, Advances in parkinsonism. Basel: Editiones Roche, 1976: 444–455.

2. Joseph C, Chassan JB, Koch ML. Levodopa in Parkinson's disease. A long-term appraisal of mortality. Ann Neurol 1978; 3: 116–118.

3. Marsden CD, Parkes JD. Success and problems of long-term levodopa therapy in Parkinson's disease. Lancet 1977; i: 345–349.

4. Marsden CD, Parkes JD, Quinn N. Fluctuations of disability in Parkinson's disease: clinical aspects. In, Marsden CD, Fahn S, eds, Movement disorders. London: Butterworth, 1982: 96–122.

5. Melamed E, Bitton V, Zelig O. Delayed onset of response to single doses of L-dopa therapy. Clin Neuropharmacol 1986; 9: 182–188.

6. Melamed E, Bitton V, Zelig O. Episodic unresponsiveness to single doses of L-dopa in parkinsonian fluctuators. Neurol 1986; 36: 100–103.

7. Yahr MD. Long-term levodopa therapy for Parkinson's disease. Lancet 1977; i: 706–707.

8. Melamed E. Initiation of levodopa therapy in parkinsonian patients should be delayed until the advanced stages of the disease. Arch Neurol 1986; 43: 402–405.

9. Markham CH, Diamond SG. Evidence to support early levodopa therapy in Parkinson's disease. Neurol 1981; 31: 125–131.

10. Melamed E, Hefti F, Wurtman RJ. Nonaminergic striatal neurons convert exogenous levodopa to dopamine in parkinsonism. Ann Neurol 1980; 8: 558–563.

11. Melamed E, Globus M, Friedlender E, Rosenthal Y. Chronic L-dopa administration decreases striatal accumulation of dopamine from exogenous L-dopa in rats with intact nigrostriatal projections. Neurol 1983; 33: 950–953.

12. Takashima H, Tsujihata M, Niwa M, Nagataki S. Effects of chronic administration of L-dopa and bromocriptine on dopaminergic metabolism in the rat striatum. Biogenic Amines 1987; 4: 15–22.

13. Brannan T, Martinez-Tica J, Yahr MD. Effects of long-term L-dopa administration on striatal extracellular dopamine release. Neurol 1991; 41: 596–598.

14. Murata M. Kanazawa I. Repeated L-dopa administration reduces the ability of dopamine storage and abolishes and supersensitivity of dopamine receptors in the striatum of intact rats. Neurosci Res 1993; 16: 15–23.

15. Opacka-Juffry J, Brooks DJ. L-dihydroxyphenylalanine and its decarboxylase: new ideas on their regulatory roles. Mov Disord 1995; 10: 241–249.

16. Hume SP, Myers R, Opacka-Juffry J, Brooks DJ. Effect of L-dopa and 6-OHDA lesioning on ^{11}C-raclopride binding in rat striatum quantified using PET. J Cereb Blood Flow Metab 1993; 13 (Suppl): 295.

17. Creese I, Sibley DR. Receptor adaptations to centrally-active drugs. Ann Rev Pharmacol Tox 1981; 21: 357–391.

18. Gerfen CR, this volume.

19. Jenner P, Tulloch I, this volume.

20. O'Leary MH, Vaughn RL. New pathway for metabolism of dopa. Nature 1975; 253: 52–53.

21. Dougan D, Wade D, Mearick P. Effects of L-dopa metabolites at a dopamine receptor suggest a basis for 'on-off' effect in Parkinson's disease. Nature 1975; 254: 70–72.

22. Marion MH, Stocchi F, Quinn NP, Jenner P, Marsden CD. Repeated levodopa infusions in fluctuating Parkinson's disease: clinical and pharmacokinetic data. Clin Neuropharmacol 1986; 9: 165–181.

23. Sage JI, Tooskin S, Sonsalla PK, Heikilla R, Duvoisin RC. Long-term duodenal infusion of levodopa for motor fluctuations in parkinsonism. Ann Neurol 1988; 24: 87–89.

24. Djaldetti R, Baron J, Ziv I, Melamed E. Gastric emptying in Parkinson's disease: patients with and without response fluctuations. Neurol 1996; 46: 1051–1054.

25. Wakabagashi K, Takahashi H, Takeda S, Ohama E, Ikuta F. Parkinson's disease: the presence of Lewy bodies in Auerbach's and Meissner's plexuses. Acta Neuropathol 1988; 76: 217–221.

26. Lanfranchi GA, Marzio L, Cortini C, Trento L, Labo G. Effect of dopamine on gastric motility in man: evidence for specific receptors. In, Duthie HL, ed, Gastrointestinal motility in health and disease. Lancaster: MTP Publishers, 1977: 161–176.

27. Schuurkes JAJ, Van-Neuten JM. Is dopamine an inhibitory modulator of gastrointestinal motility? Scand J Gastroenterol 1981; 67 (Suppl): 33–36.

28. McCallum RW, Berkowitz D. Effects of L-dopa on gastric emptying in man. Clin Res 1977; 25: 569A.

29. Graham DG. Oxidative pathways for catecholamines in the genesis of neuromelanin and cytotoxic quinones. Mol Pharmacol 1978; 14: 633–643.

30. Wick MM, Byers L, Frei E. L-dopa: selective toxicity for melanoma cells *in vitro*. Science 1977; 197: 468–469.

31. Mena MA, Pardo B, Casarejos MJ, Fahn S, De Yebenes JG. Neurotoxicity of levodopa on catecholamine-rich neurons. Mov Disord 1992; 7: 23–31.

32. Ziv I, Zilkha-Falb R, Offen D, Shirvan A, Barzilai A, Melamed E. Levodopa induces apoptosis in cultured neuronal cells – a possible accelerator of nigrostriatal degeneration in Parkinson's disease? Mov Disord, 1997; 12: 17–23.

33. Ziv I, Melamed E, Nardi N, Offen D, Barzilai A. Dopamine induces apoptosis-like cell death in cultured sympathetic neurons – a possible novel pathogenic mechanism in Parkinson's disease. Neurosci Lett 1994; 170: 136–140.

34. Hefti F, Melamed E, Bhawan J, Wurtman RJ. Long-term administration of L-dopa does not damage dopaminergic neurons in the mouse. Neurol 1981; 31: 1194–1195.

35. Melamed E, Rosenthal J. Can chronic levodopa therapy accelerate degeneration of dopaminergic neurons and progression of Parkinson's disease? In, Nagatsu T, Fisher A, Yoshida M, eds, Basic, clinical and therapeutic aspects of Alzheimer's and Parkinson's diseases. New York: Plenum Press, 1990: 253–256.

36. Perry TL, Yong VW, Ito M. Nigrostriatal dopaminergic neurons remain undamaged in rats given high doses of L-dopa and carbidopa chronically. J Neurochem 1984; 43: 990–993.

37. Blunt SB, Jenner P, Marsden CD. Suppressive effect of L-dopa in dopamine cells remaining in the central tegmental area of rats previously exposed to the neurotoxin 6-hydroxydopamine. Mov Disord 1993; 8: 129–133.

38. Ogawa N, Asanuma M, Kondo Y, Yamamoto M, Mori A. Differential effects of chronic L-dopa treatment on lipid peroxidation in the mouse brain with or without pretreatment with 6-hydroxydopamine. Neurosci Lett 1994; 171: 55–58.

39. Steece-Collier K, Collier TJ, Sladeck CD, Sladeck JR. Chronic levodopa impairs morphological development of grafted embryonic dopamine neurons. Exp Neurol 1990; 110: 201–208.

40. Melamed E, Rosenthal J, Reches A. Prenatal administration of levodopa is not toxic to fetal dopaminergic neurons *in vivo*. Neurol 1992; 42 (Suppl 3): 378.

41. Quinn N, Parkes D, Janoto J, Marsden CD. Preservation of the substantia nigra and locus ceruleus in a patient receiving levodopa plus decarboxylase inhibitor over a four-year period. Mov Disord 1986; 1: 65–68.

42. Kordower JH, Freeman TB, Snow BJ, Olanow CW. Neuropathological evidence of graft survival and striatal reinnervation after the transplantation of fetal mesencephalic tissue in a patient with Parkinson's disease. N Engl J Med 1995; 332: 1118–1124.

43. Clarke CE. Does levodopa therapy delay death in Parkinson's disease? Mov Disord 1995; 10: 250–256.

44. Bédard P, this volume.

45. Fahn S, Bressman SB. Should levodopa therapy for parkinsonism be started early or late? Evidence against early treatment. Can J Neurol Sci 1984; 11: 200–206.

CHAPTER ELEVEN

The influence of age on the use of dopamine agonists as primary symptomatic therapy

FABRIZIO STOCCHI, MD, PhD

Department of Neurosciences, University 'La Sapienza',
Rome, Italy

ABSTRACT

The use of dopamine agonists delays the onset and incidence of motor fluctuations and reduces the risk of dyskinesia in Parkinson's disease patients. Their use is strongly recommended in young patients with a high risk of developing motor complications. In patients aged 55–65 years, who may also be at risk of onset of motor complications, the rationale for the use of dopamine agonists is similar to that employed in younger patients. However, a slow titration schedule is recommended since, on balance, the minimization of side effects is likely to be more important than reducing the time to reach maximum benefit. In elderly patients, cognitive impairment and cardiovascular disease are important factors in determining the therapeutic agent. Occasionally, dopamine agonists may be combined with levodopa from the start in an attempt to gain better control of symptoms with a reduced dose of levodopa.

Once the diagnosis of Parkinson's disease (PD) has been made, it must be decided whether a patient needs to receive a symptomatic antiparkinsonian drug and which drug should be the first choice. The decision to start symptomatic treatment is based on the degree of the patient's functional impairment as determined by the particular symptoms, their severity, and the site of the body affected (dominant or non-dominant side). The presence of parkinsonian symptoms is implicit in diagnosing PD, therefore it is a question of the degree to which the patient suffers functional disability that determines whether symptomatic treatment is required. This is an individual decision and takes into account the specific needs of the patient, the philosophy of the physician, and the impact of the disease on the ability of the patient to carry out their acts of daily living.

The most important consideration in deciding when to initiate treatment is based on the capacity of the patient to maintain his or her activities of daily living. If these are compromised, early treatment is warranted. Another important factor that influences the decision as to when to start treatment is whether or not the patient is working. PD can impair job performance and threaten employability and thereby necessitates the need for early treatment. Patients with symptoms of gait impairment or postural instability must be treated relatively early as these symptoms can lead to falls and serious injury, and can seriously affect the social life of the patient. In most patients with early PD, the disease is predominantly unilateral, so that the degree of functional impairment often depends on which hand is affected. Thus patients with symptoms involving the dominant side are more likely to seek treatment. Tremor is a source of complaint for many PD patients. PD tremor tends to be asymmetric and present at rest. In most patients, tremors are cosmetic and do not induce functional impairment. Nonetheless, they may still be distressing to the patient and socially embarrassing. The patient may therefore seek treatment even though the tremor itself may not impair motor skills. Thus, the decision to start treatment weighs up many factors. Treatment may be started in a concert violinist whose minimal signs and symptoms are an important source of disability, but withheld in a farmer with more prominent parkinsonian features that do not interfere with lifestyle.

Once the decision to start treatment has been made, a specific drug has to be chosen. At this stage, amantadine or anticholinergic drugs may provide symptomatic relief for some months. Anticholinergic drugs are mainly useful in treating patients with resting tremor. Because of the high incidence of peripheral and CNS side effects (especially cognitive impairment) associated with these drugs, their use in patients over the age of 60 or with pre-existing cognitive impairment is not recommended. When disability is more advanced and a more effective therapy is required, the aims are to provide adequate control of symptoms and to adopt a strategy that is least likely to induce long-term motor complications and dyskinesias. This becomes more important in relation to the chronologic and biologic age of the patient.

YOUNG PATIENTS (AGED LESS THAN 55 YEARS)

The treatment of patients with young-onset PD is particularly problematic. These patients are especially prone to develop motor complications in the form of motor fluctuations and involuntary movements with chronic levodopa treatment.[1,2] Different authors have shown that the development of motor fluctuations and abnormal involuntary movements or dyskinesias are related to the duration and the dosage of levodopa therapy.[3,4] It has therefore been proposed that treatment with this drug should be delayed for as long as possible. This can be accomplished by the use of dopamine agonists which provide some antiparkinsonian benefit coupled with a reduced propensity for development of levodopa-related motor complications. When function cannot be adequately controlled with the agonist alone, levodopa can be added to the agonist as combination therapy. In severe cases, where the disease markedly impairs activities of daily living and patients risk losing their job, dopamine agonists may be started in combination with levodopa.

Montastruc *et al.* performed a prospective, controlled study in which PD patients were randomized to initial treatment with a dopamine agonist (bromocriptine) alone, followed by levodopa 'rescue' if necessary, *versus* levodopa alone. This study showed that bromocriptine delayed the initiation of levodopa by an average of 2.7 years and motor complications were delayed and less severe. At least one motor complication was seen in 90% of patients after 2.7 years of treatment with levodopa, compared to 56% of patients after 4.7 years with bromocriptine.[5] Moreover, animal data show that treatment with certain dopamine agonists such as ropinirole do not induce dyskinesias if the animals are not previously primed with levodopa.[6] Thus, dopamine agonist monotherapy should be the first symptomatic approach to young parkinsonian patients. However, there are some limitations with this therapeutic approach as dopamine agonists appear to be less effective than levodopa in controlling parkinsonian symptomatology.[7,8] Indeed, in a double-blind study on a large population of *de novo* parkinsonian patients, the percentage improvement in the Unified Parkinson's Disease Rating Scale (UPDRS) total motor examination score was significantly higher for levodopa-treated patients than for those on ropinirole. However, these differences are modest and may relate to disease severity. The proportion of 'responders' (UPDRS improvement of at least 30%) did not differ between groups and there was no difference between the two treatments in the Clinical Global Impression (CGI) scale for patients with early disease (Hoehn & Yahr stages I–II). In more advanced patients, a significantly higher proportion of levodopa-treated patients showed greater improvement on the CGI.[9] In another study involving a smaller number of patients, it was shown that ropinirole was as effective as levodopa in controlling parkinsonian symptoms and its effect was long-lasting.[10] Nevertheless, in most long-term studies, the effects of dopamine agonist monotherapy gradually wear off after a few years although more than 25% of the patients were still satisfactorily controlled after three years.[11]

The other problems perceived with dopamine agonist therapy are the time to reach clinical effect and the relatively high incidence of side effects in comparison with levodopa. While these side effects (nausea, vomiting, hypotension) are generally transient, they are the cause of drop-out for many patients. These unpleasant side effects can be minimized by initiating patients on a low dose of agonist and maintaining a slow titration schedule in which doses are increased no more frequently than every other day. The titration schedule may be faster in those countries where domperidone is available, and consequently the time to reach maximum benefit is reduced. The side effects associated with dopamine agonists have attracted attention because of the high drop-out rates in the early studies. However, they are relatively comparable in nature and in frequency with those seen when initiating levodopa. In the above-mentioned controlled study, 20% of patients treated with ropinirole and 14% of patients treated with levodopa required domperidone to control side effects.[9] Adverse experiences caused premature withdrawal in 8% of ropinirole patients and in 13% of levodopa patients. The compliance of patients receiving dopamine agonist treatment can be increased by the physician explaining that agonists are being started because of the possible benefit of delaying levodopa therapy and the reduced possibility of developing dyskinesias (Table 1).

Table 1: Factors influencing the use of dopamine agonists in young PD patients (aged < 55 years)	
Pros	**Cons**
Delay motor complications, dyskinesias, on-off fluctuations	Less effective than levodopa Time to reach maximum effect 2–4 weeks Side effects same as levodopa

PATIENTS AGED BETWEEN 55 AND 65 YEARS

The rationale for using dopamine agonists in this group of patients is similar to that for its use in younger patients. The aim is to reduce the cumulative exposure to levodopa and thereby possibly reduce long-term side effects. A slow titration schedule is particularly important in this population, since minimizing side effects is probably more important than the time to reach maximum benefit. At this age, patients may be less motivated than younger individuals to tolerate side effects at the beginning of treatment.

Patients who are still employed may prefer quick relief from symptoms rather than starting a slow titration of dose with a dopamine agonist. Levodopa induces more rapid relief from symptoms compared with a dopamine agonist and provides a stronger effect, especially in more affected patients. In this group of patients, the discussion between doctor and patient may be very important to understand the needs of the patient and their expectancies for future life. Eventually, a sensible proposal could be to start treatment with levodopa and to add a dopamine agonist immediately afterwards. Cognitive impairment is not common in this range of ages but it should not be underestimated. In these patients, dopamine agonists may induce hallucinations more commonly than levodopa (Table 2).

Table 2: Factors influencing the use of dopamine agonists in PD patients aged 55 – 65 years	
Pros	**Cons**
Delay motor complications, dyskinesias, on-off fluctuations	Side effects same as levodopa Time to reach maximum benefit 2–4 weeks

The concerns over development of long-term adverse effects with levodopa treatment are not as great for patients above the age of 65 years, in whom the incidence and severity of motor fluctuations and dyskinesias appear to be diminished.[2] Cognitive impairment is an important modifier in determining pharmacologic intervention in this group of patients. It can alter a patient's response to antiparkinsonian drugs, especially anticholinergics which should be avoided. In these patients, antiparkinsonian drugs may cause hallucinations, confusion and sometimes delirium. The incidence of these side effects in patients with cognitive impairment is higher with dopamine agonists than levodopa. Dopamine agonists also have an effect on the cardiovascular system, and should therefore be avoided in patients with cardiovascular disease, especially without domperidone. Levodopa itself may also interfere with the cardiovascular system but the dopa decarboxylase inhibitor present in pharmacologic preparations strongly reduces these effects. For these reasons, most physicians prefer to confine treatment to levodopa in elderly patients. Occasionally, dopamine agonists may be combined with levodopa from the start in an attempt to obtain better control of symptoms with a reduced dose of levodopa. If the patient is taking anti-hypertensive drugs, the treatment should be revised after the introduction of a dopamine agonist. In the case of patients with hypotension, dopamine agonists should be administered in combination with domperidone, but where this drug is not available, dopamine agonists should be avoided (Table 3).

Table 3: Factors influencing the use of dopamine agonists in elderly patients (aged > 65 years)	
Pros	**Cons**
Better control of symptoms in combination with levodopa	Cognitive impairment
Delay motor complications	Cardiovascular problems

CONCLUSION

The use of dopamine agonists as a first line symptomatic treatment delays the onset and incidence of motor fluctuations and reduces the risk of developing dyskinesias. Their use as initial therapy is therefore strongly recommended in young patients who have a higher risk of developing motor complications. This group of patients should be encouraged by the doctor to start treatment with dopamine agonists even if this therapy is less effective than levodopa and induces more acute side effects.

In patients aged 55–65 years, dopamine agonists should also be considered as initial therapy. In this age group, other factors must be taken into account.

For example, if the patient is still employed and is more affected on the dominant side, the doctor may consider starting treatment with levodopa and secondarily adding a dopamine agonist. Patients in this age group may be less willing than younger patients to tolerate a slow titration schedule of dopamine agonist monotherapy and combined therapy may avoid this problem.

In elderly patients, cognitive impairment and cardiovascular disease are important modifiers in determining the appropriate pharmacologic intervention. Dopamine agonists induce hallucinations and interfere with the cardiovascular system to a greater extent than levodopa/dopa decarboxylase inhibitor preparations. For this reason most physicians utilize only levodopa in this population of patients.

REFERENCES

1. Quinn N, Critchley P, Marsden CD. Young onset Parkinson's disease. Mov Disord 1987; 2: 73–91.

2. Golbe LI. Young-onset Parkinson's disease: a clinical review. Neurol 1991; 41: 168–173.

3. Fahn S, Bressman SB. Should levodopa therapy for parkinsonism be started early or late? Evidence against early treatment. Can J Neurol Sci 1984; 11: 200–206.

4. Melamed E. Initiation of levodopa therapy in parkinsonian patients should be delayed until the advanced stages of the disease. Arch Neurol 1986; 43: 405–407.

5. Montastruc JL, Rascol O, Senard JM, et al. A randomized controlled study of bromocriptine secondarily associated to levodopa in previously untreated parkinsonian patients: a 5-year follow up. J Neurol Neurosurg Psychiatr 1994; 57: 1034–1038.

6. Jenner P, Tulloch I, this volume.

7. Rinne UK. Lisuride, a dopamine agonist in the treatment of early Parkinson's disease. Neurol 1989; 39: 336–339.

8. Goetz CG. Dopaminergic agonists in the treatment of Parkinson's disease. Neurol 1990; 40 (Suppl 3): 50–54.

9. Rascol O. A double-blind levodopa-controlled study of ropinirole in patients with early Parkinson's disease. Neurol 1996; 46 (Suppl 2): 160.

10. Barbato L, Stocchi F, Monge A, Vacca L, Ruggieri S, Nordera G, Marsden CD. The long duration action of levodopa may be due to a postsynaptic effect. Clin Neuropharmacol, in press.

11. Rinne UK. Strategies in the treatment of early Parkinson's disease. Acta Neurol Scand 1993; 87 (Suppl 146): 50–53.

CHAPTER TWELVE

Neuroprotection with dopamine agonists

NORIO OGAWA, MD

Institute of Molecular and Cellular Medicine, Okayama University Medical School, Okayama, Japan

ABSTRACT

A number of complications are associated with the long-term use of levodopa, including potential neurotoxicity elicited by oxidative metabolism of the drug. Evidence from studies in mice, in PC 12 cells and in mesencephalic cell cultures has shown that the production of dopamine- and levodopa-derived cytotoxic free radicals leads to neuronal damage in the parkinsonian substantia nigra. Dopamine agonists are candidate compounds for the provision of neuroprotection in Parkinson's disease, reducing dopamine turnover and allowing a reduction in levodopa dose, thereby reducing free radical formation. Dopamine agonists may also decrease hydroxyl radical formation and scavenge both those hydroxyl radicals which are formed and nitric oxide.

Levodopa has long been considered the most effective agent for the symptomatic treatment of Parkinson's disease (PD).[1,2] Nevertheless, a number of complications are associated with the long-term use of levodopa, among which loss of efficacy and motor complications such as dyskinesias are the most severe.[3,4] There is also a growing concern that levodopa, by way of its oxidative metabolism, may be neurotoxic to the parkinsonian nigra. The disadvantages of levodopa treatment are listed in Table 1. This paper examines the proposed neurotoxic mechanisms of levodopa, and discusses the potential for neuroprotection by dopamine agonists.

NEUROTOXICITY OF LEVODOPA

Oxidative stress has been implicated in the pathogenesis of PD because of the propensity of dopamine to undergo enzymatic or auto-oxidation to form cytotoxic free radicals.[5,6] The parkinsonian substantia nigra has diminished levels of glutathione which clears peroxide and prevents formation of the hydroxyl radical.[7] In addition, there are increased levels of iron, a transition metal which promotes oxidative reactions.[8] The net result is that free radical formation is likely to occur and, indeed, there is evidence of oxidative damage to many molecules. It is unlikely that large amounts of free radicals are produced in the absence of levodopa administration because dopamine, which is a precursor for the production of free radicals, is usually present in the untreated parkinsonian brain at levels lower than 20% of normal. After administration of levodopa, however, there is a marked increase in dopamine with the risk of increased free radical formation and neuronal damage. Moreover, under some conditions, levodopa itself can be converted to levodopa radicals, as demonstrated by electron spin resonance spectrometry of oxidized levodopa.[9]

Table 1: Disadvantages of levodopa treatment

- produces levodopa radicals
- increases $HO^\bullet$ production
- antagonizes intrinsic $HO^\bullet$ scavenging activity
- decreases mitochondrial complex I activity (NADH : ubiquinone oxireductase)
- increases lipid peroxidation (in 6-hydroxydopamine-lesioned animals)
- produces apoptosis (in PC 12 cells)
- increases 8-hydroxy-2-deoxyguanosine (DNA damage)

Evidence for the production of free radicals and subsequent brain tissue damage has emerged from studies in a parkinsonian model in mice, in which lipid peroxidation is detected by thiobarbituric acid-reacting substances (TBARS). When levodopa is administered to normal mice, TBARS in the brain actually decrease, indicating lack of any toxic effect. In contrast, mice which receive 6-hydroxydopamine into the lateral ventricle to create a parkinsonian lesion, and which are then given chronic administration of levodopa, demonstrate a marked increase in TBARS levels indicative of free radical formation.[10]

Further demonstration of the neurotoxic effects of levodopa has been provided by studies in PC 12 cells[11,12] and mesencephalic cell cultures.[13] Levodopa induces apoptotic change in approximately 75% of cells. Interestingly, the changes induced by levodopa are much more pronounced than those seen following administration of the same concentration of dopamine.[11] This suggests that levodopa itself has a neurotoxic effect on PC 12 cells due to its oxidative metabolism and the formation of free radicals. This was confirmed by the almost complete abolition of apoptotic changes by the addition of glutathione, ascorbic acid or α-tocopherol. It seems likely, therefore, that the levodopa-induced neurotoxic effect is due to free radical formation or oxidative stress within the substantia nigra of PD patients.[14]

There are many candidates for neuroprotection in PD (Table 2).[15] The goal of neuroprotective therapy is to slow or halt the degenerative process in residual neurons.[16] Dopamine agonists are a candidate treatment for providing neuroprotection. Dopamine agonists which act on dopamine D_2 receptors have been shown to result in antiparkinsonian activity.[17] This same pharmacologic effect could also lead to a neuroprotective benefit.

Table 2: Possible neuroprotective therapies for Parkinson's disease

Free radical-related agents
- reduce dopamine turnover
  - restriction of levodopa dose
  - dopamine agonists (bromocriptine, pergolide)
- hydroxyl radical scavengers
  - MAO-B inhibitors (selegiline, lazabemide)
  - dopamine agonists (bromocriptine, pergolide)
- Nitric oxide radical scavengers
  - dopamine agonists (bromocriptine, pergolide)
- Spin traps
  - PBN, salicylate
- Anti-oxidants
  - α-tocopherol, ascorbic acid, EPC-K$_1$, GEPC, uric acid, β-carotene
- Anti-oxidant enzymes
  - superoxide dismutase, glutathione, glutathione peroxidase
- Iron chelators

Excitatory amino acid-related agents
- excitatory amino acid receptor blockers
- Ca^{2+} antagonists
- amantadine

Neurotoxin-related agent
- 1-methyl-TIQ

Neurotrophic factors
- brain-derived neurotrophic factor (BDNF)
- glial cell line-derived neurotrophic factor (GDNF)

PBN:	N-tert-butyl-α-phenylnitrone
EPC-K$_1$:	l-ascorbic acid 2-[3,4-dihydro-2,5,7,8-tetramethyl-2(4,8,12-trimethyltridecyl)-2H-1-benzpyrene-6-yl-hydrogen phosphate] potassium salt
GEPC:	l-ascorbic acid 2-(20β-11-oxo-olean-12-en-29-oic acid ethylester-3β-yl hydrogen phosphate) sodium salt

---

This could be achieved by agonists acting on D_2 autoreceptors to reduce dopamine turnover and reduce levodopa dosage. The potential of dopamine agonists to provide neuroprotection might be considered to result from four factors – reduction of levodopa dosage, decreased hydroxyl radical formation, hydroxyl radical scavenging, and nitric oxide (NO) scavenging.

Dopamine agonists such as bromocriptine and pergolide have been shown to be capable of scavenging hydroxyl radicals resulting from the increased dopamine levels that follow levodopa treatment.[18,19] It has been proposed recently that dopamine agonists may also be able to protect against the consequences of NO which can react with the superoxide radical to produce peroxynitrite and hydroxyl radicals and consequent cell death. We have developed an *in vitro* model for the generation of high concentrations of NO radicals by the conversion of carboxyl PTIO to carboxyl PTI by lowering the pH of NOC7.[20] Addition of pergolide or bromocriptine to this carboxyl PTIO–NOC7 system results in a decrease in the amount of free NO produced from NOC7. The NO radical-scavenging activity of pergolide is 10 times greater than that of bromocriptine. The comparative activities of pergolide and bromocriptine are summarized in Table 3. Both agents have anti-oxidant properties and can scavenge hydroxyl radicals or NO, but neither can eliminate superoxide. These results can also be seen in *in vivo* models. There is now evidence that dopamine agonists protect dopamine neurons from the consequences of an intraventricular injection of 6-hydroxydopamine in the mouse. [18,21]

Table 3: Role of dopamine agonists in oxidative stress				
Agonist	**Anti-oxidant activity**	**Scavenging activity**		
		$O_2^{\bullet-}$	$HO^{\bullet}$	$NO^{\bullet}$
Bromocriptine	++	−	++	+
Pergolide	+++	−	++	++

These observations have important implications for PD patients. They suggest that dopamine agonists may offer neuroprotective benefits by reducing the need for levodopa, by reducing dopamine turnover, and by their capacity to scavenge free radicals directly. As a body of information has implicated oxidative stress in the pathogenesis of PD, and as there is a possibility that levodopa might promote the development of oxidative stress, it is reasonable to consider the use of dopamine agonists as an alternative therapy for PD patients, particularly in the early stages of the disease. As dopamine agonists protect against the development of adverse events, it is interesting to speculate on whether their antioxidant properties may contribute to this benefit, perhaps by protecting dopaminergic terminals that regulate dopamine uptake and release.

REFERENCES

1. Marttila RJ, Rinne UK, Sirtola T, *et al.* Mortality of patients with Parkinson's disease treated with levodopa. J Neurol 1977; 216: 147–153.

2. Scigliano G, Musicco M, Soliveri P, *et al.* Mortality associated with early and late levodopa therapy initiation in Parkinson's disease. Neurol 1990; 40: 265–269.

3. Sweet RD, McDowell FH. Five years' treatment of Parkinson's disease with levodopa. Ann Intern Med 1975; 83: 456–463.

4. Lesser RD, Fahn S, Snider SR, *et al.* Analysis of the clinical problem in parkinsonism and the complications of long-term levodopa therapy. Neurol 1979; 29: 1253–1260.

5. Jenner P, Schapira AHV, Marsden CD. New insights into the cause of Parkinson's disease. Neurol 1992; 42: 2241–2250.

6. Olanow CW. A radical hypothesis for neurodegeneration. Trends Neurosci 1993; 16: 439–444.

7. Riederer P, Sofic E, Rausch W-D, *et al.* Transition metals, ferritin, glutathione, and ascorbic acid in parkinsonian brains. J Neurochem 1989; 52: 515–520.

8. Dexter DT, Wells FR, Lees AJ, *et al.* Increased nigral iron content and alterations in other metal ions occurring in brain in Parkinson's disease. J Neurochem 1989; 52: 1830–1836.

9. Ogawa N, Edamatsu R, Mizukawa K, *et al.* Degeneration of dopaminergic neurons and free radicals. Possible participation of levodopa. Adv Neurol 1993; 60: 242–250.

10. Ogawa N, Asanuma M, Kondo Y, *et al.* Differential effects of chronic L-dopa treatment on lipid peroxidation in the mouse brain with or without pre-treatment with 6-hydroxydopamine. Neurosci Lett 1994; 171: 55–58.

11. Walkinshaw G, Waters CM. Induction of apoptosis in catecholaminergic PC 12 cells by L-dopa: implications for the treatment of Parkinson's disease. J Clin Invest 1995; 95: 2458–2464.

12. Basma AN, Morris EJ, Nicklas WJ, *et al.* L-dopa cytotoxicity to PC 12 cells in culture is via its auto-oxidation. J Neurochem 1995; 64: 825–832.

13. Pardo B, Mena MA, Casajos MJ, *et al.* Toxic effects of L-dopa on mesencephalic cells cultures: protection with antioxidants. Brain Res 1995; 682: 133–143.

14. Ogawa N, Iwata E, Asanuma M, *et al.* Oxidative stress and transcription factors. In, Packer L, Hiramatsu M, Yoshikawa T, eds, Free radicals in brain physiology and disorders. San Diego: Academic Press, 1996: 131–140.

15. Ogawa N. Possible neuroprotective therapy for Parkinson's disease. Acta Med Okayama 1995; 49: 179–185.

16. Olanow CW. Early therapy for Parkinson's disease. Eur Neurol 1992; 32 (Suppl 1): 30–35.

17. Schachter M, Bédard P, Debono AG, *et al.* The role of D_1 and D_2 receptors. Nature 1980; 286: 157–159.

18. Ogawa N, Tanaka K, Asanuma M, *et al.* Bromocriptine protects mice against 6-hydroxydopamine and scavenges hydroxyl free radicals *in vitro*. Brain Res 1994; 657: 207–213.

19. Ogawa N, Nishibayashi S, Gómez-Vargas M. Free radical scavenging activity and antioxidant of pergolide. XIIth International Symposium on Parkinson's Disease, London, March 25, 1997, abstract.

20. Nishibayashi S, Asanuma M, Kohno M, et al. Scavenging effects of dopamine agonists on nitric oxide radicals. J Neurochem 1996; 67: 2208–2211.

21. Asanuma M, Ogawa N, Nishibayashi S, et al. Protective effects of pergolide on dopamine levels in the 6-hydroxydopamine-lesioned mouse brain. Arch Int Pharmacodyn 1995; 329: 221–230.

CHAPTER THIRTEEN

Dopamine agonists and the management of long-term complications in Parkinson's disease

WERNER POEWE, MD

Universitätsklinik für Neurologie,
Innsbruck, Austria

ABSTRACT

Late complications of chronic levodopa administration in Parkinson's disease result from an interaction between drug-induced changes in pharmacodynamic response and problems due to disease progression affecting multiple neuronal levels. It is important, in clinical terms, to identify risk factors which predispose patients to levodopa-related motor complications, in particular dyskinesias. The degree of disease severity seems critical in the development of levodopa-induced dyskinesias, as do the total daily dose of levodopa, the length of drug exposure and the age of the patient. The dyskinetic threshold may be increased by the administration of dopamine agonists to provide continuous stimulation of their receptors. In addition, monotherapy in early disease with dopamine agonists is associated with a significantly reduced incidence of dyskinesias and response oscillations, although long-term use of dopamine agonists may be accompanied by reductions in symptomatic improvement and tolerability. The development of new types of dopamine agonist, such as ropinirole, cabergoline and pramipexole, is aimed at improving long-term responses to this class of therapeutic agent.

The use of levodopa continues to be the gold standard of antiparkinsonian drug therapy in terms of symptomatic efficacy and tolerability.[1-3] However, the majority of patients with Parkinson's disease (PD) receiving chronic levodopa monotherapy for more than five years develop oscillations in their motor state and drug-induced involuntary movements.[4,5] Levodopa-induced dyskinesias can be as disabling as the disease itself, but are notoriously difficult to treat once they have developed. Therefore, strategies preventing the occurrence of late treatment failure due to motor oscillations and dyskinesias are among the prime issues in the development of new drug treatments for PD.

THE SYNDROME OF LATE LEVODOPA FAILURE

Late complications of chronic levodopa substitution in PD result from a complex interaction between drug-induced changes in the pharmacodynamic response and problems related to disease progression affecting multiple neuronal levels, i.e. beyond the nigrostriatal pathway. Consequently, different aspects of late levodopa failure need different therapeutic and preventive strategies and some of them are presently not amenable to drug therapy at all.

Clinical features of late levodopa failure

Response complications during chronic levodopa therapy comprise motor as well as neuropsychiatric features. On the motor side, the 'long duration response' to individual levodopa doses is progressively attenuated such that drug effects begin to wear off several hours after each dose with a predictable pattern ('wearing off' phenomenon). Abrupt oscillations between states of near-perfect motor control in 'on' phases and devastating parkinsonism in 'off' states occur in about 10–20% of affected patients as disease progresses and time under levodopa increases. 'Off' crises of the latter type may include additional non-motor features such as pain, panic attacks, tachycardia, sweating, and dyspnea, as well as confusion and hallucinosis.[4,6]

Most, if not all, patients with PD who suffer motor fluctuations are also affected by abnormal drug-induced movements. Such dyskinesias are

---

Table 1: Pharmacologic management of motor fluctuations

1. **Improve levodopa absorption and transport**
    - dietary protein reduction (<1 g/kg per day)
    - enhance gastric motility (cisapride)
    - duodenal levodopa infusions

2. **Stabilize levodopa plasma levels**
    - increase dosing frequency
    - introduce sustained-release formulations
    - add COMT inhibitors

3. **Enhance striatal dopamine concentration**
    - add MAO-B inhibitors
    - add centrally-active COMT inhibitors

4. **Add dopamine agonist**
    - orally active compounds:
        a) short half-life: bromocriptine, lisuride, ropinirole, pramipexole
        b) long half-life: pergolide, cabergoline
    - subcutaneous apomorphine (continuous or intermittent)

commonly divided into three main types: (1) 'peak-dose' or 'inter-dose' dyskinesias, which occur at times of a full motor response ('on') and are characterized by choreic, usually asymmetric, limb movements, but may also involve the face, neck and trunk; (2) 'biphasic' dyskinesias, which are linked to transition periods of onset or wearing-off of drug effects and frequently consist of a mixture of repetitive movements and dystonic elements causing bizarre twisting of the trunk and extremities; (3) 'off'-period dystonia, which is seen after the motor effect of a dose has completely worn off and typically involves asymmetric distal painful dystonic posturing of the feet.[7–9]

The therapeutic options to be considered in patients with motor fluctuations and dyskinesias are summarized in Tables 1 and 2. Treatment of problems such as progressive involvement of the axial musculature, dysarthria and flexor posture of the neck, instability and falls and, most importantly, freezing of gait is more difficult. These features are usually not amenable to dopaminergic therapy.

Table 2: Therapeutic options for levodopa-induced dyskinesias

1. Inter-dose dyskinesias

- reduce levodopa
- add/increase dopamine agonist and reduce levodopa
- switch to dopamine agonist monotherapy
- use continuous drug delivery (duodenal levodopa, s.c. apomorphine)
- try atypical neuroleptics (sulpiride, clozapine) or propranolol
- GPi pallidotomy, STN stimulation

2. Biphasic dyskinesias

- avoid sustained-release levodopa
- increase individual levodopa dose size
- switch to dopamine agonist monotherapy
- use s.c. apomorphine bolus injections
- GPi pallidotomy, GPi or STN stimulation

3. Early morning/'off' period dystonia

- bed-time levodopa sustained-release preparations
- bed-time dopamine agonists
- add baclofen, lithium
- inject botulinum toxin type A into dystonic leg muscles
- GPi pallidotomy, GPi or STN stimulation

Pathophysiology and risk factors for levodopa-related motor complications in PD

The pathophysiology underlying the development of motor response oscillations is not fully understood. The development of wearing-off oscillations is believed to be due to a progressive loss of central buffering capacity for dopamine formed from exogenous levodopa in the course of progressive nigrostriatal denervation. Peripheral pharmacokinetics then become a determining factor for the duration of the levodopa-induced motor response such that fluctuations in levodopa plasma levels are mirrored by motor response oscillations.[10-12] Such levodopa plasma level variation is determined by the drug's short half-life of about one hour plus a number of factors involved in gastrointestinal absorption, including erratic gastric emptying and competition with dietary neutral amino acids for mucosal transport of levodopa.[13] Competition between levodopa and neutral amino acids may also influence blood–brain barrier transport of the drug.[14]

While the pharmacokinetics of levodopa can explain predictable response oscillations in the setting of progressive nigrostriatal denervation, the mechanisms underlying unpredictable and abrupt 'on-off' swings are more difficult to understand. It is generally believed that they reflect pharmacodynamic changes at the dopamine receptor level.[15] The mechanisms underlying levodopa-induced abnormal involuntary movements are similarly obscure. Striatal dopamine receptor supersensitivity, imbalance between D_1 and D_2 receptor activation, and downstream changes with secondary GABAergic hypoactivity in the pallidothalamic outflow system have been proposed to play a role.[9,16,17]

From a clinical point of view, it is important to identify risk factors which predispose patients to the development of levodopa-related motor complications, in particular dyskinesias. So far, clinical studies have identified several such predisposing elements. The degree of disease severity is seemingly critical for the development of levodopa-induced dyskinesias, as demonstrated by the increasing prevalence of involuntary movements with disease progression as well as the asymmetry of dyskinesias with greater involvement of the more affected hemibody.[18] The total daily dose of levodopa as well as the length of drug exposure also play a role, although the latter is difficult to dissect from effects of disease duration. Age is the third major factor determining the risk for developing motor complications. Patients with PD of onset below the age of 45 years have been shown to develop levodopa-induced dyskinesias particularly rapidly. In one series, 40% of patients had developed levodopa-induced dyskinesias within six months of treatment and after two years 100% were affected.[19]

ROLE OF DOPAMINE AGONISTS IN PREVENTING LEVODOPA-RELATED MOTOR COMPLICATIONS

The administration of dopamine agonists is one of the cornerstones in the pharmacologic management of late levodopa motor complications (Tables 1 and 2). Numerous clinical studies have demonstrated that add-on treatment with dopamine agonists in patients with oscillations to levodopa may significantly reduce fluctuations and increase daily 'on'-time. Levodopa-induced dyskinesias may sometimes be reduced when a dopamine agonist is added, but this effect is mainly due to concomitant reductions in levodopa dose. Generally, dopamine agonists have the same dyskinetic potential when given to patients in whom dyskinesias have already been primed by levodopa exposure. This may not be true, however, when dopamine agonists can be administered to provide continuous stimulation of dopamine agonist receptors. There is now evidence from studies using continuous subcutaneous infusions with either lisuride or apomorphine showing that the dyskinetic threshold may be increased by such strategies.[20,21] Accordingly, significant decreases in the severity of pre-existing levodopa-induced dyskinesias have been observed following prolonged subcutaneous infusion of apomorphine.[21]

The main approach in the control of dyskinesias has to be preventive. A number of earlier clinical trials have demonstrated that monotherapy of early stage PD with dopamine agonists is associated with a significantly reduced incidence of dyskinesias and response oscillations in the long-term evaluation.[22,23] This has again been observed in a recent large multicenter trial in the UK comparing bromocriptine, levodopa, and levodopa plus selegiline, in which there were significantly fewer patients with motor oscillations and dyskinesias in the dopamine agonist arms after a three-year interim analysis (UK Parkinson's Disease Research Group).

In a smaller prospective open-label trial in 46 patients, Montastruc and colleagues[24] compared the five-year outcome of a group of patients treated with bromocriptine monotherapy in whom levodopa was added later, with another group treated with classic levodopa monotherapy. After five years of treatment, the incidence of motor oscillations was similar in both groups although the onset of wearing-off had been postponed in the bromocriptine arm by the time period covered by bromocriptine monotherapy. Drug-induced dyskinesias, on the other hand, had a significantly lower incidence in the bromocriptine arm despite later addition of levodopa.[24] This long-term advantage of dopamine agonist monotherapy is, however, associated with lesser degrees of symptomatic improvement and poorer tolerability compared to conventional levodopa therapy (UK Parkinson's Disease Research Group), such that only 30% of PD patients were eventually be maintained on sufficiently effective monotherapy with bromocriptine.[25]

The development of new types of dopamine agonist is aimed at improving tolerability and enhancing symptomatic efficacy to levels equivalent to levodopa. Along these lines, promising candidates have entered the scene over recent years. Ropinirole, a potent non-ergot D_2 dopamine agonist, has been shown to be of similar efficacy to levodopa in early PD (stages I and II of the Hoehn & Yahr scale).[26] Cabergoline was found to be marginally less effective than levodopa in comparative trials in *de novo* patients, but importantly possesses a long elimination half-life.[27] Pramipexole, another non-ergot dopamine agonist, is similar to ropinirole in that it has high affinity for D_3 dopamine receptors. At present it is unclear how this might translate into additional clinical benefit.

Although the role of dopamine agonists in the treatment of early PD is still controversial, there is growing consensus that PD patients with disease onset below the age of 65 should receive initial symptomatic treatment with dopamine agonists rather than levodopa in order to avoid the priming of a dyskinetic response. When the ability to offer symptomatic control wanes over the years, levodopa may be added later.

REFERENCES

1. Birkmayer W, Hornykiewicz O. Der 1-3,4, dioxyphenylalanin (=DOPA)-effekt bei der Parkinson-akinese. Wien Klin Wochenschr 1961; 73: 787–788.

2. Cotzias CG, Papavasiliou PS, Gellene R. Modification of parkinsonism: chronic treatment with L-dopa. N Engl J Med 1969; 280: 337–345.

3. Lees AJ. Levodopa – the gold standard in the management of Parkinson's disease. In, Poewe W, Lees AJ, eds, 20 years of Madopar – new avenues. Basel: Editiones Roche, 1994: 55–64.

4. Marsden CD, Parkes JD. Success and problems of long-term levodopa therapy in Parkinson's disease. Lancet 1977; i: 345–349.

5. Poewe WH, Lees AJ, Stern GM. Low-dose L-dopa therapy in Parkinson's disease: a 6 year follow-up study. Neurol 1986; 36: 1528–1530.

6. Poewe WH. Clinical aspects of motor fluctuations in Parkinson's disease. Neurol 1994; 44 (Suppl 6): 6–9.

7. Marsden CD, Parkes JD, Quinn N. Fluctuations of disability in Parkinson's disease: clinical aspects. In, Marsden CD, Fahn S, eds, Movement disorders. London: Butterworths, 1982: 96–122.

8. Poewe W, Lees AJ, Stern GM. Dystonia in Parkinson's disease: clinical and pharmacological features. Ann Neurol 1988; 23: 73–78.

9. Nutt JG. Levodopa induced dyskinesia: review, observations and speculations. Neurol 1990; 40: 340–345.

10. Gancher ST, Nutt JG, Woodward WR. Peripheral pharmacokinetics of levodopa in untreated, stable, and fluctuating parkinsonian patients. Neurol 1987; 37: 940–944.

11. Nutt JG. 'On-off' phenomenon: relation to levodopa pharmacokinetics and pharmacodynamics. Ann Neurol 1987; 22: 535–540.

12. Fabbrini G et al. Motor fluctuations in Parkinson's disease: central pathophysiological mechanisms, part I. Ann Neurol 1988; 24: 366–371.

13. Nutt JG, Fellman JH. Pharmacokinetics of levodopa. Clin Neuropharmacol 1984; 7: 35–49.

14. Nutt JG, Woodward WR, Hammerstad JP, Carter JH, Anderson JL. The 'on-off' phenomenon in Parkinson's disease: relation to levodopa absorption and transport. N Engl J Med 1984; 310: 483–488.

15. Mouradian MM, Juncos JL, Fabbrini G, Schlegel J, Bartko JJ, Chase TN. Motor fluctuations in Parkinson's disease: central pathophysiological mechanisms, part II. Ann Neurol 1988; 24: 372–378.

16. Mouradian MM, Heuser IJE, Baronti F, Fabbrini G, Juncos JL, Chase TN. Pathogenesis of dyskinesias in Parkinson's disease. Ann Neurol 1989; 25: 523–528.

17. Crossman AR. A hypothesis on the pathophysiological mechanisms that underlie levodopa- or dopamine agonist-induced dyskinesia in Parkinson's disease: implications for future strategies in treatment. Mov Disord 1990; 5: 100–108.

18. Horstink MWIM, Zijlmans JCM, Pasman JW, Berger HJC, Van't Hof MA. Severity of Parkinson's disease is a risk factor for peak-dose dyskinesia. J Neurol Neurosurg Psychiatr 1990; 53: 224–226.

19. Quinn N, Critchley P, Marsden CD. Young onset Parkinson's disease. Mov Disord 1987; 2: 73–91.

20. Baronti F, Mouradian M, Davis LT. Continuous effects on central dopaminergic mechanisms in Parkinson's disease. Ann Neurol 1992; 32: 776–781.

21. Poewe WH, Kleedorfer B, Wagner M, Bosch S, Schelosky L. Continuous

subcutaneous apomorphine infusions for fluctuating Parkinson's disease – long-term follow-up in 18 patients. Adv Neurol 1993; 60: 656–659.

22. Lees AJ, Stern GM. Sustained bromocriptine therapy in previously untreated patients with Parkinson's disease. J Neurol Neurosurg Psychiatr 1981; 44: 1020–1023.

23. Rinne UK. Lisuride, a dopamine agonist in the treatment of early Parkinson's disease. Neurol 1989; 39: 336–339.

24. Montastruc JL, Rascol O, Senard JM, Rascol A. A randomized controlled study comparing bromocriptine to which levodopa was later added, with levodopa alone in previously untreated patients with Parkinson's disease: a 5 year follow-up. J Neurol Neurosurg Psychiatr 1994; 57: 1034–1038.

25. Marsden CD. Parkinson's disease. J Neurol Neurosurg Psychiatr 1994; 57: 672–681.

26. Rascol O, Brooks DJ, Brunt ER, Korczyn AD, Poewe WH, Stocchi F. Ropinirole in the treatment of early Parkinson's disease: a 6-month interim report of a 5-year L-dopa-controlled study. Mov Disord, in press.

27. Rinne UK, Bracco F. Cabergoline in the treatment of the early Parkinson's disease. Results of the first year of treatment in a double-blind comparison between cabergoline and levodopa. Neurol, in press.

CHAPTER FOURTEEN

Adverse effects of ergot-derivative dopamine agonists

ALI H. RAJPUT, MD, FRCP(C)

Department of Medicine, Royal University Hospital, University of Saskatchewan, Saskatoon, Saskatchewan, Canada

ABSTRACT

The ergot-derived dopamine agonists include bromocriptine, pergolide and lisuride. These agents have a similar mode of action and, therefore, similar therapeutic and adverse effect profiles. Adverse effects common to all ergot-derivative dopamine agonists include central nervous system effects, such as dizziness, anxiety, hallucinations and confusion; gastrointestinal effects, such as anorexia and nausea; and cardiovascular effects, notably postural hypotension. Prolonged use of any of these agents may lead to peripheral vasoconstriction, pleuropulmonary and retroperitoneal fibrosis and erythromelalgia. In addition to the adverse effects of ergot-derived agents in general, bromocriptine may produce dry mouth, sedation, insomnia and pleural effusion in a significant proportion of recipients, particularly if therapy is prolonged. The major side effects of pergolide and lisuride have been found to be similar to those of bromocriptine.

The two most commonly used dopamine agonists in North America are bromocriptine and pergolide. Lisuride is also available in Europe. The reported adverse events depend on studies to meet regulatory agency requirements, duration of experience with the drug, types of studies, and when those studies were conducted. The long-term studies will obviously provide the most complete profile of side effects of a drug.

During the 1970s and the early 1980s, a larger dose of bromocriptine was used and dose increments were rapid. This was associated with a high incidence of acute side effects and patient drop-out. More recent practice has been to use a lower dose of the agonist and a slower schedule of titration. The acute side effects as well as the maintenance dose side effects vary according to dose and the titration schedule. Some reports are based on dopamine agonist monotherapy, while others reflect the side effects when dopamine agonists were used together with other antiparkinsonian agents.

The adverse effects common to this class of drug will be described first, and then details for individual drugs will be discussed. The ergot-derived dopamine agonists in use today share structural similarities and have a similar mechanism of action, and therefore have similar therapeutic and adverse effects profiles. The incidence and severity of adverse events vary with the titration schedule, the dosage, and the disease severity. Where literature evidence is available on these aspects, it will be discussed. Central adverse effects such as dyskinesia will be discussed elsewhere.

SIDE EFFECTS COMMON TO ERGOT–DERIVATIVE DOPAMINE AGONISTS

Central nervous system

Neuropsychiatric side effects including dizziness, anxiety, affective disorders, hallucinations, delusions, confusion and psychosis of variable severity may be seen with these drugs. Drug-induced anxiety may vary from mild symptoms, such as insomnia and jitteriness, to panic disorders. It should be distinguished from agitated depression or akathisia. Visual hallucinations or delusions, often associated with vivid dreams or disturbances of sleep on the background of a clear sensorium, may be seen. Auditory hallucinations may accompany these disturbances, but very rarely occur in isolation. Confusional state is a more common adverse effect in elderly and demented patients and in those with a previous history of a psychiatric disturbance. Atypical neuroleptics such as clozapine or risperidol may control the psychiatric side effects associated with dopamine agonists. Hypersexuality is a rare side effect and has been reported with bromocriptine and pergolide.[1]

Gastrointestinal system

Anorexia, nausea and disturbances of bowel function are reported in 20–40% of patients receiving dopamine agonists.[2–4] The incidence increases with larger doses and rapid dose titration.[5] These side effects usually occur early after initiating dopamine agonist therapy, and tolerance may develop after prolonged treatment. They are believed to be due to stimulation of the chemoreceptor trigger zone located outside the blood–brain barrier. The peripheral dopamine receptor antagonist domperidone, given at 5–10 mg before each meal, can reduce the severity of nausea and vomiting.[6]

Cardiovascular system

Postural hypotension may be an early dose-limiting factor with dopamine agonist therapy. Pre-existing autonomic dysfunction and concomitant use of levodopa can exacerbate this problem. As a rule, postural hypotension tends to occur on initiation of dopamine agonist treatment. The frequency and severity can be reduced by gradual introduction with slow increases in the dose. Manipulation of food or salt intake may also be helpful. Domperidone is less effective, as postural hypotension is believed to be both centrally and peripherally mediated. Palpitations and cardiac dysrhythmias have been reported in rare cases and will be discussed further with individual drugs.

Ergot-related side effects

Prolonged use, overdose or chronic poisoning with ergotamine can produce peripheral vasoconstriction leading to cold, pale, and numb extremities. Side effects possibly related to similar mechanisms occurring with dopamine agonists include pleuropulmonary fibrosis, retroperitoneal fibrosis, erythromelalgia and Raynaud's phenomenon. They usually occur following long-term use of relatively high doses of dopamine agonists, although some predisposed individuals may manifest them early on. Improvement of symptoms usually occurs with dose reduction or discontinuation of the drug. Prolonged vasoconstriction in poorly-vascularized tissue or an idiosyncratic immune response, with the drug acting as a hapten, have been proposed as possible pathogenetic mechanisms.[7–9]

INDIVIDUAL DRUG ADVERSE EFFECTS PROFILE

Bromocriptine

Bromocriptine was introduced for general use in 1973 and as such has the longest clinical experience of any ergot-derived dopamine agonist. Table 1 outlines the common side effects in *de novo* bromocriptine monotherapy at a mean dose of 30–40 mg. Dizziness, dry mouth, nausea, vomiting and sedation occurred with the greatest frequency. During two years of follow-up, 21% of cases were withdrawn due to adverse effects (Table 1). Severe nausea and vomiting were the most common cause of withdrawal in those who benefited from the drug. In those who tolerated the drug and were followed for two years, some side effects such as constipation remained unchanged, while others such as nausea, postural hypotension, confusion and hallucinations decreased. As noted above, a significant portion of patients discontinued the drug early because of these side effects or because of lack of efficacy. The drug profile for adverse events by the end of two years therefore does not include the same individuals. Those who had major side effects early on had already been taken off the drug before the two-year analysis. By the end of two years, some adverse effects that were not prominent earlier, e.g. palpitations, insomnia, sedation, ankle edema, coldness of extremities, erythromelalgia, dyskinesia and pleural effusions, became more common (Table 1).

In a short term study of *de novo* bromocriptine monotherapy, the adverse effect incidence and reasons for withdrawal on two different treatment regimens – low/slow dosage reaching 25 mg/day after 23 weeks and high/fast dosage reaching 100 mg/day after 23 weeks – are shown in Table 2. The incidence of withdrawal due to adverse effects was higher in the high/fast (36%) than in the low/slow (20%) group by the end of the 26-week trial.

Table 1: Adverse effects of bromocriptine*

Reason for discontinuing bromocriptine treatment over two years

All withdrawn cases	71%
Insufficient therapeutic response	46%
Withdrawal due to adverse dopamine agonist effects	21%
Severe nausea and vomiting	13%
Hallucinations and confusion	7%
Death	4%
Postural hypotension	1%

Occurrence (%) of adverse effects (AE) during the first three months of treatment with bromocriptine and at 24 months in parentheses

Common AE	Dizziness	49 (53)
	Dry mouth	39 (26)
	Nausea	31 (21)
	Sedation	26 (58)
Less common AE	Dyskinesias	17 (26)
	Anorexia	14 (0)
	Sweating	14 (16)
	Insomnia	13 (26)
	Postural hypotension	13 (0)
	Constipation	10 (11)
	Hallucinations	10 (0)
	Anxiety	7 (5)
	Confusion	7 (0)
	Erythromelalgia/cold extremities	7 (26)
	Vomiting	4 (5)
	Palpitations	4 (16)
	Pleural effusion	0 (22)
	Diarrhea	0 (0)

*Seventy-six *de novo* patients were treated with bromocriptine 30–40 mg/day (range 3.75–120 mg/day).[18]

Withdrawal due to psychiatric disturbances occurred in 13% of the low/slow group and in 9% of the high/fast group, which is comparable to other reported series treated with bromocriptine alone.[5]

Pleuropulmonary disease (pleural effusions, pleural thickening and infiltrative parenchymal lung disease) associated with bromocriptine was first reported by Rinne in 1981.[10] In this report, he reviewed 123 patients on

Table 2: Effect of dosage schedule on bromocriptine adverse effects

Incidence (%) of side effects resulting in withdrawal from study in 34 patients (27%)

	'low/slow' (n=76)	'high/fast' (n=53)
No effect	13	4
Side effects	20	36
Psychiatric disturbances	13	9
Gastrointestinal	10	19
Postural hypotension	6	4
Visual disturbances	5	2

Note: some patients suffered multiple side effects.

long-term bromocriptine therapy. Seven patients who were receiving bromocriptine 20–90 mg/day alone or in combination with other drugs developed pulmonary complications after long-term use (6–27 months). In another series,[7] eight patients developed pulmonary complications. All were males, the majority were 60 years or older and had a long history of smoking. Symptoms included dyspnea, pleuritic pain, unproductive cough, and radiologic abnormalities. The risk of symptomatic pleuropulmonary fibrosis is estimated to be 2–5% for patients on continuous bromocriptine for five years.[7] Although many of the reported cases were also taking levodopa at the time, there was symptomatic and radiologic improvement on reduction or discontinuation of bromocriptine, indicating a causal relationship. Some investigators therefore recommend a chest X-ray and pulmonary function tests prior to commencing therapy, and prompt withdrawal when respiratory symptoms develop.

Seven cases of retroperitoneal fibrosis have been reported through 1995. All of these patients were on long-term treatment (15 months to 10 years) with bromocriptine in daily doses greater than 30 mg. Such patients may present with loin pain, swollen lower limbs, or symptoms of renal failure. In view of the very rare nature of this complication, routine monitoring of renal function in all parkinsonian patients taking bromocriptine is not recommended.

Erythromelalgia, typically characterized by a symmetrical, tender, warm erythema of feet, ankles and shins was reported by Eisler et al.[11] in approximately 8% of patients after a mean duration of 13 months (two weeks to five years) on an average daily dose of bromocriptine of 101 mg (range 24–150 mg). Many patients were also taking other antiparkinsonian medications. Discontinuing bromocriptine for a mean of 10 days resulted in resolution, and re-challenge in each of two patients produced recurrence. Histology showed typical perivascular monocyte infiltration and interstitial edema. Erythromelalgia should be distinguished from amantadine-induced livedo-reticularis, where the skin is cool and dusky rather than warm and red.

A few cases are reported in the literature of bromocriptine interaction with erythromycin resulting in elevated plasma levels and toxicity.[12]

Pergolide

The side effects of pergolide are similar to those of bromocriptine. Mizuno *et al.*[13] compared patients treated with either bromocriptine or pergolide in a short-term double-blind trial and found no significant differences in the incidence of side effects (Table 3). Nausea occurred in 29.5% of the pergolide- and in 30.4% of the bromocriptine-treated group. Hallucinations were seen in 6.6% of the pergolide-treated patients and in 5.4% of the bromocriptine-treated cases.[13]

Table 3: Pergolide adverse effects		
Incidence (%) of side effects during short-term double-blind treatment with either bromocriptine or pergolide[13]		
Side effect	**Bromocriptine alone (n=49)**	**Pergolide alone (n=49)**
Nausea	30.4	29.5
Hallucinations	5.4	6.6
Cumulative incidence (%) of side effects during open-label treatment with pergolide alone and with the later addition of levodopa. Follow-up two to four years.		
Side effect	**Pergolide alone (n=34)**	**Pergolide + levodopa (n=28)**
Nausea	17.6	17.9
Vomiting	8.8	3.6
Anorexia	26.5	14.3
Epigastric discomfort	17.6	28.6
Dry mouth	23.5	25.0
Headache	23.5	21.4
Dizziness	17.6	21.4
Delusions	8.8	10.7
Hallucinations	14.7	21.4
Postural hypotension	8.8	10.7

In combined data from clinical trials involving 1200 patients (Table 4), adverse events resulted in withdrawal from treatment in 27% of patients. This is comparable to bromocriptine adverse effect-related withdrawal, although a proportion of the side effects may well have been due to concomitant medications. The most frequent side effects which were significantly more common than placebo were nausea, dizziness, hallucinations and constipation (Table 4).

Table 4: Pergolide adverse effects (%) in a placebo-controlled trial*		
Side effect	**Pergolide**	**Placebo**
Nausea	24.3	12.8
Dizziness	19.1	13.9
Hallucinations	13.8	3.2
Rhinitis	12.2	5.4
Confusion	11.1	9.6
Constipation	10.6	5.9
Somnolence	10.0	3.7
Postural hypotension	9.0	7.0
Insomnia	7.9	3.2
Anxiety	6.4	4.3

* Six-month placebo-controlled trial of pergolide in PD. Data from Eli Lilly, cited by Langtry and Clissold.[19]

Cardiac dysrhythmias were noted on pergolide in one study[14] while another double-blind study did not support pergolide cardiac toxicity.[15] Patients with pre-existing heart disease on high dose pergolide (>3 mg/day) may be at increased risk of cardiac rhythm abnormalities[14] and therefore need closer observation.

Abnormalities of liver function tests may occur in very rare cases and one case of retroperitoneal fibrosis has been reported in a patient taking pergolide.[16]

Lisuride

Lisuride is a semi-synthetic ergot derivative. In addition to its potent dopamine agonist effects, lisuride has high affinity for serotonin receptors, a short mean plasma elimination half-life and is water-soluble. Hypotension, gastrointestinal intolerance and psychiatric disturbances occur with approximately the same frequency as with other ergot-derivative dopamine agonists. A comparison of bromocriptine with lisuride noted a similar side effect profile.[17] Increased appetite was reported in six patients (21%) which may be related to the action of the drug on serotoninergic receptors.

References

1. Uitti RJ, Tanner CM, Rajput AH, Goetz CG, Klawans HL, Thissen B. Hypersexuality with antiparkinsonian therapy. Clin Neuropharmacol 1989; 12: 375–383.

2. Olanow CW, Alberts MJ. Double-blind controlled study of pergolide mesylate in the treatment of Parkinson's disease. Clin Neuropharmacol 1987; 10: 178–185.

3. Hoehn MM, Elton RL. Low dosages of bromocriptine added to levodopa in Parkinson's disease. Neurol 1985; 35: 199–206.

4. Lees AJ, Stern GM. Sustained bromocriptine therapy in previously untreated patients with Parkinson's disease. J Neurol Neurosurg Psychiatr 1981; 44: 1020–1023.

5. UK Bromocriptine Research Group. Bromocriptine in Parkinson's disease: a double-blind study comparing 'low-slow' and 'high-fast' introductory dosage regimens in *de novo* patients. J Neurol Neurosurg Psychiatr 1989; 52: 77–82.

6. Agid Y, Pollak P, Bonnet AM, L'Hermitte F. Bromocriptine associated with a peripheral dopamine blocking agent in the treatment of Parkinson's disease. Lancet 1979; i: 570–572.

7. McElvaney NG, Wilcox PG, Churg A, Fleetham JA. Pleuropulmonary disease during bromocriptine treatment of Parkinson's disease. Arch Intern Med 1988; 148: 2231–2236.

8. Demonet JF, Rostin M, Dueymes JM, Ioualalen A, Montastruc JL, Rascol A. Retroperitoneal fibrosis and treatment of Parkinson's disease with high doses of bromocriptine. Clin Neuropharmacol 1996; 9: 200–201.

9. Bowler JV, Ormerod IE, Legg NJ. Retroperitoneal fibrosis and bromocriptine. Lancet 1986; ii: 466.

10. Rinne UK. Pleuropulmonary changes during long-term bromocriptine therapy in the treatment of PD. Lancet 1981; i: 44.

11. Eisler T, Hall RP, Kalavar KA, Calne DB. Erythromelalgia-like eruption in parkinsonian patients treated with bromocriptine. Neurol 1981; 31: 1368–1370.

12. Nelson MV, Berchou RC, Kareti D, LeWitt PA. Pharmacokinetic evaluation of erythromycin and caffeine administered with bromocriptine. Clin Pharmacol Ther 1990; 47: 694–697.

13. Mizuno Y, Kondo T, Narabayashi H. Pergolide in the treatment of Parkinson's disease. Neurol 1995; 45 (Suppl 3): 13–21.

14. Liebowitz M, Lieberman AN, Neophytides A, Gopinathan G, Goldstein M. The effects of pergolide on the cardiovascular system of 40 patients with Parkinson's disease. Adv Neurol 1983; 37: 121–130.

15. Kurlan R, Miller C, Knapp R, Murphy G, Shoulson I. Double-blind assessment of potential pergolide-induced cardiotoxicity. Neurol 1986; 36: 993–995.

16. Jimenez-Jimenez FJ, Lopez-Alvarez J, *et al*. Retroperitoneal fibrosis in a patient with Parkinson's disease treated with pergolide. Clin Neuropharmacol 1995; 18: 277–278.

17. LeWitt PA, Gopinathan G, Ward CD, *et al*. Lisuride versus bromocriptine treatment in Parkinson's disease: a double-blind study. Neurol 1982; 32: 69–72.

18. Rinne UK. In, Fahn S, Calne DB, Shoulson I, eds, Advances in Neurology 37: Experimental therapeutics of movement disorders. New York: Raven Press, 1983: 141–150.

19. Langtry HD, Clissold SP. Pergolide – a review of its pharmacological properties and therapeutic potential in Parkinson's disease. Drugs 1990; 39: 491–506.

CHAPTER FIFTEEN

High dose pergolide monotherapy for the treatment of severe dyskinesias in Parkinson's disease

JUAN R. SANCHEZ-RAMOS, PhD, MD

University of South Florida College of Medicine and
James Haley Veterans' Affairs Hospital,
Tampa, Florida, USA

ABSTRACT

Dopamine agonists have been in use for approximately 20 years, although none of the agonists currently in use has proven to be as effective as levodopa/carbidopa (LD/CD). However, a subset of Parkinson's disease patients exists who become supersensitive to the dyskinesiogenic effects of levodopa and cannot tolerate even a small dose of LD/CD. In these patients, dyskinesias may be eliminated, without a diminution of antiparkinsonian efficacy, by the use of high-dose pergolide monotherapy. In the present small-scale study, all patients receiving high-dose pergolide without LD/CD, or with minimal morning LD/CD, reported greatly improved control of parkinsonian symptoms, were free of troubling dyskinesias and were able to function at a higher level in everyday activities (some even able to resume full-day working). Controlled clinical trials should be undertaken to further our understanding of factors predictive of patients likely to benefit from high-dose pergolide monotherapy.

Dopamine agonists have been in use for approximately 20 years, and none of the agonists currently in use has proven to be as effective as levodopa/carbidopa (LD/CD). However, 20–30% of Parkinson's disease (PD) patients have been satisfactorily maintained on agonist monotherapy for more than three years.[1] Those patients show a markedly decreased incidence of fluctuations and dyskinesias compared to patients maintained on LD/CD alone.[2] Some authors have suggested that early treatment with combinations of LD/CD and dopamine agonists has similar efficacy to high dose LD/CD but with a lower incidence of side effects, including fluctuations and dyskinesias.[3] Others have contended that early combination therapy does not prevent later clinical fluctuations and dyskinesias.[4] Whether or not early combination therapy obviates later development of dyskinesias is thoroughly discussed in other chapters in this volume.[5,6] We wish to bring attention to the usefulness of high dose pergolide monotherapy for some patients with advanced disease and severe motor fluctuations.

Predictable wearing-off phenomena and peak-dose dyskinesias can sometimes be lessened with sustained release LD/CD, infusion of levodopa or apomorphine and combined therapy with LD/CD and a dopamine agonist, but there still remains a subset of PD patients, usually with younger age of onset, who become supersensitive to the dyskinesiogenic effects of levodopa. These patients often cannot take even a small dose of LD/CD, i.e. 50 mg, without experiencing intense and complicated dyskinesias. We have been able to eliminate dyskinesias without diminishing antiparkinsonian efficacy in these severe patients by using high dose pergolide monotherapy. Our experience with high dose pergolide monotherapy in 13 cases is summarized here.[7] These patients were selected for treatment with pergolide monotherapy due to the presence of incapacitating dyskinesias elicited by small doses of LD/CD, and absence of dementia. Thirteen patients (2% of all PD patients seen in one year by the author) were treated with high dose pergolide monotherapy. All patients were examined and followed by the same neurologist for at least one year from the start of pergolide administration.

The characteristics of 13 patients (six men/seven women) successfully treated with high dose pergolide monotherapy are listed in Table 1. The

Table 1: High dose pergolide in advanced PD patients with severe dyskinesias		
	Pre-pergolide	**Post-pergolide**
No. of patients	13	13
Male/female	6M/7F	–
Age (years)	65.9 ± 6.5	–
Duration of disease (years)	12.9 ± 3.35	–
Hoehn & Yahr 'on'	2.8 ± 0.8	2.4 ± 0.9
Hoehn & Yahr 'off'	3.86 ± 0.8	3.91 ± 0.7
'Off' time (%)	26.5 ± 21.3	16.1 ± 24.2
Dyskinesia duration (years)	5.8 ± 1.83	–
Dyskinesia (% of day)	70.9 ± 13.1	13 ± 7.3*
AIMS score	32.5 ± 4.5	7.15 ± 8.81*
Levodopa/24 hour (mg)	825 ± 489	98.1 ± 105.3*
Bromocriptine (mg)	16.8 ± 13.8 (n = 6)	–
Pergolide/24 hour (mg)	–	6.5 ± 2.1

* Comparison of pre- and post-pergolide variable was statistically significant using Student's t-test ($p < 0.05$). Table reprinted with permission.[7]

average age was 65.9 years and duration of disease was 12.9 years. Motor complications from LD/CD had been documented for an average of 5.8 years and were present for about 70% of the day. Patients experienced clinical fluctuations ('off' >25% of the day) and complicated, incapacitating dyskinesias (>50% of the day). The objective in all patients was to gradually withdraw LD/CD and bromocriptine therapy while at the same time slowly introducing pergolide. In general, the regimen was modified by an increase in pergolide of a half-tablet of 0.25 mg (0.12 mg) every three to four days, and a concomitant decrease of LD/CD by 50/12.5 mg every three to four days. This transition period occurred very gradually and for most patients took approximately three to four months to attain the optimum schedule where the patient could be functional without dyskinesias and with decreased total hours in the 'off' state. The interval between pergolide doses was three to four hours. This titration period was difficult to tolerate by both patient and physician. Increases in patient complaints during the transition period caused a follow-up by phone at least once a week. The most common complaints during the transition period included increases in dyskinesias, prolonged 'off' periods, increased difficulty performing daily activities, light-headedness, and digital paresthesia (one patient). A single patient had an episode of delusions and hallucinations requiring pergolide dose reduction.

Eight of 13 patients were able to discontinue LD/CD for periods of days to weeks but because of morning akinesia that could not be alleviated by pergolide alone, these eight patients eventually resorted to using low single doses of LD/CD upon arising in the morning. The average total daily LD/CD dose was decreased to 12% of the pre-pergolide total daily dose (mean levodopa = 98.1 mg). The remaining five patients were able to remain LD/CD-free (for six to 18 months). These patients also noted mild akinesia that could be improved with addition of amantadine and anticholinergic drugs to the pergolide regimen. Bromocriptine was withdrawn completely in all patients. The average total daily dose of pergolide attained was 6.5 mg (±2.1), distributed throughout the waking day at three- to four-hourly intervals. The highest dose used as monotherapy was 10 mg/day. Other antiparkinsonian medications used by this group were as follows: 11 of 13 patients used amantadine 100 mg b.i.d., six used trihexyphenidyl (2 mg t.i.d.) and the five patients who remained LD/CD free used amantadine (100 mg b.i.d.) and trihexyphenidyl (2 mg t.i.d.).

All patients using high dose pergolide without LD/CD (or with minimal morning LD/CD) reported greatly improved control of symptoms of PD, and were free of troubling dyskinesias (Table 1). The patients were able to function at a higher level in everyday activities and more importantly several patients were able to work full days at their jobs. The AIMS scores were significantly improved, (32.5 to 7.15) and the percentage of the day the patients were dyskinetic decreased dramatically from 70.9% to 13%. Moreover, percent 'off' time was improved from an average of 26% to 16% of the day. Most importantly, patients felt that freedom from incapacitating dyskinesias was the most striking benefit from this regimen.

Discussion

The purpose of these studies was to demonstrate that dyskinesias can be eliminated or significantly reduced without loss of control of PD symptoms using high dose pergolide in advanced patients with complicated management problems. The doses used for this purpose were two to three times greater than the highest doses recommended for combination therapy. Most neurologists and patients are aware that introduction of pergolide as an adjunct to LD/CD will often increase the incidence and severity of dyskinesias (especially 'peak-dose' dyskinesias), unless LD/CD is reduced. Once dyskinesias are present following chronic LD/CD treatment, it is believed that dopamine agonists will also produce dyskinesias and so most neurologists use agonists exclusively for treatment of 'wearing off' or 'end-of-dose' phenomena relatively early in the disease. It has been reported that pergolide may be particularly useful for end-of-dose dystonia,[8] but there is only one prior report in the literature describing improvement of dyskinesias in advanced cases treated with pergolide monotherapy.[9] These investigators reported benefits of pergolide monotherapy in advanced patients even though withdrawal from LD/CD and introduction to pergolide was abrupt, unlike the gradual transition used in the present study. Pergolide monotherapy was also attempted in late-stage PD.[10] Twenty-six patients with late-stage severe management problems were given 0.4 to 15 mg pergolide per day. In all subjects, attempts were made to establish monotherapy with pergolide. Among 14 patients taking LD/CD, complete withdrawal was achieved in only one patient. However, 11 of 26 patients improved with addition of pergolide, both objectively and subjectively. Patients with dose-related fluctuations responded best with addition of pergolide while those with non-dose-related fluctuations were minimally helped. On optimal pergolide therapy, and with reduction in dose or withdrawal of LD/CD and bromocriptine, the frequency and severity of dyskinesias were similar to those before pergolide, unlike our experience. It is important to note, however, that these patients remained on LD/CD, albeit at lower doses.

We have shown that high dose pergolide can be used to treat some individuals with incapacitating dyskinesias. Clearly, it is not easy to get a patient dependent on LD/CD to substitute it for pergolide, despite its unpleasant adverse effects (dyskinesias). Many experts in PD believe that dependence on levodopa in this situation is both physiologic and psychologic. It may be suggested that substitution of pergolide for LD/CD is akin to substituting methadone for heroin in an opiate addict. Pergolide compared to LD/CD, like methadone compared to heroin, has a longer latency of onset and thus is less likely to produce a reinforcing effect associated with 'kicking in' which may analogous to the rapid onset of a subjective feeling of well-being elicited by heroin self-administration. Those few patients who are able to tolerate higher doses of pergolide and are able to be weaned from LD/CD are likely to exhibit a smooth motor response without disabling dyskinesias.

We suggest that controlled clinical trials be undertaken to permit greater understanding of factors that predict which patients with advanced disease will benefit from pergolide monotherapy. This is an opportune time to initiate these studies since the surgical procedure of pallidotomy appears to be especially effective in diminishing clinical fluctuations and dyskinesias.[11] Given the irreversible nature of the surgical procedure, and its questionable effectiveness over the long term, it would be of interest to compare pallidotomy with high dose pergolide monotherapy in controlling severe clinical fluctuations.

ACKNOWLEDGMENT

Supported, in part, by the National Parkinson's Disease Foundation, Miami, Florida, USA

References

1. Marsden CD. Parkinson's Disease. J Neurol Neurosurg Psychiatr 1994; 57: 672–681.

2. Rascol O, this volume.

3. Rinne UK. Dopamine agonists as primary treatment in Parkinson's disease. Adv Neurol 1986; 45: 519–528.

4. Weiner WJ, Factor SA, Sanchez-Ramos JR, Singer C, Sheldon C, Cornelius L, Ingenito A. Early combination therapy (bromocriptine and levodopa) does not prevent motor fluctuations in Parkinson's Disease. Neurol 1993; 43: 21–27.

5. Tolosa E, Marin C, this volume.

6. Poewe W, this volume.

7. Facca A, Sanchez-Ramos J. Pergolide monotherapy in complicated Parkinson's disease. Mov Disord 1996; 11: 327–329.

8. Factor SA, Sanchez-Ramos J, Weiner WJ. Parkinson's disease: an open-label trial of pergolide in patients failing bromocriptine therapy. J Neurol Neurosurg Psychiatr 1988; 51: 529–533.

9. Mear J-Y, Barroche G, de Smet Y, Weber M, L'Hermitte F, Agid Y. Pergolide in the treatment of Parkinson's disease. Neurol 1984; 34: 983–986.

10. Lang AE, Quinn N, Brincat S, Marsden CD, Parkes JD. Pergolide in late-stage Parkinson's disease. Ann Neurol 1982; 12: 243–247.

11. Laitinen LV. Pallidotomy for Parkinson's disease. Neurosurg Clin N Am 1995; 6: 105–112.

CHAPTER SIXTEEN

General discussion on clinical experience with dopamine agonists

Bonuccelli: One of the concerns about using dopamine agonists that is continuously raised is the perception that dopamine agonists are associated with increased risk of side effects in comparison to levodopa. However, in a large Italian study, we found fewer side effects with dopamine agonists than with levodopa alone.

Tolosa: Another interesting point is that the pharmacokinetic and pharmacodynamic half-lives of the dopamine agonists may be different. For example, both cabergoline and pergolide have long half-lives but, practically, they need to be administered two to three times daily in order to sustain clinical efficacy.

Jenner: This may relate to the fact that some of these drugs act through their metabolites. Alternatively, when we measure the half-life using radioisotopes, we are really measuring the half-life of the radioactive drug which includes its metabolites. Its real half-life may be shorter.

Sanchez-Ramos: Yet another misunderstood feature is the notion that high doses of agonist are poorly tolerated. In fact, in our study we substituted pergolide for levodopa in doses greater than 10 mg per day. Using this approach, we found that the drug was well tolerated and there was a reduction in the incidence of dyskinesia and motor fluctuations.

Bédard: In your study, Dr. Rascol, could patients have been on levodopa before randomization? If so, this might account for some of the dyskinesias seen in your dopamine agonist group.

Rascol: You are correct. Some of the dyskinetic cases in the ropinirole group had received levodopa before entering the study and therefore may have been primed, as was seen in the monkey experiments.

Leenders: Is there any difference in the incidence of psychiatric side effects with ropinirole as compared to the ergot dopamine agonists?

Rascol: Ropinirole is a cleaner drug than currently available dopamine agonists. It stimulates only the D_2 and D_3 receptors, does not stimulate serotonin or norepinephrine receptors and it is a non-ergot. While it is only my subjective impression, I believe it has fewer psychiatric side effects than ergot agonists such as bromocriptine. We were struck by the observation that in early patients the drug was well tolerated and had clinical effects more or less comparable to levodopa.

Olanow: More important than efficacy comparisons with levodopa is whether dopamine agonists such as ropinirole will be associated with a reduced incidence of motor complications. In this regard, the three- and five-year endpoints will be critically important.

Rascol: I agree.

Brücke: How do you explain the reduced incidence of psychotic side effects in a drug that stimulates the D_3 receptors?

Jenner: The role of D_3 receptors in psychosis is unclear. It is the D_4 and D_5 receptors that have been primarily implicated in the development of psychosis.

Melamed: I am interested in the fact that ropinirole is associated with increased somnolence.

Rascol: This may not be a specific phenomenon and may be a general effect of dopamine agonist receptor stimulation. Both levodopa and dopamine agonists cause sleepiness.

Tolosa: Somnolence frequently occurs during the day due to lack of sleep at night which is a common problem in PD. I feel drug-induced somnolence is not a common problem.

Rascol: I disagree. This is a problem that we frequently encounter with dopaminergic stimulating agents. Interestingly, patients who receive intravenous infusions of levodopa will often fall asleep while they are receiving the medication and apomorphine is frequently associated with yawning.

Olanow: In comparison to currently-marketed dopamine agonists, ropinirole has been much better studied in early disease and offers a better opportunity to definitively define the role of dopamine agonists in the early treatment of PD.

Tolosa: Is a transdermal preparation of a dopamine agonist being considered ?

Jenner: Transdermal administration is possible, but the effect of continuous administration of a dopamine agonist must be carefully considered from the point of view of both benefits and side effects. Such an approach could offer the benefit of providing more continuous and therefore physiologic dopamine receptor stimulation. I am impressed with the recent results from Japan where good antiparkinsonian results were obtained with transdermal lisuride applied as a cream. On the other hand, patches are difficult to formulate, poorly tolerated by many patients and difficult to titrate on an individual basis.

Gerfen: Nonetheless, transdermal delivery of a dopamine agonist could offer the possibility of testing continuous treatment with D_2 agonists, based on existing preclinical models and theories.

Bédard: That is true, as pulsatile administration of levodopa or a dopamine agonist is preferentially associated with the development of dyskinesias.

Olanow: The FIRST study tried to address this issue by comparing the effect of initiating treatment with standard Sinemet® versus a sustained release formulation (Sinemet CR®). After five years of treatment, there was no difference whatsoever in the incidence or prevalence of motor complications between groups. However, Sinemet CR® was only administered twice daily and therefore did not achieve a condition comparable to continuous levodopa administration. Therefore, an experiment testing pulsatile versus continuous administration of levodopa or a dopamine agonist as initial therapy for PD remains to be performed. In such a study, it might be preferable to utilize levodopa in combination with a COMT inhibitor to further stimulate continuous delivery.

Melamed: The stomach is of paramount importance and may play a major role in delivering levodopa to the brain in a continuous and predictable fashion. Levodopa is absorbed in the small intestine and alterations in GI transit time can influence levodopa absorption and central availability. This is crucial in patients with advanced disease who presumably have impaired central storage and decreased capacity to buffer fluctuations in peripheral levodopa concentration. There is also some evidence to suggest that levodopa influences GI motility and in this regard chronic treatment may alter its own kinetics.

Bonuccelli: The use of agents that improve GI motility such as cisapride and domperidone may improve levodopa absorption and lead to an enhanced clinical response.

Melamed: There are many subtypes of response fluctuations and some of these may be explained by a gastric mechanism. For example, a 'no-on' response in the afternoon is likely to be due to impaired GI delivery of levodopa to the small intestine and may be helped by prokinetic drugs such as you describe, as well as by crushing the tablet, taking plenty of water, or adding a COMT inhibitor.

Olanow: Do dopamine agonists influence their own kinetics?

Melamed: I do not know and these types of experiments looking at the effects of the different antiparkinsonian drugs on one another should be performed.

Obeso: Dr. Stocchi, you describe the effect of age on your decision-making with regard to using dopamine agonists and particularly ropinirole. How safe is ropinirole from the cardiovascular standpoint and describe for us, if you will, what are the preferred doses and how long it takes to get to the desired dose.

Stocchi: The cardiologists at my hospital have not had problems with ropinirole and say that it is the safest dopamine agonist they have studied to date. In my experience, the effective doses of currently-available dopamine agonists are 15–30 mg of bromocriptine, 1.5–3 mg of lisuride, 2–4 mg of pergolide, and 12–15 mg of ropinirole. The time to reach the effective dose, and the titration schedule employed, depend on whether or not domperidone is used. With domperidone, doses can be increased daily and an effective dose is reached within 15–20 days. Obviously it would be necessary to proceed more slowly if domperidone is not available. Using this approach, side effects are not common and do not appear to be more severe than occur with initiation of levodopa.

Tolosa: In your experience, do the majority of PD patients respond to dopamine agonists?

Stocchi: The majority of patients do respond but the dose is very important. Occasionally it is necessary to increase the dose substantially above usual levels in order to obtain a satisfactory response. This may be worth doing if this approach reduces the likelihood of developing levodopa-related adverse effects.

Sanchez-Ramos: We have utilized such an approach in patients with severe motor complications secondary to levodopa and have had good results with doses of pergolide as high as 17 mg per day. However, these doses are taken round the clock, and patients do not receive more than 2.5 mg at each dose. These patients noted a dramatic reduction in their levodopa-induced dyskinesia when they were switched from high dose levodopa to high dose agonist with only small amounts of levodopa.

Poewe: We have had similar experiences. Some of our long-term pump patients who got fed up with the equipment over the years have been switched to pergolide monotherapy with success.

Rajput: I have found that addition of amantadine to a full dose of levodopa alleviated dyskinesias in 25% of patients.

Olanow: That may be due to the capacity of amantadine to block NMDA receptors and effectively induce chemical pallidotomy. Papa and Chase have recently reported in *Annals of Neurology* that NMDA receptor antagonists can diminish dyskinesia in monkey models and Greemayre suggested that these agents may effectively be inducing a chemical pallidotomy. Dr. Rajput, how many of the side effects were significantly different to placebo?

Rajput: The major side effects I have had with high dose dopamine agonists are psychiatric side effects, sleep disturbance, skin rashes and retroperitoneal or pulmonary fibrosis.

Obeso: What percentage of patients actually succeed in being stably controlled by switching from levodopa to monotherapy to treat levodopa 'off' periods ?

Sanchez-Ramos: A very small percentage. Patients need to be sharp and free from dementia, and clinicians need to spend much time with them. When patients do succeed, they are still quite functional although tolerance does develop. This is the final step before surgery.

Rascol: In a very recent study, we tested a D_1 selective agonist intravenously in PD patients whom we switched off. With the D_1 agonist we were able to switch them on again as effectively as with levodopa, but with less dyskinesia. This was an acute challenge, and we know very little about D_1 agonists in man.

Poewe: Has there been any success with switching to bromocriptine or lisuride monotherapy? There are only anecdotal reports that pergolide therapy has been successful.

Olanow: We have been able to substitute high dose bromocriptine (100–150 mg per day) for levodopa, and showed increasing antiparkinsonian benefits as the dose was increased. Bromocriptine was well tolerated.

Sanchez-Ramos: Patients should never have the feeling of being 'on', of experiencing the immediacy of the effects of levodopa. This should be saved until all other alternatives have been exhausted.

Melamed: What percentage of patients will tolerate large amounts of bromocriptine or pergolide ?

Olanow: In our studies, all patients were screened for psychiatric problems or dementia and excluded if they had problems. In the group that we studied, high doses were well tolerated but only a few were functionally improved. It is logical to ask how high one can go before introducing levodopa therapy, particularly if dopamine agonists reduce the likelihood of developing adverse effects, and have a putative neuroprotective effect.

Melamed: How many patients stop using the dopamine agonist, regardless of the dose?

Olanow: Several studies show that as many as 90% will eventually withdraw and cannot be maintained on dopamine agonist monotherapy. There is a tendency, however, to stop the monotherapy at a fixed point, and we need to determine whether higher doses of the agonist are actually associated with additional benefit.

Tolosa: That would have to be done in a controlled manner, in view of possible side effects associated with increased dosage.

Rascol: The mean daily dose of bromocriptine in our studies was 50 mg. We have increased de novo patients to 80 and 90 mg with domperidone without major problems. More than 80% of patients reach doses of more than 40 mg per day. In the Montastruc study, the drop-out rate for lack of tolerance was only two or three of 30 patients receiving bromocriptine. We increase the dose progressively, usually reaching 30 mg within the first 6–12 months. If patients tolerate it, the dose can be increased up to 90 mg per day. We add levodopa when required. After five years, the majority of patients receive levodopa as an adjunct treatment but in significantly smaller doses than a control group treated with levodopa alone. Using this approach, there is a significant difference in terms of the long-term side effects.

Olanow: We certainly see more psychosis with dopamine agonists; it was the commonest cause of drop-out in the pergolide study. However, patients developing psychosis are generally those who develop a dementia, so they are predisposed. The dose can always be reduced if problems occur. At least we have an opportunity with the dopamine agonists to explore an alternative strategy that permits a delay in the introduction of levodopa, where studies show convincingly that levodopa is associated with a variety of adversities.

Rascol: The problem of psychosis can be managed more easily by following the patients and adjusting the dosage accordingly, rather than waiting until they start hallucinating.

Poewe: Many clinicians have the impression that levodopa-induced psychosis differs from agonist-induced psychosis, in that with the former the vivid dream pre-stage is longer. Frank, paranoid hallucinosis takes longer to develop. With dopamine agonists, paranoid hallucinations may appear more quickly. Do you agree ?

Rascol: I have not noticed any significant difference, as my experience varies from one patient to another.

Obeso: Most of the patients who will develop psychosis are actually in polytherapy, so it is difficult to be certain which drug is primarily responsible. My feeling is that problems arise from the addition of a combination of drugs.

Melamed: We are trying to put some order to the rich and enormous repertory of hallucinosis and psychosis in these patients. We also see equal or similar psychotic problems with levodopa and dopamine agonists, but one has more time to detect their development with levodopa. But once hallucinosis has occurred, however benign, the patient carries the potential to switch to paranoia or confusion immediately.

Sanchez-Ramos: Another predictor besides dementia is when the sleep cycle is completely deranged. This is invariably a problem with pergolide, but patients can be protected with clozapine which is a safe hypnotic and sleeping pill. Therefore we should not be dissuaded by the potential for development of hallucinosis because it can be prevented by the right combination of dopamine agonist therapy and protection from adverse dopaminergic events with clozapine.

Stocchi: If we were to recommend maximum doses for the treatment of PD, we would suggest up to 60 mg of bromocriptine, between 6 and 10 mg of pergolide, and between 4 and 6 mg of lisuride, doses which can easily be achieved in a PD clinic. In my experience with ropinirole, 24 mg per day can be used easily. One of the more tedious problems with dopamine agonists is somnolence. Finally, there are differences in terms of dyskinesias induced between pergolide, apomorphine and other D_2 agonists when they are added to levodopa. Addition of pergolide or apomorphine to levodopa generates more dyskinesias than lisuride or high dose ropinirole. A pure D_2 agonist can reduce dyskinesia more easily than a mixed D_1/D_2 agonist. I find that lisuride reduces dyskinesias more than apomorphine even though apomorphine is able to switch the patient on, whereas lisuride cannot.

Olanow: Sleep disturbances are extremely common in PD and are under-appreciated. They actually occur in about 80% of patients who are analyzed electroencephalographically and by specific questioning. Over half of patients do not mention sleep disturbances to their doctor.

Tolosa: It is not always the case that patients who develop hallucinations on dopamine agonists are those who are going to develop dementias. Some young patients with hallucinations do not develop dementia if the drugs are modified or stopped. It might therefore be worthwhile to define dementia in PD patients, since neurological testing will reveal some kind of cognitive dysfunction in almost all patients.

Rascol: In response to Dr. Stocchi's point on maximum dosage, it is puzzling and disappointing that after 20 years of bromocriptine usage as an effective antiparkinsonian drug, we still do not know the optimum dose to prescribe. When psychosis develops, the first drug to be withdrawn is deprenyl, then the dopamine agonist, then levodopa.

Tolosa: Are there any problems with ondansetron?

Melamed: With ondansetron, we wanted to determine if psychosis could be treated by means other than dopamine receptor blockade. All strategies involving blockade of dopamine receptors with neuroleptic-like drugs (except clozapine) prevent levodopa-associated psychosis but cause deterioration of PD. Clozapine could be working via blockade of D_4 receptor subtypes but it is an unclean drug and also blocks a variety of 5-HT receptors. Ondansetron is very selective for 5-HT_3 subtype serotoninergic receptors, and improves psychosis, particularly the visual hallucinosis. But it will not be the only solution, since parkinsonian psychosis is governed by several mechanisms including dopaminergic, serotoninergic and possibly enkephalinergic elements. It will be interesting to treat patients who develop psychosis following a dopamine agonist with either clozapine or ondansetron, to elucidate the biochemical mechanisms for this psychosis and determine if it differs from levodopa-induced psychosis. Additionally, dopamine agonists may not be clean, and may act on serotoninergic receptors as well.

Olanow: Even with the new dopamine agonists currently being tested, the incidence of psychosis appears to be the same as the other agonists, suggesting that the mechanism is likely to be dopaminergic.

Rascol: In our ongoing controlled study in early de novo patients, ropinirole does not yet appear to show significantly less psychosis after six months. The same is true for bromocriptine. It is essential that the three-year follow-up data are collected. However, after treating a patient with ropinirole for seven to eight years, I have observed less psychosis, although this remains unproven. It is possible that more than 120 patients per group are required to show differences in this population after three years.

Tulloch: Dr. Ogawa, you indicate that pergolide and bromocriptine have antioxidant effects, but these are seen at concentrations of 20mM. Further, the nitric oxide scavenging activity of pergolide you describe occurs at 50mM. These concentrations seem high.

Ogawa: Free radicals are difficult to detect because they react quickly with other molecules and it may be impossible to detect them under normal conditions. Against this background, free radical scavenging activity can be shown with a free radical-producing system using sophisticated technology such as electron spin resonance to detect oxidized molecules and radical species. This is what we have done with pergolide and bromocriptine. This is different from traditional pharmacology where trapping techniques are employed with agents such as salicylates. A high concentration of the dopamine agonist is required in our experiments because of the very high concentration of radicals being produced and the need to detect these species on ESR.

Scarlato: If dopamine agonists are free radical scavengers and provide neuroprotection, can they be used in the treatment of other neurodegenerative diseases such as Alzheimer's disease?

Ogawa: It may be possible, because they have been shown to provide neuroprotective effects in the hippocampal CA1 region after transient ischaemia. However, this has never been addressed in a clinical trial or in models of neurodegenerative diseases.

Leenders: Do dopamine agonists accumulate in the striatum as does levodopa?

Ogawa: Dopamine agonists do accumulate in the striatum and in this regard may be neuroprotective because of their capacity to stimulate autoreceptors and decrease dopamine release and turnover.

Obeso: Before closing this discussion, may I ask Dr. Tolosa what are his practical criteria in choosing one dopamine agonist over another when prescribing?

Tolosa: As stated earlier in this symposium, there is no consensus of opinion on whether a given profile of dopamine receptor stimulation is an important consideration with respect to efficacy. We do not know either if a partial agonist may be more efficacious than a full dopamine agonist in the various stages of the illness, and it is still unclear from a practical point of view if those agonists with a longer half-life, e.g. pergolide, are more effective than those with shorter half-lives. Several trials suggest that the various agonists, and in particular bromocriptine and pergolide, are not dramatically different in their clinical effects in equipotent doses. The choice of an agonist when prescribing is, therefore, somewhat arbitrary. I believe most of us prescribe those dopamine agonists we are more familiar with. In Spain, bromocriptine has been on the market for a long time and is widely prescribed, unlike pergolide which has only recently become available. For reasons which remain unclear, lisuride is not very popular. As a final comment, if one agonist does not work, I often try another one. I do not combine two orally administered agonists in a given patient, but I often add subcutaneous or intranasal apomorphine to patients receiving an ergot agonist.

CHAPTER SEVENTEEN

Future studies

ANTHONY H.V. SCHAPIRA, DSc, MD, FRCP

Department of Clinical Neurosciences, Royal Free Hospital School of Medicine, London, UK

ABSTRACT

An understanding of the etiology and pathogenesis of Parkinson's disease (PD), particularly that of dopaminergic cell death, underpins future research in the development of both symptomatic and neuroprotective strategies. Present treatment is largely symptomatically-based and is only partially effective, often resulting in complications such as dyskinesias during levodopa therapy. Furthermore, levodopa may sensitize basal ganglia to induce motor fluctuations which would prompt its use only in patients who fail on alternative therapies. While dopamine agonists have proven effective in the control of parkinsonian symptoms, their role is now evolving beyond that of purely symptomatic relief, with the prospect of monotherapy, particularly in early PD. A potential neuroprotective role for these agents in the prevention of dyskinesias and in the retardation of dopaminergic cell death in the substantia nigra is also a promising development. Neuroprotection may result not only from reduction in levodopa dosage, but also from the direct antioxidant effect of the dopamine agonists. Further work is required to (1) confirm that motor fluctuations do not develop in patients given only agonists and never levodopa, (2) assess whether selectivity occurs in the effects of specific agonists, (3) determine whether agonist actions may be enhanced by agents such as selegiline or COMT inhibitors, and (4) to discover whether rotation of dopamine agonists is helpful in maintaining their effect over a long period.

The introduction of the dopamine agonists in the treatment of Parkinson's disease (PD) has enabled a significant improvement in the control of parkinsonian symptoms. The role for dopamine agonists, however, is now evolving past their use simply for symptomatic relief. Adjuvant therapy with levodopa is now being superseded by the prospective use of dopamine agonists as monotherapy, particularly in the initial stages of PD.[1] A potential neuroprotective action of dopamine agonists, not only in terms of preventing the development of levodopa-induced dyskinesias but also in retarding the rate of dopaminergic cell death in the substantia nigra, is an obvious area for future research.

An understanding of the etiology and pathogenesis of PD, and the physiology and pharmacology of the basal ganglia, underpins future research into the development of both symptomatic and neuroprotective strategies in PD. Our current concepts on etiology embrace both genetic and environmental factors. The recent mapping to chromosome 4 of a gene causing autosomal dominant parkinsonism will provide the means to define the molecular genetic and protein chemical basis for at least one method by which selective dopaminergic cell death may be induced.[2] Although this will provide valuable insight into how selective neuronal populations may be targeted for premature death, its relevance to the majority of patients with idiopathic PD remains to be established.

An increasing body of opinion accepts that PD is probably a heterogeneous disorder in etiological terms but with common clinical and pathological end-points. In this respect it is probably the pathogenesis of dopaminergic cell death that will provide the most important clues to the development of new treatment (symptomatic) strategies. Thus, much research is focused on understanding the relevance of oxidative stress and damage, and of mitochondrial dysfunction, to the sequence of events that terminate in neuronal cell death in the substantia nigra. Understanding this sequence of events and their precipitants will enable the development of treatments to intervene in this pathway to provide a protective action.

Present treatment is for the most part symptomatically based with only selegiline having a potentially neuroprotective action, although this remains hotly debated.[3] Symptomatic treatment itself is only partially effective and may result in complications both in the short and the long term. Short-term advances in the therapy of PD are presently focused on broadening the range of medications available with an increase in mechanisms of action available for choice. This has included the development of controlled-release formulations of levodopa, an increased range of dopamine agonists with different receptor subtype agonist profiles, additional monoamine oxidase inhibitors and catechol-O-methyl transferase inhibitors (COMT).

One important question regarding dopamine agonists, that may be answered in the near future, is that of which is the best receptor agonist profile for these drugs. Recent developments have focused on using D_2 agonists although there is some information that a combination of both D_1 and D_2 agonism is beneficial. However, the incorporation of an agonist action on D_3 or D_4 receptor subtypes may limit side effects, and paradoxically may provide benefit for some of the non-dopaminergic aspects of PD. To date, very little work has been undertaken on pure D_1 agonists.[4,5] This is because previous work with such agents was severely limited by side effects. Attempts to circumvent this, however, may provide agents that can usually be added to the antiparkinsonian armamentarium.

NEUROTOXICITY

There has been much discussion on the potential neurotoxicity of dopamine turnover. Dopamine is oxidized to neuromelanin and this is associated with increased free radical generation. Thus, it might be expected that levodopa therapy would at least exacerbate the oxidative stress and damage already observed in the PD substantia nigra and potentially might be the cause of this damage. This theory would propose that melanized neurons would be more at risk of damage than non-melanized neurons. However, there is evidence both for and against this hypothesis. *In vitro* studies have documented dopamine toxicity,[6–9] but *in vivo* studies have failed to show increased dopaminergic cell death with levodopa use.[10,11] Dopamine can be shown to cause mild mitochondrial complex I inhibition in rats, but this is reversible.[12] The observation that patients with multiple system atrophy, who have been given doses of levodopa in concentrations and for durations comparable to parkinsonian patients yet who fail to have any mitochondrial complex I defect, suggests that this interaction may not play a primary role in the biochemical abnormalities of the parkinsonian nigra.[13]

In the context of the potential toxicity of levodopa therapy, the use of dopamine agonists has not been associated with neuronal toxicity. Indeed, there is some evidence that dopamine agonists may have a direct antioxidant effect. For instance, apomorphine has been shown *in vitro* to have an antioxidant action although similar studies failed to confer the same activity on pergolide.[14] Clearly this is an area which needs further work and might add some validity to the claims that dopamine agonists may have some neuroprotective action.

NON-RESPONDERS

It is often quoted that up to a third of patients with idiopathic PD will not respond to dopamine agonists at all, and even in responders only a small proportion will be able to remain on dopamine agonists as monotherapy for more than 12 months. The proportion of non-responders is on reflection rather high, and a similar figure used to be quoted for levodopa. It is now clear that a high proportion, if not all, of the non-responders to levodopa have an alternative diagnosis. This may to some extent also be the case with dopamine agonists. The limit on the use of agonists as monotherapy may be related to an unwillingness to exceed the stated maximum dose. Some studies have shown that when used in high dose, up to 60% of patients may be maintained on agonists alone for up to three years. Thus, further work needs to be undertaken to assess the therapeutic ceiling for agonists. Unwanted effects of agonists usually appear early on in treatment and can be circumvented with the adjuvant use of anti-emetics (e.g. domperidone) and by slow and gradual increase in the dose. The development of neuropsychiatric side effects often requires a reduction in dose or the withdrawal of the drug. In those patients who are able to tolerate agonists well, however, it should be possible to continue increasing dosage and improve therapeutic response.

The development of motor complications with the use of levodopa is well documented. It has been suggested that even a single dose of levodopa may sensitize the basal ganglia to subsequent motor fluctuations. If true, then this would add considerable weight to the argument that levodopa should be reserved for those patients who fail on agonist therapy. Naturally, there will be exceptions to this suggestion, particularly in those patients who develop PD late in life for whom the development of motor fluctuations may be of no practical relevance.

Work on the use of agonists as combination therapy with levodopa to delay or attenuate the development of motor fluctuations has produced conflicting results.[15,16] Nevertheless, it seems appropriate to at least use agonists for a levodopa-sparing effect. The effective use of dopamine agonists as monotherapy has much to recommend it in this respect. Further work needs to be done to confirm that motor fluctuations do not develop in those patients given only agonists and never levodopa, even in therapeutic tests. A supplementary question is whether all agonists might be the same in providing any neuroprotective action or in preventing the development of motor fluctuations. There may, for instance, be some selectivity along these lines with respect to the dopamine receptor profile of the agonists. Furthermore, it would be interesting to know whether the effect of dopamine agonists can be augmented by other drugs. There is some evidence that the action of bromocriptine may be enhanced by selegiline. It would be valuable to know whether the action of other agonists can also be enhanced by selegiline or such other agents as the COMT inhibitors.

Clinical practice has often shown that some patients do better on one type of agonist than another. The question arises as to whether rotation of dopamine agonists is helpful, particularly should the therapeutic action of one agonist begin to fail. Thus, rotating agonists with actions on different dopamine receptor subtypes may be beneficial. Alternatively a judicious combination of agonists with different receptor profiles may also prove of value.

Table 1: Future studies on the use of dopamine agonists

CLINICAL
1. Define most effective receptor agonist profile, e.g. D_1/D_2; D_1; D_2; with or without D_3/D_4.
2. Determine maximum dose-response/tolerance profile.
3. Early use with later addition of COMT inhibitors and avoidance of levodopa.
4. Alternate agonist use.

NEUROPROTECTION
1. Comprehensive *in vitro* and *in vivo* studies on neuroprotective action of agonists against specific toxins.
2. Define antioxidant effect of agonists, and determine any relationship to structure required for receptor selectivity.

Table 1 lists some areas of agonist research that are currently being explored or may be undertaken in the short term. The present emphases on the clinical application of agonists are directed towards defining the optimum agonist receptor profile and determining the place for agonists in the sequence of PD treatments. Demonstration that early agonist use with selegiline, and the avoidance of levodopa, prevents or delays the onset of dyskinesias will be a major advance. This needs to be combined with the provision of sufficient symptomatic relief, possibly through the use of higher doses of agonists. Demonstration of any neuroprotective action of agonists will reinforce their early use. Thus, more extensive studies in tissue culture and in animal models must be undertaken to define this property more clearly.

References

1. Montastruc JL, Rascol O, Senard JM, Rascol A. A randomized controlled study comparing bromocriptine to which levodopa was later added, with levodopa alone in previously untreated patients with Parkinson's disease: a five-year follow-up. J Neurol Neurosurg Psychiatr 1994; 57: 1034–1038.

2. Polymeropoulos MH, Higgins JJ, Golbe LI, Johnson WG, Ide SE, Di Oro G, *et al.* Mapping of a gene for Parkinson's disease to chromosome 4q21–q23. Science 1996; 274: 1197–1199.

3. Kieburtz K, Shoulson I. Treatment of Parkinson's disease with deprenyl (selegiline) and other monoamine oxidase inhibitors. In, Olanow CW, Jenner P, Youdim M, eds, Neurodegeneration and neuroprotection in Parkinson's disease. London/San Diego: Academic Press, 1996: 47–54.

4. Braun A, Fabbrini G, Mouradian MM, Serrati C, Barone C, Barone P, Chase TN. Selective D_1 dopamine receptor agonist treatment of Parkinson's disease. J Neural Transm 1987; 68: 41–50.

5. Jenner P. The rationale for the use of dopamine agonists in Parkinson's disease. Neurol 1995; 45 (Suppl 3): S6–S12.

6. Mena MA, Pardo B, Casarejos MJ, Fahn S, de Yebenes JG. Neurotoxicity of levodopa on catecholamine-rich neurons. Mov Disord 1992; 7: 23–31.

7. Michel PP, Hefti F. Toxicity of 6-hydroxydopamine and dopamine for dopaminergic neurons in culture. J Neurosci Res 1990; 26: 428–435.

8. Mytileneou C, Hans SK, Cohen G. Toxic and protective effects of L-dopa in mesencephalic cell cultures. J Neurochem 1993; 61: 1470–1478.

9. Ziv I, Zilkha-Falb R, Offen D, Shirvan A, Barzilai A, Melamed E. Levodopa induces apoptosis in cultured neuronal cells – a possible accelerator of nigrostriatal degeneration in Parkinson's disease? Mov Disord 1997; 12: 17–23.

10. Hefti F, Melamed E, Bhawan J, Wurtman RJ. Long-term administration of L-dopa does not damage dopaminergic neurons in the mouse. Neurol 1981; 31: 1194–1195.

11. Perry TL, Yong VW, Ito M, Foulks JG, Wall RA, Godin DV, Clavier RM. Nigrostriatal dopaminergic neurons remain undamaged in rats given high doses of L-dopa and carbidopa chronically. J Neurochem 1984; 43: 990–993.

12. Przedborski S, Jackson-Lewis V, Muthane U, Jiang H, Ferreira M, Naini AB, Fahn S. Chronic levodopa administration alters cerebral mitochondrial respiratory chain activity. Ann Neurol 1993; 34: 715–723.

13. Gu M, Gash MT, Cooper JM, Wenning GK, Daniel SE, Quinn NP, Marsden CD, Schapira AHV. Mitochondrial respiratory chain function in multiple system atrophy. Mov Disord, in press.

14. Gassen M, Glinka Y, Pinchasi B, Youdim MBH. Apomorphine is a highly potent free radical scavenger in rat brain mitochondrial fraction. Eur J Pharmacol 1996; 308: 219–225.

15. Rinne UK. Early combination of bromocriptine and levodopa in the treatment of Parkinson's disease: a five-year follow-up. Neurol 1987; 37: 826–828.

16. Olanow CW, Fahn S, Muenter M, Klawans H, Hurtig H, Stern M, *et al.* A multicenter double-blind placebo-controlled trial of pergolide as an adjunct to Sinemet in Parkinson's disease. Mov Disord 1994; 9: 40–47.

Search for Consensus

The role of dopamine agonists in the treatment of Parkinson's disease – a discussion and search for consensus

Olanow: During this conference we have addressed the basic science and the clinical issues that are relevant to the use of dopamine agonists in the treatment of Parkinson's disease (PD). We will now initiate a general discussion to see how we can utilize that information in order to better treat our PD patients. Specifically, we will determine where there is, and where there is not, consensus. We will not attempt to generate an algorithm for the general treatment of PD and will not specifically consider the wide range of available drug therapies, surgical interventions, and non-pharmacologic approaches including patient education that comprise the current therapeutic armamentarium for treating PD. We will assume that patients defined as having PD do in fact have this disorder and will not consider the criteria for making this diagnosis. Rather, we will focus exclusively on the use of dopamine agonists in the treatment of PD with particular emphasis on patients in the early stages of the disease. For the purposes of the discussion, the early stages of the disease will be defined as that period before patients begin to develop adverse events (usually within the first two to five years after diagnosis). We will consider the role of dopamine agonists in two groups of patients – (1) the *de novo* patient, who has never been exposed to levodopa, and (2) patients who have not developed motor complications but are taking or have previously taken levodopa.

Let us begin with an example – a *de novo* PD patient who has never received antiparkinsonian therapy and is now deemed to require symptomatic treatment. Should we initiate therapy with levodopa or a dopamine agonist? Let us see if we can get some consensus on what people would do at this stage of treatment. Does this audience believe that the scientific evidence presented during the course of this conference is sufficient to warrant initiating symptomatic therapy with a dopamine agonist rather than levodopa in the routine case? Could you raise your hand if you agree with this approach?

[241]

Olanow: Let us now entertain a discussion of those factors that must be taken into account in applying this recommendation to specific PD patients.

Gershanik: I think age considerations are a factor in deciding what medication one should start with, as was so nicely reviewed by Dr. Stocchi in this volume. There are significant levodopa-related complications that occur in young patients that are much less likely to occur in elderly patients with equal disease duration. In a patient below the age of 55 years, I would definitely consider a dopamine agonist, whereas in a patient 65 years or older, I would not consider a dopamine agonist as the first option because of the potential for side effects.

Melamed: What about the patient between the ages of 55 and 65? This is the commonest age of onset for PD that we see in the clinic.

Gershanik: In our study comparing early *versus* late onset cases we considered young onset to be below 45 years and late onset to be older than 65 years. Thus, we have information concerning these groups of patients. I do not know what happens with the patients in between and think that it is a tough decision to make.

Stocchi: I believe that we should try to start with a dopamine agonist in patients under 65 years because their life expectancy is longer and we know from many studies that they have less risk of developing motor fluctuations and dyskinesias if they start with a dopamine agonist instead of levodopa. Over the age of 65 years, one could start with levodopa, but I would definitely consider starting with an agonist or a combination of levodopa and an agonist in younger patients.

Obeso: Does anyone have any evidence indicating that PD evolves differently in patients presenting in the different age groups?

Gershanik: There is a paper coming out in *Movement Disorders* in which we prospectively compared the effects of an acute pharmacologic challenge with levodopa in young *versus* late onset cases of PD. There was a definite difference in the pattern of response to levodopa and in the severity of the dyskinesias and motor fluctuations in these patients. So in our experience, there is definitely a difference.

Obeso: But is there an underlying reason based on differences in biochemical or pathological features? For example, it appears that patients with young onset PD progress at a slower rate than older patients despite the fact that motor complications are more prevalent and presumably a relatively greater degree of neuronal loss must have occurred for clinical features to emerge at a young age.

Gershanik: I have not seen any paper dealing with changes in the underlying pathology or pharmacology that can explain the difference in clinical performance.

Olanow: It is known that older PD patients have a higher incidence of cortical pathology and Alzheimer's-type changes than younger patients. Whether similar differences between young and old patients exist in the SNc or in other basal ganglia regions is not known.

Gershanik: There is no hard evidence in that regard. In our study we evaluated patients of different ages but with the same duration of disease. For example we compared patients 40–60 years of age with those who were 60–80 years of age and who each had a disease duration of approximately 20 years. So neither life expectancy nor duration of the treatment accounts for these differences. They behave differently because of the age of onset.

Tolosa: I would like to disagree slightly with Drs. Gershanik and Stocchi. I think the age of onset is important, for the reasons that have been already given, but if you have a patient aged 45–55 years with disability that affects quality-of-life and employability, I think that starting on a dopamine agonist may not be justified. I would start such a patient with levodopa and consider adding an agonist later. In my opinion, some patients need more potent treatment than can be provided by an agonist alone.

Gershanik: I agree entirely with Dr. Tolosa. I talked about age consideration as a first factor. A second consideration has to do with the degree of disability and the effect of that disability on activities of daily living or employment. In these cases, perhaps one should think about early combination treatment in which you introduce a low dose of levodopa and add a dopamine agonist shortly thereafter so as to avoid increasing the dose of levodopa.

Olanow/Obeso: We choose to employ dopamine agonists in the early stages of the disease based on animal studies and some clinical trials indicating that, in comparison with levodopa, these drugs have a reduced propensity to induce motor complications. These studies also indicate that the likelihood of developing motor complications following levodopa administration is directly related to the degree of underlying disease severity. Thus, patients who have more severe disability might be precisely those who would most benefit from the early use of a dopamine agonist as monotherapy. It is also reasonable to consider that higher doses of agonists could be tested as a means of obtaining a satisfactory clinical benefit before resorting to levodopa.

Stocchi: We should also clarify that it does not take that long for a young patient to reach a therapeutically effective dose of a dopamine agonist. Our studies suggest that this occurs in *de novo* patients in approximately 12 to 24 days. This is not a particularly long time even if the patient is working. In Europe we have the advantage of being able to use domperidone (20–40 mg/day). This permits us to escalate the dose more rapidly. In a recent trial of ropinirole, we enrolled 35 *de novo* patients with a variety of professions including lawyers and doctors. None of them dropped out because of lack of efficacy. In the modern era, *de novo* patients generally do not wait to go to the doctor until they are so disabled that they have problems at work. I agree that if a patient is threatened with loss of employment, it would be better if they could have a treatment that acts rapidly. However, even levodopa takes approximately 12 days to reach maximum benefit, so I do not see enough of a difference to warrant not using a dopamine agonist in these patients.

Olanow: You indicate that it takes 12–24 days to see benefit with an agonist and 12 days with levodopa. In our experience, we take longer with either group of drugs in order to minimize the risk of side effects.

Stocchi: I think domperidone makes the difference as it permits a more rapid titration schedule. We use it with agonists and with both standard and controlled-release formulations of levodopa.

Albanese: One should bear in mind that age is a relative issue, not an absolute one. The problem is how old the patient is physiologically and how they are progressing in general terms. Compliance must also be considered as this can be a problem if the dopamine agonist is introduced too rapidly. We also introduce agonists more slowly than what Dr. Stocchi describes. In my experience it takes two months and maybe more to reach the optimal level.

Rascol: I think it is difficult to say that one can reach a stable dose within any defined period of time. Patients are titrated until their parkinsonian condition is optimized. Some patients have mild problems and it is not good to go too quickly. Others are severely impaired and require more rapid improvement so the titration schedule needs to be faster. I agree that, in general, patients nowadays visit a doctor or neurologist with only minor functional impairment and there is plenty of time to reach the effective dose.

Leenders: We examined the significance of disease duration and age of onset in PD. We discovered that the older the age of onset, the greater the degree of frontal lobe pathology and impairment in neuropsychologic function whereas increased disease duration correlated more closely with greater basal ganglia pathology. Interestingly, the two did not correlate with each other and there was no interaction. This means that the age of onset of the disease but not duration should be a determining factor for whether or not you start agonists, since agonists are associated with a relatively high degree of psychologic and psychiatric complications.

Olanow: Has anyone done a study in which *de novo* patients were randomized to receive an agonist *versus* levodopa and proven that agonists have more psychiatric side effects than does a bioequivalent dose of levodopa, particularly in patients in the early stages of PD?

Oertel: We are doing a double-blind placebo-controlled study of levodopa *versus* pergolide and the only data I can give at the moment is that the drop-out rate in both groups is the same.

Gershanik: I think that one cannot define a specific time interval for the introduction of an agonist in a given PD patient. In our group, we never take 12 days or 24 days to reach a stable dose. The time and the dose are dependent on the response of the patient and the degree of improvement and this cannot be strictly defined. Another point that we should consider is the cost and number of medications that we recommend for a PD patient. Many of us would consider using a putative neuroprotective agent, a dopamine agonist, domperidone and later levodopa. It may be hard to convince a mildly disabled patient that they need to take three to four medications for something that might happen in the future.

Rascol: In an ongoing double-blind controlled study, we could not detect any difference in the drop-out rates between patients randomized to ropinirole *versus* levodopa. In fact there was a slightly higher incidence of drop-outs at six months in levodopa-treated patients. Thus, side effects do not preclude starting untreated PD patients on treatment with a dopamine agonist.

Poewe: There is one aspect that we have not mentioned in our discussion so far that I think is pertinent. Levodopa responsiveness is one of the criteria for diagnosing PD and differentiating it from the atypical parkinsonian syndromes. So, having agreed that dopamine agonists should be the first symptomatic treatment for some PD patients, should there still be a levodopa test to confirm the diagnosis and, if so, should it be a single dose of levodopa or several weeks of treatment?

Olanow: If the animal data are correct and even a single dose of levodopa can prime for the development of dyskinesia, then even a test dose of levodopa could be potentially harmful and would be best avoided. I think we should at least consider avoiding levodopa entirely until such time as nothing else will control the patient. This is a very important area for study.

Poewe: I agree with you. This would probably require revision in the diagnostic criteria for definition of study populations, even in *de novo* patients.

Obeso: In *de novo* patients, all that might happen if we did not perform a levodopa test is that we would increase the incidence of false positive diagnoses. This is addressed by the randomization procedure and is far less significant than potentially priming a patient to develop motor complications. In fact, many PD experts do not rely on this test anyway.

Gershanik: I agree. Many studies of *de novo* PD patients such as DATATOP have been done without using levodopa as a diagnostic test and in practice this is done every day. One does not start every single parkinsonian patient on levodopa to be sure that he or she has PD.

Olanow: Plus, in the early stages of the disease if the patient has only mild severity it may be difficult to detect a levodopa response.

Oertel: May I ask Dr. Bédard, is a single dose of apomorphine capable of inducing priming?

Bédard: Because apomorphine is a very short-acting drug, I believe that in contrast to the longer-acting dopamine agonists, it is capable of inducing priming. However, there is no reason why a test with a longer-acting dopamine agonist would not be just as good as a test with levodopa for confirming the diagnosis. For scientific purposes I think it would be preferable to start with a long-acting agonist from the very beginning without doing a levodopa test.

Melamed: It is important to study the effects of the first doses of levodopa. If one dose of levodopa can cause priming, then we have a lot of trouble, but we do not know for certain that this is the case. It is the same issue as whether a single dose of a neuroleptic drug primes the patient later on for the development of tardive dyskinesia which I believe it can.

> **The audience was polled and the large majority indicated that they would not rely on a levodopa or apomorphine test in deciding whether to initiate a patient with very mild disease on symptomatic therapy with a dopamine agonist or levodopa.**

Olanow: Let me make another point. In the United States only 6% of PD patients receive dopamine agonists during their first five years of treatment. So, although we have unanimously agreed that dopamine agonists should be considered as primary therapy in all but some subsets of PD patients, dopamine agonists are not being used in the vast majority of patients with early disease.

Rascol: When you look at what is known in clinical pharmacology and what is happening in the routine practice of medicine, there is often a big difference. It is very clear that there is a discordance in the results of published controlled trials and everyday practice patterns. So, we have to find a way to speed the time for the results of laboratory research and clinical trials to impact on clinical practice.

Tolosa: What you have said is true, namely that therapies that have been proven to be effective can take months or years before they are applied by general practitioners. However, the notion of using dopamine agonists as early or even primary therapy in PD has been around for a long time. I think the delay in its application in the clinic results from this concept not having been conclusively established in clinical trials. I think this will be necessary if this treatment approach is to be implemented in practice.

Albanese: Will prescribing patterns change when the COMT inhibitors become available?

Rascol: From the viewpoint of the general neurologist and internist, managing PD will become increasingly confusing as so many new drugs are now becoming available. We will also have to consider the potential impact of one drug upon another. For example, in the study comparing ropinirole with bromocriptine, for an unexplained reason selegiline interacted with the results. We now have many drugs to consider and it will be impossible to perform clinical trials on all possible combinations. For these reasons a treatment approach using dopamine agonist monotherapy may be highly desirable and appealing to practitioners because it is relatively straightforward.

Melamed: I need a push to change my attitude. I do not like levodopa, but I have no choice but to use it. I know all the problems that it can cause but I need to have more information about the use of dopamine agonists in *de novo* patients – their acute effects, their long term effects, and their interaction with levodopa. In the general neurological community, I think most neurologists start patients on levodopa but would be willing to employ dopamine agonists if clinical trials validated the laboratory and preliminary clinical data suggesting that dopamine agonist drugs are associated with a reduced risk of developing levodopa-related motor complications.

Damier: Some neurologists favor using early combination therapy with levodopa plus an agonist. While levodopa has been shown to produce a priming effect, maybe if the dose is reduced or is given with an agonist it would not induce this priming effect. We do not have scientific evidence that early combination with low doses of levodopa is not as good as agonists alone. For these reasons, I start with both levodopa and an agonist at the same time.

Olanow: If you believe that, why would you not still prefer to start with just the agonist as monotherapy and hold the levodopa until the patient needs it, whether it be three months or three years? Most physicians would be reluctant to introduce two drugs simultaneously.

Stocchi: Dr. Olanow, how many of your private patients do you start with a dopamine agonist in your private office? This is the real test of what a doctor really thinks. I personally start more than 60% on dopamine agonists. If you explain to patients what you are doing, the compliance is very high. In Italy there is another phenomenon. The *de novo* patient, most of the time, arrives already informed by the Patients Association about the potential risks of levodopa treatment and they look at you in a strange way if you start them on levodopa. Patients are much more informed today about the potential risks of levodopa.

Gershanik: One cannot generically say one does not like levodopa; one does not like levodopa at a certain point in time and in a certain population of patients. There are also many confounding factors when it comes to talking about how many patients you treat with dopamine agonists. Considering reimbursement policies in Argentina, it costs my patients approximately $20 a month if I start with amantadine *versus* $400 a month for pergolide. So, I cannot start 60% of my patients on dopamine agonists if they do not get reimbursement.

Rascol: If cost is a limiting factor in the choice of a drug, then one has to consider the cost over the course of the disease. Pharmacoeconomic studies can factor in the relative contribution to the overall cost of patient care of the higher price of a dopamine agonist and the relative savings associated with reduced motor complications.

Albanese: Only 5% of early PD patients are treated with dopamine agonists. But if 95% of parkinsonian patients were started on treatment with dopamine agonists, it is likely that the cost of these drugs would markedly decrease.

Tolosa: Another confounding factor is where one practices. For example, I work in an area of Barcelona where we see a lot of elderly parkinsonian patients. Maybe we should rephrase the question – how many of us would treat young, mildly affected parkinsonian patients that do not have economic problems with a dopamine agonist?

Obeso: It is interesting to consider that there is often a dissociation between the theoretical, scientific position and the routine office practice.

Olanow: Let us then address some of the modifiers that influence your choice of drug in starting treatment for a PD patient. The first one is age. It has been suggested that, in general, dopamine agonists should be used in patients 55 years of age and under and levodopa in patients 65 years of age and older.

Obeso: Can we then be more specific? I would suggest initiating therapy with a dopamine agonist in all patients under the age of 65 years.

Rascol: In our ongoing ropinirole study the maximal age for entry was 75 years. In general, the older patients did not have trouble tolerating the agonist and have shown good clinical benefit. I think it depends very much on how healthy your patient is and whether or not there is cognitive impairment.

Olanow: I use physiologic rather than chronologic age in making the decision as to whether to introduce a dopamine agonist. Some people at age 70 years are active and fit and I would have no hesitancy in using a dopamine agonist in these patients. Others at age 60 are already slowed mentally and I would be reluctant to use an agonist. What primarily drives my thinking in regard to age is the presence or absence of neuropsychiatric problems such as cognitive impairment or hallucinations.

Obeso: So we might summarize by saying that age is a modifying factor but this must be considered in the light of the physical and mental status of the patient.

Poewe: In spite of the lack of controlled clinical data, I am convinced that I should do all I can to avoid levodopa. I agree though that it is more difficult in older people especially if there is evidence of dementia.

Olanow: So, let us see if there is consensus.

> **The audience was polled and there was unanimous agreement that a dopamine agonist is the drug of choice for initiating treatment in PD patients less than 55 years of age. All but one participant indicated they would also initiate treatment with a dopamine agonist in PD patients between the ages of 55 and 65 years if there was no cognitive impairment or psychosis. Most favored using levodopa as initial treatment in patients older than 65 years although several argued for initiating treatment with an agonist if there was no cognitive impairment. They agreed that cost was a factor and that in many circumstances, it might not be possible to abide by this approach because of financial considerations.**

Olanow: So is there general consensus on this point of view. Let us now consider disability. If a patient is experiencing disability that impairs their capacity to maintain their activities of daily living or employability, would that influence your choice of the initial medication?

Tolosa: If the patient is disabled by parkinsonian features, I would change my strategy. I prefer to introduce levodopa in these patients if they have disability such that a more rapid-acting and effective treatment is necessary. Whether the dominant side is affected is an important factor in making this determination.

Stocchi: One thing we know from our double-blind study comparing ropinirole to levodopa is that there was no difference in their response to treatment or in their functional status after treatment. So why should you use levodopa just because the patient is more disabled if you can, at least initially, obtain the same results by using a dopamine agonist?

Ogawa: May I suggest treating severe patients with dopamine agonists and if benefits are unsatisfactory, substituting another type of dopamine agonist that might provide better relief of symptoms rather than increasing the dopamine agonist to maximum doses?

Rascol: If there is a potential benefit in the long term, even if it is only for a small percentage of patients, and if they can be adequately controlled with dopamine agonist monotherapy even for a short time, why should we not start with the dopamine agonist and then add levodopa as an adjunct when patients have reached the maximum tolerated dose of the agonist? What you find is that some patients do fine on monotherapy for years, while others will receive adjunct levodopa after six months. I do not find any good reason to deviate from this treatment plan of starting with a dopamine agonist.

Olanow: This raises an interesting point. Laboratory studies in parkinsonian monkeys demonstrate that even a single dose of levodopa is enough to prime the animals for the development of dyskinesia even if levodopa is subsequently replaced by a dopamine agonist. In contrast, when therapy is started with a dopamine agonist such as ropinirole and levodopa is avoided, the animals experience comparable motor benefits without the hyperactivity or dyskinesias that characterize levodopa treatment. If we believe that this same situation is likely to exist in PD patients, we should make every effort to avoid levodopa as the first drug, even if the patient is experiencing disability. If the agonist cannot provide satisfactory clinical control, then levodopa can be added as an adjunct. Alternatively, the dose of the agonist can be increased to levels above those traditionally employed in practice, which in our experience may provide additional benefits and are generally well-tolerated. If increased doses of the agonist cannot be tolerated or it is evident that further dose increases do not provide satisfactory benefit, then levodopa can be added as an adjunct. I realize that there are cost issues involved, but if this can be established to be the preferred treatment approach, I am confident that drug companies could provide pills containing large amounts of medication at a reasonable cost.

Rascol: I agree with that philosophy and I would even apply that strategy to patients with severe disease. In such cases I may try to increase the dose at a faster rate in order to achieve a more rapid improvement. For example, I frequently increase the dose of bromocriptine to 60 or 80 mg per day and only add levodopa if the patient does not do well. In our controlled study, patients were randomized to start therapy on levodopa or an agonist. Patients initiated on the agonist had a delay in onset and a reduced incidence of motor complications compared to levodopa-treated patients even though patients had comparable levels of control. After five years of treatment, approximately 30% are doing perfectly well on high doses of the agonist alone and have developed no motor complications. So even if it is only a small proportion, I think that this treatment approach gives patients the opportunity to have this type of response.

Bédard: I also agree. The risk of developing motor side effects starts from the moment levodopa is added. In other words, levodopa used in a combination therapy might produce the same problems as levodopa monotherapy.

Olanow: Another point that could be considered is the potential neuroprotective effect of dopamine agonists. In the laboratory, levodopa induces neurodegeneration while dopamine agonists protect dopaminergic neurons both in tissue culture and in animal models of parkinsonism. Dopamine agonists have the potential to induce these benefits in PD patients because they decrease the need for levodopa, decrease dopamine turnover through stimulation of dopamine autoreceptors, and have the capacity to act as free radical scavengers.

> **The audience was polled regarding how disease severity influences the introduction of symptomatic therapy for PD patients. The majority indicated that they would still initiate treatment with a dopamine agonist and if necessary either increase the dose above currently employed levels or add levodopa as an adjunct.**

Olanow: Let us now consider whether there is a difference in the magnitude or quality of the response that is obtained with levodopa *versus* a dopamine agonist.

Rascol: It is generally believed that levodopa is more potent than dopamine agonists and is generally preferred by patients. However, can anybody give me a good scientific reason why a dopamine agonist should be less effective than levodopa? Apomorphine is very effective.

Tolosa: I cannot give you any scientific reason but my experience, and everything I read, suggests that monotherapy with dopamine agonists is not as effective and is less well-tolerated than levodopa.

Olanow: In MPTP-lesioned monkeys, the behavioral responses are comparable when they were treated with levodopa, bromocriptine and ropinirole (see Chapter 6). Have we increased the dose of agonist sufficiently in PD patients to know that you cannot attain the same level of benefit as with levodopa?

Rascol: I agree. We believe that the benefit:risk ratio is probably in favor of levodopa but I am not sure that this has really been demonstrated.

Gershanik: But on the other hand, there is no scientific evidence that a dopamine agonist that is as potent as levodopa in relieving the symptomatic status of the patient would not produce dyskinesias and fluctuations in the long term. Animal studies have all been relatively short-term.

Rascol: I totally agree. There is a general belief that dopamine agonists are less effective than levodopa, which I am not sure is true. But concerns about long-term side effects need to be considered.

Damier: Maybe levodopa induces psychologic effects that explain why patients like levodopa and are different to what is seen with a D_2 agonist, even though motor benefits may be comparable. For example, with pallidal stimulation, our patient had a normal motor score but still missed levodopa. Are there any studies comparing the effect of levodopa and D_2 agonists on depression?

Rascol: There are no available controlled data. Ropinirole was thought to be effective in animal models of depression but I am not sure if the drug has been studied for this indication in patients.

Stocchi: In the experiment we did with ropinirole and levodopa, a blind evaluator could not detect any difference between the two drugs in terms of efficacy in *de novo* patients. I think we have to clarify this point. *De novo* patients respond perfectly well to dopamine agonists. The effect of dopamine agonists wears off with time, but so too does the effect of levodopa. This may correlate with a loss of endogenous dopamine and may represent the loss of D_1 receptor stimulation. So, at this stage we need to add a small amount of levodopa to replace the D_1 stimulation.

Aquilonius: I think it is very important to solve some of these very important questions by designing, perhaps in collaboration with industry, new types of studies which attempt to reproduce the preclinical findings in monkeys. Relatively small numbers of patients should be put on steady-state concentrations of levodopa or an agonist with objective measurements of what is really happening. We could then base our discussion on a more scientific level.

Gershanik: When we talk about wearing off, are we talking about the duration of the response or the magnitude of the response? In our experience with acute levodopa challenge tests, there is a reduction in the duration of the benefit but not in the magnitude of the response. With dopamine agonists, there is loss in both the magnitude and duration of the response. I think it has to do with the need for at least some endogenous dopamine to provide D_1 receptor stimulation in order for a relatively pure D_2 agonist to be effective.

Olanow: Perhaps we could move on to consider how to introduce dopamine agonists.

Albanese: I would favor introducing them slowly in order to minimize the risk of side effects and drop-out. Double the time suggested by drug companies.

Gershanik: I would agree but it depends on the individual patient. Should we start with domperidone in every single patient in order to be able to increase the dose faster or not? In my own practice with bromocriptine, I start with 1.25 mg per day and increase the dose every five days, without domperidone. It takes me about 60 days to get to the desired dose.

Melamed: One of the reasons why I am reluctant to start a dopamine agonist in a young patient is the side effects. Syncope and orthostatic hypotension etc. are quite common. Although I cover them with domperidone, it is frequently problematic. The question that I have is if one challenge fails, should we rechallenge or regard this as a treatment failure? Patients themselves are very wary of trying the drug again after such a phenomenon.

Olanow: I think this is a good point. When treating early onset patients, my main concern is to get them to tolerate the drug the first time and not try to rush. In general, there is no urgency and one can easily take 30 to 90 days to get a patient on to a satisfactory drug. I agree that once patients have had a bad reaction, they frequently will not take the drug any more.

Tolosa: My feeling is that slow titration over six to 12 weeks is best. If the patient develops nausea one can add domperidone.

Rascol: There is an ongoing study comparing three different titration schedules for ropinirole. The more rapid titration was associated with increased side effects, with or without the addition of domperidone.

Melamed: Does the addition of domperidone influence orthostatic hypotension as well as nausea and vomiting?

Rascol: No, because central factors are probably involved. In healthy volunteers pretreated with domperidone, a single dose of levodopa induced a significant reduction in the plasma level of norepinephrine indicating a central effect. It is not clear if this is due to a D_1 or a D_2 effect.

Delwaide: I see a problem with this 'slow' strategy because it takes a long time. When you meet the patient for the first time it is important to gain their trust by getting an early benefit. The delay for me is not a good thing.

Olanow: In our clinic, waiting six weeks or longer for a benefit is not a problem. I explain to the patient what we are doing and why and they seem to accept that. It might be more of a problem in the hands of a general neurologist where, if they do not obtain a rapid benefit, they may move on to another doctor. I think that is all the more reason why a group such as ours needs to make recommendations so that the general neurologist can consider all of the facts. I would not like, for example, to increase the likelihood that a patient will develop adversity because I want to get a result in two weeks as opposed to six weeks.

Obeso: The next question is how high do you go and can this be done relatively quickly?

Gershanik: I do not want to be a pioneer. There are no good studies and I do not have a lot of experience with high doses. I think it is important though to define how high we should go before we say that we have failed or that we have reached the optimal response.

Obeso: Cotzias suggested increasing the dose of dopamine agonists until the patient develops side effects. Fortunately, he used this approach with levodopa because his initial dose was 5 mg per day and benefits were not seen until much higher levels were employed.

Rascol: We have performed a study with ropinirole and demonstrated a dose-dependent increase in clinical response. We did not see a specific ceiling effect.

Brücke: It has been mentioned several times that we should try to increase the dose of the dopamine agonist above levels routinely employed. These drugs come in relatively small doses so to do this, patients would have to take large numbers of tablets which they may be reluctant to do.

Olanow: You make a good point. But if it can be shown that higher doses can safely provide additional benefits for PD patients, then companies could manufacture tablets containing a high dose of the dopamine agonist. Because the actual amount of medication in the pill usually does not meaningfully affect the cost, these pills could be sold for a reasonable price.

Poewe: I think as a general statement we should use the same principles that we do in epilepsy. That is, for any one drug in PD, one must go to the highest tolerated dose before one can be sure that the potential of the drug has been fully exploited.

Obeso: What would be a high dose of bromocriptine? Between 80 and 120 mg?

Olanow: A dosing study has really never been done and there are potentially individual variations. It does seem reasonable to apply the pharmacologic principle of using the lowest dose that will provide a satisfactory response and to continue to raise the dose until side effects develop or it is evident that the drug provides no additional benefit.

Tolosa: There may be legal problems with that strategy, because if you put out these recommendations, neurologists may end up prescribing 20 mg of pergolide, and if that patient commits suicide or kills his wife, there may be problems for the doctor because he recommended a dose that is higher than used in general practice. This is an important issue but it ought to be studied before specific recommendations are put forward.

Olanow: Perhaps the one thing we really have not addressed is what to do if a patient has been assigned to levodopa and now requires additional medication. Would we continue to add levodopa or would we now supplement with a dopamine agonist? This point may have been largely answered by our earlier discussions in which we agreed that if levodopa primes for motor complications it might be best to utilize an agonist from the onset of treatment. Does it follow, therefore, that if somebody is already on levodopa it is better to add a dopamine agonist rather than to increase the dose of levodopa?

Bédard: It is our experience in patients on rather large doses of levodopa and who have already developed prominent motor side effects that decreasing the dose of levodopa and replacing it with a dopamine agonist produces a better clinical profile. This approach is supported by numerous studies including Dr. Olanow's study with pergolide. So on that basis I think it is certainly preferable to combine the two rather than pushing up the dose of levodopa.

Gershanik: But again, the same considerations and limitations apply. This is because if a 75- or 80-year old patient who has been on levodopa needs to supplement medication, I would push up the dose of levodopa, whereas for a younger patient I would add a dopamine agonist if they are healthy and there is no significant cognitive impairment.

Rascol: My feeling is that the dose of the agonist needs to be high enough. A lot of studies have not given positive results because the amount of dopamine agonist used is too small.

Tolosa: I think that it makes sense adding a dopamine agonist in this situation, with the modifiers you suggested, but there is not enough information at present to say that this is what has to be done. I would like to see a good study that shows that this is really the right thing to do. I would then feel more comfortable in adding an additional drug to patients already on levodopa as well as perhaps selegiline and a COMT inhibitor.

Rascol: I agree that long-term studies are required. In our study comparing an agonist with supplemental levodopa to levodopa alone, we have shown that after five years the agonist group has fewer motor complications in the form of motor fluctuations or dyskinesias. However, when the motor complications first occur, they are not very troublesome. Longer follow-up is required before we can say with absolute certainty that it is better to use the agonist as first line therapy and adjunct levodopa, or start with levodopa and adjunct with an agonist.

Albanese: It seems to me that we are all coming to a more or less common view. Namely, that we should identify those patients who can be treated with dopamine agonists as primary therapy and add levodopa when they cannot be controlled. If they already take levodopa, then a dopamine agonist should be added. The minority of patients, such as the elderly or cognitively impaired, will be managed with levodopa alone.

Leenders: Every year for the last 10 or 12 years these same issues come up and still there is no way to decide. Could you summarize what real information there is now upon which to base a decision?

Olanow: One of the problems is that we are forced to make decisions every day without the necessary clinical data. Certainly laboratory studies in parkinsonian monkeys indicate that dopamine agonists have a reduced propensity to induce motor complications in comparison to levodopa (see Chapters 5 and 6). We are also beginning to understand the molecular biology of how levodopa might prime for the development of these motor complications (see Chapter 3). There are also preclinical studies showing that dopamine agonists have neuroprotective effects in tissue culture and in *in vivo* models (see Chapters 2 and 12). It is in the clinical area that we really lack information. Several studies do point to the benefits of using dopamine agonists early in the treatment of PD but they have not been carried out with satisfactory rigor and long-term, prospective, randomized, double-blind studies are required (see Chapters 8 and 9). There are two purposes of this conference. One is to see if there is a consensus in what we do, and the other is to make recommendations as to what studies we should do to get the necessary data. It is clear that long-term studies in untreated PD patients are required in which patients are randomized to:

1. levodopa as initial therapy – with increasing disability, continue to increase the dose;
2. levodopa as initial therapy – with increasing disability, supplement with a dopamine agonist;
3. dopamine agonist as initial therapy – with increasing disability, continue to increase the dose;
4. dopamine agonist as initial therapy – with increasing disability, supplement with levodopa.

End points for such a study could include clinical response and the latency and frequency of developing motor complications.

I think the issues that we have raised now could very well have been raised 10 or 12 years ago but they were not resolved. Several things have changed since then. Firstly, there is more basic scientific information supporting the use of dopamine agonists as primary therapy in PD, as mentioned above and outlined in this volume. Secondly, two new dopamine agonists will be introduced to the market in 1997. These are the first agonists to be extensively studied in the early stages of the disease. Based on these interests, it is more likely that corporate sponsors will provide the funding necessary to perform these studies and answer these important questions.

Olanow/Obeso: Perhaps this would be a good point to summarize the results of this session in which we have sought to determine where there is consensus in the use of dopamine agonists.

● It is the consensus of this group that the optimal treatment for initiating symptomatic treatment in a PD patient is a dopamine agonist. This is based on existing laboratory and clinical information indicating that such an approach can provide symptomatic benefits and is more likely to delay or avoid the motor complications associated with levodopa therapy and possibly even disease progression.

● There is general support for the notion of increasing the dose of a dopamine agonist beyond the traditional upper limits, so as to maximally delay the introduction of levodopa for as long as possible, based on the potential of levodopa to prime for the development of motor complications. Most would favor initiating treatment with low doses and escalating the dose gradually in order to minimize acute side effects associated with dopamine agonists.

● There are several modifying factors that would influence how this treatment strategy is put into effect in general practice. Foremost among these is age. At 55 years of age and younger, there is consensus that all would start with a dopamine agonist; at 65 years and over, the majority favor introducing therapy with levodopa for reasons of both increased risk of neuropsychiatric side effects and the reduced incidence of motor complications in older patients. For patients between 55 and 65 years, all but one participant would favor introducing therapy with a dopamine agonist but would be influenced by the patient's physiological age and cognitive function.

● Severe disability or threatened loss of employment would influence most to start with levodopa in the hope of obtaining a more rapid response, but others felt that the same could be accomplished with a dopamine agonist, particularly if it is combined with domperidone. It was also pointed out that the full extent of benefit that can be obtained with a dopamine agonist titrated to its maximum tolerated level remains to be determined.

● The clinical presentation would influence many. If a patient has dementia, the large majority would not favor introducing a dopamine agonist, because of the belief that levodopa has a better risk:reward ratio in this population of patients.

● Cost is an important factor that might limit the widespread use of dopamine agonists both because of the price of the drug and because of the reimbursement policies of many insurance companies and health care providers.

- All agreed that if a patient was receiving therapy with levodopa and experienced worsening disability, they would add a dopamine agonist rather than continue to raise the dose of levodopa except in the very elderly or in patients with cognitive impairment.
- Finally, it was universally agreed that whatever treatment strategy is chosen, it should be discussed with the patient and the philosophy behind why a particular approach was chosen explained.